AAI-4494

Rites of Execution

Rites of Execution

Capital Punishment and the Transformation of American Culture, 1776–1865

LOUIS P. MASUR

New York   Oxford
OXFORD UNIVERSITY PRESS
1989

Oxford University Press

Oxford   New York   Toronto
Delhi   Bombay   Calcutta   Madras   Karachi
Petaling Jaya   Singapore   Hong Kong   Tokyo
Nairobi   Dar es Salaam   Cape Town
Melbourne   Auckland
and associated companies in
Berlin   Ibadan

Copyright © 1989 by Louis P. Masur

Published by Oxford University Press, Inc.,
200 Madison Avenue, New York, New York 10016

Oxford is a registered trademark of Oxford University Press

Library of Congress Cataloging-in-Publication Data

Masur, Louis P.
Rites of execution : capital punishment and the transformation of
American culture, 1776–1865 / Louis P. Masur.
p.   cm.
Includes index.
ISBN 0–19–504899–7 (alk. paper)
1. Capital punishment—United States—History.   2. Executions and
executioners—United States—History.   I. Title.
HV8699.U5M36 1989   88-22719
364.6'6'0973—dc19   CIP

2 4 6 8 10 9 7 5 3 1

Printed in the United States of America
on acid-free paper

For Jani and Benjamin

Acknowledgments

Books are as much the products of collaborative as individual effort, and this book could not have been completed without the financial assistance provided by several institutions and the intellectual and emotional support furnished by numerous friends.

I am grateful to the history department at Princeton University for a generous Fellowship that made it possible for me to attend graduate school, and for awarding me a Post-Doctoral Fellowship that provided time off from teaching in the fall of 1987. A Whiting Foundation Fellowship held in 1983–84 allowed me complete the writing of my dissertation. In the summer of 1982, the American Antiquarian Society awarded me a Frances Hiatt Fellowship; I would like to thank Nancy Burkett, John Hench, and the rest of the staff at AAS for all their help. A summer stipend from the National Endowment for the Humanities and a research grant from the Academic Senate of the University of California, Riverside, allowed me to complete the research for this book. Finally, a Regents Faculty Fellowship from UCR provided financial support for the final revisions.

My deepest intellectual debt is to Daniel Rodgers. Over the last eight years, conversations with him in classrooms and offices, over lunches and walks, through letters and notes, have helped make me a more imaginative historian and this a better book. Many others at Princeton shared in the enterprise of creating an intellectual community, one with a not-half-bad softball team. I have benefited enormously from the guidance provided by James McPherson, Stanley Katz, and John Murrin. I am especially indebted to Douglas Greenberg for his friendship, encouragement, and good taste.

A number of other colleagues and friends evaluated some portion of this project at various stages, or simply improved life in Princeton. I am grateful to John Carson, Elizabeth Clark, Gregory Dowd, Daniel Ernst, Gerald Grob, Thomas Knock, Alice Lustig, James Oakes, Laura Porter, Peter Sahlins, and Robert Tignor. Nancy Light deserves special thanks for typing an early draft of the manuscript into the computer. My colleagues at Riverside have been extremely supportive, and I am indebted to Edwin Gausted, Sharon Salinger, and Charles Wetherell for their comments on assorted chapters. John Phillips's critical skills have improved the manuscript, while his expertise at racquetball and lowball has left me both poorer and happier.

At Oxford University Press, Sheldon Meyer expressed early interest in my work, and Rachel Toor and Stephanie Sakson-Ford have guided the manuscript to publication with great skill.

I should also like to thank Louis Knafla for permission to reprint portions of my article, "The Revision of the Criminal Law in Post-Revolutionary America," *Criminal Justice History* 8 (1987): 21–36.

There is not an idea in this book, and hardly any in my head, that has not been discussed with Thomas Slaughter over the past nine years. For a long stretch of that time we met weekly over dinner and drafts, and debated such issues as what to think of Benjamin Rush, how to construct a historical narrative, and whether it is appropriate to root for a baseball team whose owner is less than admirable. There is not a sentence in this book that has not been scrutinized and improved by James Goodman, who became a valued friend the moment he fell asleep while I was presenting a paper in New York, and who continues to wonder with me just how free we are to make our own destiny and why there is no eatable pizza in Southern California.

Some family and friends have had as little as possible to do with this book, and are all the more appreciated as a consequence. I owe a special debt of gratitude to Sarah and Seymour Masur, Herbert Mallin, Bruce Rossky, and David Reis. Mark Richman asked lots of probing questions about Chapter 1, and then proceeded to hit my fastball over the center field fence, something he has done regularly since 1973. I am lucky that I have always been able to share my hopes and anxieties with my brother, David Masur, who has a sweet jump shot and a generous heart.

My final debt is also my greatest. After all these years, Jani Masur continues to provide equal measures of balance, understanding, humor, and chocolate ice cream. Long ago, she taught me that it made no sense to postpone until the future what we can enjoy in the present. Admittedly, I went kicking and screaming into marriage and fatherhood. But every day, Jani and Benjamin show me that love is wild, love is real, and that is why this book is for them.

Riverside   L.P.M.
June 1988

Contents

Rites of Execution

Introduction

Between the seventeenth and nineteenth centuries, Western societies abandoned public executions in favor of private punishments. If public death for a variety of capital crimes typified the seventeenth century, solitary confinement in penitentiaries and private executions only for first-degree murder characterized the nineteenth century. The transition was guided by a reconceptualization of the causes of crime and the purposes of punishment. The shift from public, external, physical forms of punishment toward private, internal, psychological modes of discipline embodied the triumph of new sensibilities and the reconstitution of cultural values throughout the Western world.[1]

The origins of the movement away from capital punishment are difficult to date precisely. In the seventeenth century, the Anglo-American world began to rely less frequently on the death penalty. To be sure, scores of crimes were considered capital offenses, but execution rates for those convicted of capital crimes generally remained well below 50 percent. A number of legal procedures served to mitigate the law's potential harshness. These included the plea of benefit of clergy by defendants, the return of partial verdicts by juries, and the discretionary power of prosecutors. As applied, the criminal law enabled hundreds of condemned prisoners to sidestep the gallows.[2]

The criminal law in practice prevented the indiscriminate use of the death penalty. In addition, essayists in the seventeenth century began to assail capital punishment. In the 1640s some Englishmen, most notably Levellers, demanded the abolition of the death penalty. The argument of the Levellers, and later the Quakers, was primarily a religious one. "If the power of life and death be only in the hand of the Lord," one critic insisted, "then surely he is a murderer of the creation that takes away the life of his fellow creature man, by any law whatsoever." For the next century, jurists and social critics occasionally condemned capital punishment, not only on religious grounds but also as an ineffective deterrent, a violation of the ideal of proportionality in sentencing, and a breach of the increasingly widespread belief that the criminal could be reformed.[3]

In the late eighteenth century, capital punishment became the subject of extensive public conflict. Reformers no longer accepted informal mechanisms of mitigation internal to the legal system. They pressured legislators to revise the very laws themselves so that robbers, burglars, rapists, and counterfeiters could not be executed for their crimes. Activists helped design alternative punishments for those malefactors who previously might have hanged. Widespread condemnations replaced isolated criticisms of capital punishment. Enlightenment concepts of balance, proportionality, and humanity in systems of punishment combined with a faith in the reformation of the criminal and redefined sensibilities about public space and social order to make capital punishment a repugnant practice. Many called for the total abolition of the gallows, while, in response, others ardently defended execution day.

Nowhere was the debate over the death penalty and the drive to find alternative punishments more compelling than in the United States. The early American criminal justice system also protected some prisoners from the gallows, and early American history had its share of critics of capital punishment, among them William Penn and Thomas Jefferson. But with the American Revolution, the problem of capital punishment assumed greater importance. In the context of the Enlightenment and the age of revolutions, theorists reconsidered what they had always known—that punishments were bound up with moral and political philosophy, with questions of the nature and power of the state. As patriots fought and won independence, as they set about creating a new republic, they self-consciously examined the place of the death penalty in society. By the time the last revolutionaries passed from the scene, little remained of the older rituals of punishment.

This study examines the conflict over capital punishment and the transformation of American culture between the Revolution and Civil War. Prior to the 1780s, a criminal could be executed for any of a number of offenses; afterwards, only first-degree murder was a capital crime in most

Northern states. In the 1790s, a new institution, the penitentiary, punished with solitude those who previously might have been hanged. These changes were not simply a byproduct of the Enlightenment. Instead, ideas derived from republican ideology, liberal theology, and environmentalist psychology combined with the experience of the American Revolution to trigger an opposition to the death penalty in America. Condemnations of the death penalty marked the emergence of a new understanding of crime and punishment. Essayists argued that social influences, not depravity, caused crime and that reformation, not retribution, should govern punishments.

By the 1830s, legislatures throughout the Northeast transferred executions from the town commons to behind prison walls. The rise of the penitentiary and the transition to prison hangings coincided with the emergence of a middle class that valued internal restraints and private punishments. The formation of middle-class sensibilities, characterized by a suspicion of the public arena, disgust with seemingly senseless cruelty, and a desire to withdraw into an exclusive social setting, constituted a central chapter in the transformation of American culture between the eighteenth and nineteenth centuries. It was a change not unique to American society, but one experienced by most Western cultures. The shift in rituals of punishment and attitudes toward discipline in the United States, however, had its own logic and history. This is the story of how these changes came about in America.[4]

From endings, historians discern beginnings. Studying change over time requires that we know what happened before we can explain how it happened and suggest what it means. Accordingly, this book begins with a case study of the ritual of execution day and the campaign against capital punishment in antebellum America. The opening chapter discusses an episode that occurred at a time when hangings took place in prisons, when the well-honed rhetoric of activists more often than not overreached its influence, and when middle-class assumptions about public behavior, human character, and social progress held great sway. If the case gives only a hint of the conflict rooted at the center of the debate over capital punishment, a conflict over competing visions of politics, religion, and society, it is because by 1850 the transformation in the rites of execution had become institutionalized and the opposition to the death penalty had stalled.

From the vantage point of the gallows in the late eighteenth century, one would not have imagined the changes that loomed on the horizon. Chapter 2 examines the design of execution day in the Revolutionary era as a spectacle of civil and religious order, as a performance directed by magistrates and ministers and involving the condemned themselves. The spectators who gathered by the gallows participated in an exhibition that served as warning and celebration, as both a deterrent to potential subvertors of republican and Christian values and a representation of communal identity and individual salvation. Yet even as it assuaged some anxieties, the ritual of execution day revealed other tensions in the social order. Those whom the state hanged tended to be young, black, or foreign. The identity of the condemned helped prevent dissent on hanging day, yet at the same time made it more difficult for authorities to convince spectators that unless they obeyed civil and divine law they too would end their days upon the gallows.

Not everyone thought hanging day desirable. In the context of a war that augmented fears over social order and provided an opportunity for the creation of republican, Christian institutions, the gallows came under attack. Chapters 3 and 4 discuss the origins of an organized opposition to the death penalty and the invention of the penitentiary in America. The argument against capital punishment hastened the revision of the criminal law and experimentation with new forms of punishment. When activists settled on solitude as the most effective regimen of discipline, they selected a punishment supple enough to satisfy both those who dreamed of reforming criminals and those who wanted to terrorize them. Although the new penal regime did not, as some had hoped, reclaim and restore criminals to the community, the opposition to the gallows and experimentation with the penitentiary marked the initial movement away from public, capital punishments.

The transformation in rituals of punishment culminated with the institution of private executions in the 1830s. Within several years, legislatures redesigned a ritual that had been embedded in American culture for two centuries. Legal hangings continued, but only within the confines of the jailyard. The creation of private executions, analyzed in Chapter 5, was an act charged with multiple meanings: it marked the triumph of a certain code of conduct and set of social attitudes among the middle and upper classes; it symbolized a broader trend toward social privatization and class segmentation; it turned the execution of criminals into an elite event centered around class and gender exclusion rather than communal instruction; and it provided some social critics with additional proof that despite the apparent democratization of Jacksonian society, America was drifting back into despotism.

Private hangings did not curtail the opposition to capital punishment. Throughout the 1830s and 1840s reform organizations emerged and conflict over the death penalty raged. Chapters 6 and 7 assess the commitment to social activism and analyze the competing visions of man and society lodged at the core of the debate over the gallows. The opponents of capital punishment were idealists and perfectionists, politicians and professionals; all were also mortally afraid of social vice and disorder. Many of them joined reform associations to advance their careers; others labored in obscurity and poverty, trying to reshape the world by aiding a few convicts. For the most part, all believed they were fighting to eliminate forever an inhumane, unjust, ineffective punishment. While these opponents of the death penalty thought of man as moral, educable, and savable, supporters of capital punishment viewed man as sinful, corrupt, and depraved. Thus, the debate represented nothing less than a fundamental division within the Victorian world view, a struggle over reforming individuals and reclaiming souls or restricting vice and re-establishing the moral government of God.

As an exercise in cultural history, this book takes beliefs seriously. Ideas cannot be separated artificially from the so-called reality of society. Beliefs are themselves tangible and meaningful; thoughts are actions. Rituals, as cultural performances and dramatic representations, constitute a text that provides another window onto ideological assumptions, social relations, and collective fictions. Ideas and rituals, however, are neither conceived nor employed in a vacuum. They simultaneously create and exist in contexts, and these contexts are crucial to describing how cultural assumptions and practices change as and when they do. Cultural history must remain sensitive to ideas and contexts, belief systems and social behaviors, and the interrelationships between them.[5]

Of course, ideas and society, divorced from individuals, are little more than abstractions. The debates and transformations discussed in the following pages are dependent upon the lives of famous, infamous, and altogether obscure persons. Examples include Washington Goode, a sailor convicted of a crime he may not have committed and to whose defense anti-gallows activists rallied; Thomas Mount, the most notorious bandit in post-Revolutionary America, who mocked republican values and went eagerly to the gallows; Benjamin Rush, physician and signer of the Declaration of Independence, who led the opposition to the death penalty and supported the penitentiary, but who died disconsolate and confused over the reforms he had promoted; George Barrell Cheever, a Presbyterian minister who defended the death penalty and possessed a bookmark embroidered with the hanging scene; and Charles Spear, Universalist minister and prominent opponent of the gallows, who devoted himself to reform both for the sake of mankind and for his own quest for fame. Through individuals such as these we can perceive more clearly the ritual of execution day and the problem of capital punishment in America between the Revolution and the Civil War.

The transformation of American culture was completed long before the opponents of capital punishment became frustrated and ennervated by their inability to secure the abolition of execution day. That in the end these social activists were keenly disappointed by some of the changes they promoted, and that the gallows continued to stand, says as much about the constraints imposed on reform as the reformers' ability to transform culture. Reformers thought they could reshape society, but it was the changing culture in which they played a part that determined the consequences of reform. Whatever the intentions of its advocates, the invention of the penitentiary, the abolition of public executions, even the formation of reform organizations themselves were the products and implements of a middle-class culture that dreaded vice, craved order, advocated self-control, and valued social privacy. Remnants of that culture persist long after the ideas and contexts that helped shape their origin have become obscured. What follows is a story about reform and punishment, about ritual and culture, about ideas and sensibilities that seem both surprisingly remote and terribly familiar.

1

Ritual and Reform
in Antebellum America

Put the scaffold on the Common,
Where the multitude can meet;
All the schools and ladies summon,
Let them all enjoy the treat.
What's the use of being "private"?
Hanging is a righteous cause;
Men should witness what you drive at,
When you execute the laws.

Anti-gallows poem (1849)

I

But for the scream of "Murder! Murder!" on a rainy June night in 1848, Washington Goode would have remained in the shadows of antebellum society and on the periphery of the written historical record. As it is, little is known about the twenty-nine-year-old black sailor's life whose case galvanized Boston for several months in 1849. A cook aboard the barque *Nancoockee,* Goode passed his time when in port within the environs of the boarding houses and drinking cellars on the north side of the city. At the four corners that constituted Richmond and Ann streets, an area referred to as "the Black Sea" because of the concentration of blacks and sailors pocketed there and the district's reputation as a "place of profligacy," someone fractured black seaman Thomas Harding's skull and plunged a knife nine inches deep between his ribs. Nearby, an officer arrested Washington Goode for the murder of his fellow mariner.[1]

Goode's trial began on New Year's Day, 1849, before the Supreme Judicial Court, which held exclusive jurisdiction in capital cases. The case made compelling reading, and the newspapers of Boston covered

9

the trial and reported the efforts made on Goode's behalf. Presiding over the court proceedings were Chief Justice Lemuel Shaw and Associate Justices Samuel Sumner Wilde and Richard Fletcher. One of the most influential jurists in nineteenth-century America, Shaw, during his tenure as Chief Justice between 1830 and 1860, rendered numerous key decisions that helped shape American law and jurisprudence. Shaw's court cleared the way for an instrumentalist law that promoted economic competition. Shaw's court expanded the police powers of the state. Shaw's court also upheld segregation in schools, denied protection to fugitive slaves, and curtailed the free speech of critics of religion. It was in Shaw's Supreme Judicial Court, acting as a trial court, that Washington Goode found himself a defendant charged with murder.[2]

In his opening remarks to the jury, the attorney for the Commonwealth, Samuel D. Parker, drew upon a rhetoric which prosecutors in murder cases have often employed: he bemoaned the increase in "crimes of violence" and the simultaneous relaxation in the use of stern punishments. Parker played on the juror's sympathy by reminding them of the "premature grave" that held Harding's "mouldering body." And he appealed to their fears that "those nightly haunts of vice and dissipation where homicide and robbery flourish," if not contained, would spread to engulf all respectable Bostonians.[3]

From the witnesses he called, Parker painted a picture of jealousy and drunkenness leading to murder. The previous summer Goode began seeing Mary Ann Williams. Sources are not clear about Williams's identity, but it is likely she too was black. Although married, Williams's husband had been away two years and during his absence she engaged in a number of casual affairs. The defense characterized her as a "vile prostitute"; from her testimony, however, she emerges as an independent woman who "kept home" and refused "to be ruled by anybody."[4]

On the night before the murder, Goode visited Williams's house and while there asked about a silk handkerchief in her possession. She told him it was a gift from Thomas Harding, whom she had been seeing since spring. In a rage, Goode tried to burn the handkerchief but Williams intervened. The gift had some value to her as it was the only present Harding had given her after a month of being together and washing clothes for him. Goode tore the handkerchief, threw it to the floor, and bolted out the door.[5]

The next day Harding visited Williams and asked what happened to his handkerchief. After she told him, a witness heard Harding claim that he would ask Goode to pay for the damaged article. Within the drinking cellars and dancing rooms along Richmond Street that night Goode said he heard Harding was after him and that he was prepared for an encounter. Armed with a sailor's common sheath knife and fortified with strong drink, Goode was heard to declare that before the night ended he would make "Rome howl."[6]

In the restricted environs of Richmond and Ann streets, Goode, Harding, and Williams encountered one another at Harris's cellar between 10 and 11 o'clock on the night of June 28. No one recalled whether Harding or Goode arrived first, but when Williams entered Goode slapped her with his open hand and shoved her to the floor. At the time, Harding was in another room. When told Goode was looking for him, customers heard him reply, "Let him come. That's what I want." Goode left Harris's first; Harding followed shortly thereafter. Less than half an hour passed before the "dark, big-whiskered man" Harding was dead.[7]

No one saw Goode crack Harding's skull and stab him between the ribs. One witness claimed to have observed "the person of the man who struck the blow but not his face." It was "his belief" that the murderer was Washington Goode, though under cross-examination the witness admitted that Goode was probably "fooling" when he talked so bravely in the cellar. Another witness, a boarder in the area, heard blows struck and a voice cry, "God damn you, I got my revenge." The witness testified that the voice sounded like Goode's, though he "would not swear positively that it was his." A third witness only viewed Goode running down the street and observed a white man standing near the entrance of Johnson's cellar when he heard the cry of "murder." Others claimed that a figure seen walking away from the crime site had on a tarpaulin hat; Goode wore such a hat that evening. By 4 a.m. on the night of the murder, the Captain of the North Watch had located Goode at his uncle's boarding house on Southark Street. According to the arresting officer, when found Goode declared, "I have only one life, you may do with it as you please."[8]

After four days of testimony, the attorneys began presenting their closing arguments. Goode's defense attorneys, William Aspinwell and Edward Hodges, pleaded that their client was innocent. Hodges addressed the jury over the course of two days. He began by impressing upon them the deep responsibility each juror would suffer if Goode were found guilty, executed, and later proved innocent. What a terrible burden of conscience they would feel for having consigned Goode to a "disgraceful and untimely death." Hodges began to discuss the appropriateness of capital punishment generally, but Parker objected on the grounds that the jury was there only to listen to "evidence and facts relative to the case, and not to the propriety of commutation or alteration to the laws." Shaw upheld the objection, stating counsel was "out of order to discuss the ex-pediency or justice of the death penalty."[9]

Hodges then shifted grounds. He condemned the source of the testi-mony against Goode as unworthy of consideration in a case of life and death. The testimony of the residents in the neighborhood of "the Black Sea" was contradictory, inconsistent, and "hopelessly false." In a region where "prostitution and infamy exist in all hours of the day and night, it was impossible for the fair image of truth to emanate." In addition to the "disreputable source" of the testimony against Goode, Hodges asked the jury to consider that the defendant acted well within his rights to carry a weapon "in order to defend himself against a man whose threats had made him afraid." The desire to make "Rome howl" was offered in a jocular manner only; Goode's comments to the night watch resulted only from his being pressed. Finally, the prosecution had presented vague and circumstantial evidence. Goode was in the area of the murder, but so were others. That Goode's dress matched that of someone seen walking away from the area was a thin connection on which to convict a man of murder. After five hours, Hodges concluded his address by leaving the defendant "in the hands of the jury, and the hand of his God."[10]

Following a brief recess, the jury listened to the counsel for the Com-monwealth for nearly three hours. Parker argued that a man could be positively identified even without viewing his face. Matters of gait, voice, and dress made it clear that Goode had struck the deadly blows. The defendant had a knife in his possession that could have accounted for Harding's mortal wound. The only other person in the vicinity was an "Irishman" further down the street. In response to the defense's argu-ment, Parker claimed there was no reason to disbelieve the testimony "though coming from Ann street." Goode not only had motive to kill Harding, he also had threatened him. The murderer had been heard to declare "I got my revenge," and revenge was precisely what Goode was after. Finally, the prisoner's response to the officers when they confronted him "implied proof of guilt." Parker concluded that the jury, if it were to perform its duties properly, could not bring in a verdict other than murder.[11]

Shaw offered Goode an opportunity to speak in his defense. The sailor was about to reply but his counsel, who had described Goode earlier as a representative of "a benighted and downtrodden race," claimed the de-fendant had nothing to say. Shaw instructed the jury that it was their responsibility to decide whether or not Goode had killed Harding and, if so, whether he had done so with malice. The jury deliberated for thirty-five minutes and found Washington Goode guilty of murder.[12]

After several postponements, the Supreme Judicial Court reconvened and Shaw passed sentence. The jurist lamented Goode's immersion into a depraved environment where "vice holds out a premium to passions of the worst kind." He especially condemned Goode's use of alcohol which undoubtedly placed the sailor into an intoxicated state that overwhelmed all sense of reason. Finally, Shaw disparaged Goode's association with "an abandoned married woman, whose husband was yet alive."[13]

"Sensible that it is not our own voice that pronounces it, but that of the law," Shaw sentenced Goode to death. He hoped Goode's "situation" would serve as an example to youth to avoid the path of vice. Described by the newspapers as being choked with emotion, the sixty-eight-year-old justice encouraged the doomed convict to prepare himself for the transition "from time to eternity." If Goode's mind had been "neglected in youth," then he should make use of God's ministers on earth to find "comfort in the prospect of the great change" that awaited him. Goode bore the sentence, in a courtroom that seemed "as quiet as a tomb," with a silence and fortitude that some characterized as suggesting a "careless air of indifference."[14]

Shaw's address had encapsulated the core social values of a conservative, mercantile, and Whig elite. The concern with environment revealed an uneasiness with the dangerous classes and a faith that proper education could save those predisposed to vice. The members of Shaw's class embraced temperance as a favorite reform; in their eyes, drunkenness served far less as a sympton of social alienation than as a cause. The sober, intact Christian family stood at the center of their moral vision. By immersing himself in "the Black Sea," and by drinking and maintaining an adulterous relationship, Goode had placed himself outside the boundaries of acceptable behavior that circumscribed Shaw's universe. For others, similar environmental and social beliefs would lead them to oppose the death penalty as failing to reform the criminal. Shaw, however, had little difficulty in supporting capital punishment. By doing so, he departed from the position taken by many of his fellow Unitarians who participated actively in the movement to abolish the death penalty. But Shaw respected and loved the law. It was the law, according to him, that pronounced sentence, and it was the law that remanded Goode to the Leverett Street Prison to await execution on May 25.

II

Coming as it did in the midst of a national debate over capital punishment, Goode's case served as a rallying point for anti-gallows activists

in Massachusetts. In March, after Governor George Briggs rejected defense counsels' application for commutation of Goode's sentence, the
Massachusetts Society for the Abolition of Capital Punishment appointed
a committee "to take means for saving, if possible, this poor man from
the Gallows." In addition to Goode's attorneys, Aspinwell and Hodges,
Wendell Phillips, Charles Spear, Walter Channing, Samuel May, Robert
Rantoul, Jr., Ellis Gray Loring, James Freeman Clarke, and other politicians, ministers, and reformers volunteered to serve.[15]

As one of its first acts, the committee issued a broadside designed to
attract public attention for Goode's case. Titled "Shall He Be Hung?,"
the full text appeared on lamp posts and building walls, and an abbre-
viated version was published in the *Liberator*. Goode, the broadside declared, had been convicted on "circumstantial evidence of the most flimsy
character." No one witnessed the struggle that resulted in Harding's death.
Someone near the scene wore clothes that resembled Goode's attire that
evening, but any testimony as to personal identity, especially on a night
that was "pitchy dark, rainy, and foggy," was "utterly unreliable."[16]

The authors of the broadside, most likely John Spear and Wendell Phillips, suggested that only the Governor's desire to test the question of
whether the death penalty could be inflicted in Massachusetts explained
the state's determination to send Goode to the gallows. No one had been
hanged in Boston since 1836; opponents of capital punishment took this
as evidence of a shift in public sentiment away from the death penalty.
No greater indication of this could be found, they felt, than in the "determination of many of our jurors" not to become "some accessory to the
destruction of human life." One editorial invited all those who doubted
the community's enlightened attitude to attend the Supreme Judicial Court
when it was about to impanel a jury: "They will find that a great number
of summoned jurors are rejected by the Commonwealth because they are
opposed to taking life for murder." If Goode's execution could be prevented, activists believed that the death penalty would in effect be eliminated in Massachusetts.[17]

According to reformers, the state not only wanted to demonstrate its
support for capital punishment and its power to inflict the penalty of death
according to the law, but the Governor also decided to select Goode's
case as the moment to make a stand against reform because the condemned man was black. No issue played a greater role in the efforts to
save Goode than the question of race. The broadside implored readers
that it should "not be said that the last man Massachusetts suffered to be
hung was a colored man . . . one whom society most preeminently in-

jures—doomed with such inevitable certainty, to ignorance and vice, by cruel prejudice and wicked statutes, in almost every part of the country—the child of an abused race." The *Boston Herald* speculated that, if a "white man who had money" committed the murder, he would not have been executed. What better victim for the state to choose in order to gain public support for capital punishment than a black man? Through Goode's case, then, reformers not only summarized their opposition to the gallows but also expressed their sympathy toward blacks, "a race systematically excluded from most of the influences which soften and elevate man," and even their opposition to racism. The broadside concluded by announcing a petition campaign and inviting the public to attend a meeting on Goode's behalf.[18]

On Friday, April 6, a "monster gathering" assembled at the Tremont Temple to discuss capital punishment and how best to save Goode from the gallows. At 7:30 the "full, spirited" audience settled and heard the first speaker, William Henry Channing. Unitarian clergyman and transcendentalist, Channing had recently completed a three-volume biography of his famous uncle, William Ellery Channing. The minister commented on how timely it was that they be assembled on Good Friday, and he insisted that Goode's case must be considered in the light of "Christian Justice."[19]

Rather than theological considerations, however, Channing focused on environmental conditions as mitigating factors in Goode's case, assuming Goode had indeed committed the murder. As a sailor, Goode inhabited a closed world of rough companions and authoritarian relations. "Christian Justice" had not been kind to Goode. Rather than sanctifying him with purity and temperance, "it has baptized him with the lava of intemperance, and the leprosy of licentiousness." Rather than "self-command, rectitude, usefulness, benevolence," Goode had learned "passion, brutal indulgence, self-will, violence, inhumanity." Channing had provided a list of attributes one would expect from any liberal, middle-class reformer in the mid-nineteenth century. Alluding to the religious occasion on that day, Channing concluded that to hang Goode was neither to redeem the lost, not restore the fallen.[20]

Wendell Phillips spoke next. On this occasion he did not wish to discuss the general issue of the abolition of capital punishment. Phillips thought it abhorrent that the Governor selected Goode through which to set an example, and he began by discussing the particulars of the case. Phillips reminded the audience that Goode was not a hardened criminal. If he committed the murder, about which there was much doubt, it was not "in cold blood," not with "deliberate purpose," not as "the climax of a long list of atrocities." Rather, strong drink led Goode to threaten Harding just as Harding had sworn vengeance on Goode.[21]

In general, Phillips proceeded, Goode must be viewed as "the victim of the worst social influences" rather than a "hardened villain." As a black man "the doors are shut against him—he has a separate school, a separate church; other people were ashamed to be associated with him, and by the law he was ostracized." If anything, Goode was a hero, not a criminal, for he had once helped a slave escape bondage in Missouri. "Poor and degraded," a product of the South where the "very heart of the colored man is torn out of his bosom and trampled under foot," Goode deserved sympathy and instruction, not the gallows and the grave.[22]

As others spoke they reiterated the themes of Goode's likely innocence, the problem of race, the environmental origins of crimes, and the need to reform rather than execute. One minister alerted the audience that, in supporting Goode, they would be accused of "morbid sentimentality" by those in favor of "rigid justice"; they should take pride, however, in their efforts to save the Commonwealth from a stain of blood that could never be washed away. The meeting concluded just after 10 o'clock. Some two hundred persons signed petitions requesting commutation of Goode's sentence by the executive, and it was announced that similar meetings would take place across the state.[23]

Charles Spear, Universalist minister and a leading opponent of capital punishment, returned from the gathering optimistic about Goode's chances and thrilled by the commitment to reform evident in the Boston community. That evening he commented in his diary that "four years ago such a meeting would not have excited half the interest. What a change! Here is a whole community raised up to sympathize with a friendless negro." After the Tremont Temple meeting, efforts on Goode's behalf accelerated. In addition to the Boston meeting, meetings for the commutation of his sentence were held in Worcester, New Bedford, Lyon, Lowell, and Mansfield. The petition campaign also made encouraging progress. Overjoyed at the public response, Spear wrote Governor Briggs that "in about *seventeen days,* more than *twenty-three thousand* names were obtained." Spear admonished Briggs that "you can sentence a poor, friendless, moneyless negro to the scaffold," but the gallows would not stand much longer.[24]

Many of the petitions on Goode's behalf simply used the succinct form recommended by the *Prisoner's Friend* that "we the undersigned ask for a commutation of punishment in the case of Washington Goode." Other petitions were more revealing. John T. Hilton and "118 other colored citizens of Boston," urged upon the Governor's attention that Goode "belongs to a race against whom a cruel prejudice paralyzes his effort for self-improvement, shuts the halls of the Lyceums against him, banishes him to separate schools and churches . . . and deprives him of the best means of education." It seemed "peculiarly hard and unjust" that a victim of racial prejudice and social inequality should be hanged. Another petition, from whites who had known Goode ten years earlier when he lived in Chambersburg, Pennsylvania, attested to his fine character and commented, in words suggestive of their own attitudes towards blacks, that "he always seemed to be good natured and obedient."[25]

Just as Goode had advocates, Briggs too had supporters. At a debate on capital punishment held at the Boston Latin School, supporters of the gallows, in particular, representatives of the city's orthodox clergy, asserted that "the right to inflict Capital Punishments can be proved to spring from a divine source." Since civil government was derived from divine government, and the laws of God demanded death, the state had an obligation to impose and carry out the death penalty. Calvinist ministers defended capital punishment as "one of the chief safe-guards of society," and condemned reformers for feeling "more pity for the blood-dyed murderer, than for his innocent victim." Amazed by what he viewed as the extremism of orthodox rhetoric, William Lloyd Garrison reprinted in the *Liberator* articles from the evangelical press chastising the reform community for false philanthropy. The *New York Evangelist* expressed concern for the victims and berated the activists for doing their best "to stand between the criminal and justice." If the reformers had their way, the editorial fumed, "Goode the murderer" would be "cared for and tenderly cherished," and society would become a "paradise for rogues."[26]

For the most part, the state's supporters did not publicly urge the hanging of Goode. Charles Spear noted that only one petition with nine signatures requested that the sentence against Goode be carried out. He tried to turn the question of Goode's fate into a public referendum, and took great pleasure in recording the "vote for the hanging Goode" as "ayes, 9, noes, 24,400." By mid-April, there was great hope among Goode's advocates that his death sentence would be commuted. In addition to the petitions and the decade since the last execution, reformers who tended to cast a wishful eye on the political scene thought Briggs unlikely "to risk his reputation against a growing public sentiment which everywhere in New England is frowning upon the gallows, as an unnecessary, anti-Christian, and barbarous method of disposing of criminals."[27]

The anti-gallows interpretation of legislative activity also gave Goode's supporters reason to feel optimistic. In 1846 and again in 1849 Briggs

himself, in his annual address, requested that the Legislature examine the
feasibility of the abolition of the death penalty for all crimes except first-
degree murder. The joint special committee on the abolition of capital
punishment commented that "vast numbers of petitions, for the repeal of
all enactments, legalizing the infliction of death, have been presented
. . . during the current session." Although the committee report did not
go on to recommend the elimination of capital punishment entirely, anti-
gallows activists appeared with high expectations before the Governor
and his council in late April to plead for the commutation of Goode's
sentence.[28]

Among those who spoke before the executive council were William
Aspinwell and Wendell Phillips. From the outset, Goode's defense attorney assured the council he would not discuss the abstract issue of the
propriety of capital punishment. Aspinwell insisted the crime committed
was not murder in the first degree. If Goode attacked Harding, "he did
so while laboring under such a feeling of injury, after such repeated threats
by the slain man, and while his sense of right and wrong was so deadened
by intoxication, as greatly to mitigate the character of the crime." Phillips
added that, if Goode had been tried under the new law being considered
by the legislature, he would not be executed. Aspinwell further argued
that, given the character of the witnesses and the circumstantial evidence
on which the conviction was based, it would be a grievous wrong to
punish Goode capitally. "There is not a single fact proved which is not
perfectly consistent with Goode's innocence," Aspinwell asserted.[29]

In conclusion, the attorney and the activist once again raised the issue
of race. Phillips pointed out that, since the state did not allow blacks to
sit on juries, Goode did not have a fair trial. Aspinwell thought that Goode,
as a black man, "had not that degree of moral accountability which makes
him as guilty as thousands of others would have been in his place." The
attorney thundered, "You brought them [slaves] from a state of barbarism
into an intelligent society, but you left their hearts as you found them,
stirred by the vague impulses of passion. While you surrounded them with
all the temptations to wrong, you gave them no moral powers of resistance; and when they have yielded, you have had no mercy upon them.
I speak now of what *America* has done."[30]

To be sure, there was tension in reformers' attitudes toward race. Many
of them shared in a paternalistic ethos that characterized the way in which
most whites thought about blacks in nineteenth-century America. Edu-
cating and elevating blacks to the middle-class ideal seemed at least as
important as guaranteeing blacks the right to participate fully and equally

in society. For others, egalitarian ideals and environmentalist assumptions did not translate into a vision of an interracial society. Still, the arguments put forth on behalf of Goode represented a challenge to the racism and segregation that permeated the antebellum North.[31]

Despite the "powerful and conclusive" appeal made on Goode's behalf, the Governor and council rejected the request for commutation of sentence to life imprisonment. "A pardon here," they claimed, "would tend toward the utter subversion of the law." Goode's supporters viewed the refusal as nothing less than a repudiation of democratic principles. A protest against the council's decision demanded the petitions of more than 20,000 citizens be respected. The people's right "to a voice and a just influence in the administration of public justice" requires that the "legal murder" of Washington Goode not take place.[32]

There is little doubt that reformers were sincere in their belief that the people of Massachusetts joined them in calling for the commutation of Goode's sentence. Far more likely, most citizens supported capital punishment in principle and, to the extent that they followed the case, thought Goode guilty and cared little about the life of one transient, black seaman. Perhaps sensing public support, the executive did not respond to the appeal. As a devout Baptist, Governor Briggs undoubtedly supported the death penalty for murder. Goode was to be hanged as scheduled on May 25. Distressed and disappointed, the reformers concluded that Goode was to be executed for two reasons. The "first is because he is 'a negro'— and the second is to sustain an 'evangelical' dogma in regard to capital punishment." Racial prejudice and orthodox religion, long the enemies of humanity and benevolence, would triumph again. The death of Goode, they predicted, would be an odious day long to be remembered.[33]

III

Rain poured onto the streets of Boston throughout the morning of Friday, May 25. Anticipating a huge crowd assembled outside the jail, authorities erected the gallows in the northernmost corner of the prison yard, hidden from the windows and roofs of the rowhouses lining Leverett street. But from Colting and Wall streets, "the gallows could be seen very plain with its rope and cap dangling in the breeze." For a public never entirely pleased with the institution of private executions, any opportunity to view the hanging was to be pursued. That morning, hundreds assembled outside the prison hoping for a glimpse of the scheduled execution. Some young entrepreneurs rented window space for one dollar per ticket, and rum shops in the vicinity did especially brisk business on the stormy day. With some consternation, newspapers noted that "men and women, *boys and girls*" jockeyed for clear sightlines.[34]

Reports of incidents outside the prison portrayed the crowd as filled with "rabble" making comments both "vulgar and profane." One spectator claimed that "Scriptures say that the d---d black scoundrel ought to be hung." Another screamed "give us a look at the son of a b---h," while a third hollered "tear down the wall, and let us see his d---d black face." So intent were some to witness the hanging that "a strong posse of policemen was required to keep the walls and roofs of the jail buildings from being scaled by the crowd."[35]

Not everyone was eager to view the hanging. One daguerreotypist, with offices near the jail, closed his shop, shrouded it in crape, and posted a placard that read "A Brother is to be Hanged." A butcher claimed to have refused as much as twenty dollars for access to his windows. He expressed concern that his customers would no longer buy from him, but resolved he did not care, for "this is downright murder." Charles Spear locked the offices of the *Prisoner's Friend* and left the following note on the door: "A man to be killed. No business till the killing is over!"[36]

Dismayed that their efforts on Goode's behalf had apparently failed, reformers denounced the impending private execution with sarcasm and bitterness. On the morning of the execution, Horace Greeley editorialized in his New York paper that "it is absurd that an act which is claimed has a beneficial effect on the public, should be performed in secrecy, or its benefits confined to a small number of privileged individuals." He concluded that those considerations which forbade executions from occurring in public view should prevent their taking place altogether. Less temperately, Garrison protested that Goode was to be "strangled in a corner of a jail yard." One newspaper recommended that "Briggs and his Council, or the deluded priests who are clamoring for the wretch's blood, be compelled to perform the duties of gallows builders and hangmen."[37]

Prior to Goode's scheduled execution, the disgust with cruelty and concern with humanity led one writer to inquire whether, if Goode's sentence was not commuted, his suffering might not be eased by the use of chloroform before the hanging. It was the sheriff's responsibility only to make certain that the "punishment of death be inflicted by hanging the criminal by the neck until he is dead." Nothing in the statute prevented the sheriff from exercising discretion in taking whatever measures necessary to alleviate the convict's pain. Introduced in 1846, anesthesia in its various forms had quickly spread through the medical profession. Since "either ether or chloroform is now universally used by surgeons in painful operations, shall not the convict share also the advantage of this benign discovery[?]," the writer wondered.[38]

An essay in the *American Whig Review* a year prior to Goode's case developed an argument for the use of chloroform in hanging. What preserved society in a civilized state, G. W. Peck maintained, was "manners" and "true refinement." Peck, a music and literary critic who was also a member of the Massachusetts Bar, was concerned with the "social health" of America. His was a vision of society where the "good and the wise" could peacefully transmit their "spiritual wealth"; most important in allowing for this was a condition of "healthful quietness necessary to refinement."[39]

Given his desire for social quiet and tranquility, Peck might have found the execution of criminals offensive, but he did not oppose capital punishment. According to him, criminals clotted the arteries of the well-refined social body. To have sympathy for the murderer was to "inoculate ourselves with bad blood." But Peck's sensibilities led him to inquire whether the execution of the criminal "must be made more painful than absolutely necessary." Provided that the death continues to be "fearful and shameful," the pity and compassion felt by all mannered people should be allowed to operate. "Why should not we," Peck wondered, "now that science has found a means of alleviating extreme physical suffering, . . . allow the benefit of it to the miserable wretches whom we simply wish to cast contemptuously out of existence?" Chloroform would permit the criminal an easy rather than a violent death, a calm rather than a horrid one. Where science has furnished a means of avoiding unnecessary pain, even in the case of murderers, it would be "against good manners" and "unbecoming to civilized Christian people" not to use it.[40]

With his emphasis on social well-being and betterment, his faith in the advancement of science, and his concern over the place of cruelty among the well-mannered and refined, Peck touched upon key elements in the Victorian world view. The invention of anesthesia encapsulated sensibilities that considered pain, suffering, brutality, and even death itself as antithetical to the higher ideals of humanity, compassion, and benevolence. It was no accident that Walter Channing, who participated in the humanitarian reforms of the day including the opposition to capital punishment, had also written a central text on *Anesthesia in Obstetrics,* though it is uncertain whether he pushed for the use of ether on Washington Goode. If the state were to continue to execute criminals, then it must at least mitigate the prisoner's ordeal. The use of anesthesia, like private

executions, helped to sustain the illusion that, though the hanging occurred, decorum, propriety, and civility were preserved, the control of
vicious passions effectuated.[41]

Several years after Goode's case, Wendell Phillips commented on the
desire to find "the easiest mode of taking life" as evidenced by giving
chloroform to condemned criminals from "motives of humanity." Rather
than trying to kill humanely, why not forsake the taking of life altogether?
he wondered. By giving up the rack and the wheel, society had "come
down one step" from severe and cruel punishments. Why not come down
two, he asked, and adopt imprisonment? Why not come down three and
make the prisons over into "moral hospitals?" Why not come down four
and put the criminal "under the influence of some community of individuals who will labor to waken again the moral feelings and sympathies
of his nature?" Phillips had made the argument many times before: the
sensibility and civility of the nineteenth century demanded not cruelty and
inhumanity but morality and community. By successive approximation,
society could erase criminality not by seeking ways to take life humanely
but by allowing the "favorable community," by which Phillips meant the
"moral and intellectual elite of the state," to reclaim and redeem deviants.[42]

As the date of his execution neared, the suggestion that Goode be given
anesthesia received no further discussion. In the days preceding the
scheduled hanging, Goode repeatedly declared his innocence to the clergymen who were granted access to his cell. The idea of being hanged
"like a Pirate" especially troubled Goode, who reportedly had fought for
Zachary Taylor in Florida and, as a former soldier, knew well the dis-
honor associated with being hanged. What a contrast, one advocate of
the commutation of Goode's sentence noted, that Taylor was now President and Goode was "to be hung on the gallows."[43]

At midnight on the twenty-fifth, guards heard Goode struggling in his
cell. Filled with despair, Goode was attempting to suffocate himself by
stuffing a corner of his blanket in his mouth. Guards unwrapped him only
to discover his bed and body "bathed in blood." Somehow, most likely
while having his cell cleaned, Goode obtained a piece of glass which he
used to hack at the veins near his elbow. To make the veins protrude,
Goode had tied cords around the upper part of his arms. The prison doctor
rushed in and managed to stop the flow of blood; the irony that the physician had "preserved the prisoner for a more terrible death in the morning" was not lost upon observers. Following the doctor's efforts, Goode
began violently to vomit "tobacco, paper, and other substances which he
had swallowed" in an effort to poison himself. He endured the few hours
until dawn sick and restless.[44]

At 8:45 in the morning, a procession formed to accompany Goode to the gallows. Although a private execution, over one hundred persons stood within the jail yard to observe the hanging. These witnesses "comprised some of the most respectable citizens of Boston." Unfortunately, except for representatives of the press, several observers who carried the title of "Captain" or "Major," and a few attorneys who had no direct involvement in the case, we cannot determine the identity of these privileged spectators. In the driving rain, they took their places on each side of the posts and chains that created a lane from the mortar of the jail to the unplaned timber of the gallows.[45]

The ceremony began outside Goode's cell with an address by Reverend Taylor, who prayed that Heaven would pardon the condemned for his crime, blessed the sheriff and his officers for enacting the law, and hoped no further crimes would stain the Commonwealth. The assembly then sang a hymn. Throughout Taylor's sermon, and the hymn that encouraged the condemned to "cheerful leave this mortal shore," Goode drifted in and out of consciousness. Unable to walk from exhaustion and loss of blood, Goode was strapped into a chair with his arms and legs pinioned. The condemned man requested water, and, at 9:30, the sheriff led the procession to the gallows with Goode carried by two constables. He was lifted onto the platform, placed over the drop, and had the rope adjusted around his neck. Sheriff Everleth read the warrant signed by the Governor, who was reported to be out of town attending a Baptist convention in Philadelphia. The sheriff asked Goode if he had any last words, but the sailor only moaned. His "eyes were upturned toward the skies and fixed vacantly upon the void above" when the deputy sheriff drew a white hood over Goode's face. At 9:45, the drop fell and Goode's body, still fastened to the chair, plunged several feet. Those nearest the gallows heard his neck snap. The body hanged twenty-five minutes before physicians examined it and pronounced Goode dead. The doctors wanted the corpse for dissection, but the sheriff turned the body over to Goode's uncle, who took his nephew back to the house on Southark Street where nearly a year earlier Goode had been awakened and arrested.[46]

A victim of prejudice in life, Goode was also discriminated against in death. The deacons of the black churches refused to allow services for Goode in their institution. Instead, a service was held in the same tenement where Goode's body was sent after the execution. Resting in an open, black walnut coffin purchased with funds raised from the black community, Goode "was robed in a neat white shirt, with standing collar and white neckerchief." A gathering of relatives, ministers, and neighbors participated in the service and took solace that Goode was done "toiling in this weary world of ours." A dense crowd waited outside for the coffin to appear and a procession formed to escort the body to the city burial ground.[47]

The "Leverett Street Tragedy" took place during "Anniversaries Week," that time each year when reform organizations gathered to review their efforts and rekindle enthusiasm for their causes. At a meeting on capital punishment held in Boston, angered activists again condemned the politicians for ignoring the wishes of the people, chastised the theologians for encouraging retribution, chided the community for its morbid curiosity, ridiculed the contradictions embedded in private executions, and lamented that a poor, innocent black man had been executed. They expressed their fear that the hanging of Goode destroyed respect for human life in the hearts of thousands and their concern that, if the state was allowed to deprive a person of life, then what was to prevent it from rightfully removing all else that belonged to a citizen? Reflecting upon the scene enacted on the twenty-fifth, one witness wished never to see again "the rain, the solemn stillness of the hour, the gloomy and wretched group, and the sad occasion . . . of this spectacle of misery and woe."[48]

2

The Design of Public Executions in the Early American Republic

> The event which calls us together is an awful and effecting dem-
> onstration of the danger of sin—a warning to hold our passions and
> appetites in constant subjection to reason—to cultivate fixed prin-
> ciples of honesty, justice, and benevolence—to be consistently strict
> in obeying the laws of God, and our country. . . . Such awful ex-
> hibitions are designed that others may see and fear—Go not to that
> place of horror with elevated spirits, and gay hearts, for death is
> there; justice and judgment are there; the power of government dis-
> played in its most awful form is there.
>
> NATHAN STRONG, *The Reasons and
> Design of Public Punishments* (1777)

Sometime in the afternoon of Wednesday, October 20, 1790, authorities
executed Joseph Mountain, a thirty-two-year-old black man, before a crowd
of thousands on the green in New Haven, Connecticut. Earlier in the day,
a procession threaded its way from the jail to the First Church, where an
overflowing assembly heard the Reverend James Dana deliver a sermon
entitled "The Intent of Capital Punishment." The pastor chose as his text
Deuteronomy 19:19,20: "So shalt thou put evil away from among you.
And those who remain shall hear and fear, and shall henceforth commit
no more any such evil among you." Dana addressed the multitude "of
all orders and characters" on the civil and religious necessity of capital
punishment and stressed the "excellence" of virtue and the "turpitude"
of vice. The pastor encouraged true repentance and warned of "destruction from God." Toward the close of the sermon Dana preached to Mountain directly. "In about three hours," he informed the prisoner, "you must
die—must be hanged as a spectacle to the world, a warning to the vicious."[1]

Following the church service a procession formed to escort Mountain
to the hanging scene. His arms pinioned and a coiled rope around his

neck, the prisoner trudged to the gallows erected on the green guarded by a company of militia and attended by clergymen. The sheriff and his deputies accompanied on horseback. A cart containing a coffin and a ladder followed the prisoner; had he so desired Mountain might have chosen to ride atop his own coffin. A throng of people closed the procession. Upon reaching the gallows, the sheriff read aloud the death warrant. As a chorus sang hymns, Mountain probably paused to pray and to deliver his last words to those within hearing distance. The sheriff pulled a white cap over Mountain's face. At a precise moment in the afternoon he gave a signal, and, with a shove, the prisoner was "launched into eternity." The body dangled for three-quarters of an hour before a guard cut it down and delivered it to the family, friends, or physicians who claimed it.

Magistrates and ministers designed public executions in the early American Republic as displays of civil and religious authority and order, as a "spectacle for Men and Angels." The spectators who gathered on execution day viewed, heard, and read a variety of messages about the culture they lived in and the behavior expected of them. It was a day on which civil and clerical figures appeared in a public ceremony before a congregation of thousands to display their authority and to convey the values they believed most fundamental to the preservation of the moral and social order of the community. The condemned also had a crucial, carefully circumscribed role to perform in the theater of execution.

As a civil ceremony, the execution exhibited the authority of the state. It sought to bolster order and encourage conformity to a republican code of social values. As a religious ceremony, ministers used hanging day to remind the crowd of its own mortality and to demonstrate that God alone could redeem the sinful. Ministers instructed spectators that the truly penitent could earn salvation. Execution day served as both a warning and a celebration. At the gallows the crowd received a lesson on the consequences of crime and sin; on hanging day civil and clerical figures offered proof that society worked properly and that God saved souls. Anyone who dissented from the proceedings did so subtly and infrequently.

Social leaders transmitted the meanings of execution day in oral, written, and dramatic form. The gallows procession and accompanying ritual represented the authority of magistrates and ministers. The execution sermon and the formulaic lives, last words, and dying confessions of the prisoner articulated the lessons to be learned from the spectacle. Printed versions of the sermons, confessions, and other gallows ephemera, which sold as pamphlets and broadsides on execution day and often contained woodcuts of the hanging scene, helped disseminate the message of the hanging through the crowd and across the region. The extent to which spectators internalized, reformulated, rejected, or ignored the intended meaning of the ritual is unclear. What is certain is that hanging day embodied political, theological, and cultural assumptions that mattered dearly to social elites in the early Republic.

I

It should come as little surprise that the overriding civil theme of execution day was the preservation of order. Above all else, authorities designed public hangings as a demonstration of the power of government and a warning to those who violated the law. Society punishes, one minister explained, "for the great purpose of preserving, in peace and safety, our property, our life, our civil and sacred rights and privileges. . . . We are bound by love and duty to each individual and the whole community, to support the order of society." Another minister emphasized the consequences of disorder: "In civil society, the wicked would walk on every side, and the cry of the oppressed be in vain, the foundations would be destroyed, confusion and misery would prevail were punishment, capital punishment, never executed." By choosing to stand outside the prescribed rules for moral, law-abiding behavior, the criminal seemed to undermine the stability of society. On execution day, authorities condemned actions that were perceived as rebellion against civil government (the state) and mounting disobedience to moral government (the church).[2]

Social leaders have always been preoccupied with the problem of disorder, but the anxieties of Americans seemed especially acute in the last quarter of the eighteenth century, and not without good reason. The act of Revolution not only triggered a war that raged for seven years and brought turmoil to many areas of the country but it also created a nation and government which, according to patriots, demanded the vigilance of the people for its survival. Loyalists, both real and imagined, posed a continual threat to the fragile Republic; thousands were imprisoned "on suspicion of their being inimical to America." As the war progressed, barely latent political, social, and geographic tensions erupted into manifest conflicts. According to patriot leaders, it seemed for a time as if the people had become totally unwilling to obey "any sort of order," and had become "addicted to corruption and venality."[3]

The fears over social decay and disorder were intensified by the constant chant of the republican hymn. Republican values centered on the idea of public virtue, the belief that an individual's passions must yield to the good of the community and that self-abnegation must come before self-interest. Accordingly, evidence of the lack of virtue augmented concerns that the newly risen nation would rapidly fall. Thomas Cope, a prominent Philadelphia merchant, offered a typical expression of these worries in his diary. Cope confided that "virtue is said to be the basis of a republic. If so, I fear ours is fast approximating toward its grave. . . . Moral virtues are giving place to gross depravity, licentiousness & corruption." Social anxieties did not abate after the war was won; Cope penned his thoughts in 1801. Already sensitive to the instability of republics, social leaders found in events such as the Shays' and Whiskey rebellions additional evidence that the virtue and order of the people had not been secured to their satisfaction.[4]

The messages transmitted on execution day expressed these elite concerns heightened by war and the creation of a new polity. At the execution of Moses Dunbar in 1777 for treason, Nathan Strong, pastor of the first Church at Hartford, delivered a sermon in which he denounced vice and decried actions he thought contributed to the subversion of civil harmony and the corruption of those virtues essential to winning the Revolutionary War and forming a government. A "prodigious concourse of people" heard the minister lament "that so many are insensible to the veneration and punctual obedience due to the laws of the land":

> That people are not far from destruction who disobey the public acts of their own government—who endeavor artfully to elude the institutions of their own legislature—who think themselves better judges of safety, and the means of preservation than the collected wisdom of the whole—who are generally become so avaricious as to prefer the smallest interests of their own, to the most capital and sacred interests of the state. . . . Let such persons . . . be warned by the proceedings of this day and do no more so wickedly. . . . Is there not reason to think, that those who knowingly injure the State by fraud, avarice and oppression, would plunge their swords into its bowels, if they had courage to face danger? . . . [They] commit those political sins which must be punished by the halter and the gallows. . . . When you look thereon, learn the venerableness of state and civil government—the sacred nature of the laws made to protect liberty and property, and our obligations to obedience.[5]

Strong's explication of the civil meaning of the execution relied on language that was essentially Whig and republican, and had its roots in seventeenth-century New England notions of moral obedience to divine government and the jeremiad tradition. His image of swords driven into bowels echoed John Wilkes's speech in Parliament against permitting Englishmen "to sheath their swords in the bowels of their fellow subjects." When he denounced those who, like the criminal, chose avarice over the interests of the nation, Strong expressed a fundamental tenet of republican ideology—public virtue demanded the sacrifice of private interests for the common good. Those who did not comply, Strong argued, must be severely punished.[6]

Strong intended his sermon as a warning to spectators that individuals such as Moses Dunbar, who battled the state, must lose. He expected citizens to "love . . . venerate . . . obey . . . honor" the law, not "elude . . . disobey . . . injure" the country. Many civil and religious leaders argued that only public executions could control the disordering effects of independence, war, and the establishment of government. "To attain the end of civil government is it not . . . necessary to punish the vicious?" asked one participant at Harvard's commencement in 1787. Only by zealously guarding against the corrupting power of criminals would the new Republic be protected from internal invasion at the very moment it was besieged by external enemies. Only the death penalty, they insisted, could preserve virtue and, in so doing, secure the survival of the Republic.[7]

The execution of two rebels, John Bly and Charles Rose, at Lenox, Massachusetts, in December 1787 affords a prime opportunity to probe further the message of civil order transmitted on execution day. In 1786 disgruntled citizens, many of them farmers who were deep in debt, heavily taxed, and facing loss of their property through foreclosure, rose in armed protest throughout western Massachusetts. These regulators closed down courts within the commonwealth and fought troops who marched west to battle them. Defeated at Springfield in February 1787 by a government force of several thousand men, the rebels dispersed but continued to harass citizens linked to the government. The insurrection, known as Shays' Rebellion, subsided by the summer of 1787.[8]

Most of the condemned Shaysites received pardons or commutations from the Governor, but not before prompting a discussion over whether or not the State should execute captured insurgents. At Northampton on June 21, 1787, the entire "parade of death" to the gallows was enacted until the sheriff read a reprieve for convicted rebels Jason Parmenter and Henry McCullough. James Sullivan, who defended several of the insurgents, argued for clemency for Parmenter on the grounds that "peace and tranquility could be restored without sanguinary examples." The mock execution, he later told the executive council, "was so far from exciting opposition to legal authority, that a gloomy silence and solemn awe at the power of government were universally exhibited." "Even Britain," the counsel remarked, "whose sanguinary disposition daily gluts the grave with legal consignments" offered clemency in similar cases. Sullivan concluded that, if he thought for a moment that the hangings would excite opposition, he would favor a sentence of death. But since there was no "public advantage" to executing the insurgents, and because the State had "sunk into the arms of peace and tranquility," he recommended full pardon.[9]

Samuel Adams viewed the matter differently. "In monarchies," he observed, "the crime of treason and rebellion may admit of being pardoned or lightly punished; but the man who dares to rebel against the laws of a republic ought to suffer death." Only good, he believed, would come from a demonstration of the strength of the state; only public executions, he insisted, could re-establish lapsed virtue and secure the order of a traditionally fragile republic. Ezra Stiles, president of Yale College, agreed. "Should none be executed, Government is not established & the matter will be all to be disputed over again by the Sword; but if only one should be executed the point is settled."[10]

Not everyone concurred with Adams's and Stiles's views. In Philadelphia that same year Benjamin Rush, physician and signer of the Declaration of Independence, proposed the abolition of capital punishment entirely. In part, Rush feared in public executions the onset of a destructive cycle. The State hanged criminals to control disorder. Executions, however, by brutalizing and demoralizing spectators, generated more crime, resulting in additional executions. The very act designed to preserve the Republic, Rush argued, violated republican principles and would in time contribute to its extinction. For authorities in Massachusetts, however, the acuteness of Shays' Rebellion muted any argument over capital punishment.[11]

The actions of the insurgents horrified Adams and Sullivan. Typical of social leaders, they feared for the commonwealth, and sought to guarantee that rebellions against the authority of the state, no matter how they were justified, would never again occur. It is ironic that some twelve years earlier, John Hancock, who served as Governor following the crisis, and Samuel Adams had both been singled out to suffer death by the British. Then they were the rebels and not the authorities. Both Adams and Sullivan later served as Governors of Massachusetts. Sullivan's hopes fed the myth of a conciliatory, peaceful end to the insurrection, while Samuel Adams's fears led the state to execute two Shaysites, John Bly and Charles Rose.

Political authorities in Massachusetts hanged Bly and Rose for robberies committed during the rebellion and not for treason. That distinction allowed the state to display its authority without inciting further opposition. That is also the most likely reason why citizens in western Massachusetts, as far as we can ascertain, did not disrupt the execution, even though Shaysites had earlier threatened revenge should the Governor execute anyone for treason. The gallows literature that emerged from the spectacle, however, demonstates that by executing Bly and Rose civil authorities intended to send a message to western Massachusetts and to those people who might consider rising against the state again.[12]

On the morning of December 6, 1787, two hundred and fifty men escorted Bly and Rose to the meetinghouse in Lenox. The path that brought Bly to the gallows covered much ground if not many years. He was only twenty years of age and had been with Shays since early on. When General Benjamin Lincoln and his troops entered Berkshire County, many of the "rebels," Bly among them, fled. He found his way to New York, but he was twice captured, returned to Massachusetts, and released. Back in New York, Bly heard "great stories that Shays was coming down [from Vermont to Massachusetts]. I took orders to raise men and join him." During the spring and summer of 1787, Bly and a party of men stole weapons from supporters of the government.[13]

Charles Rose, under orders from an officer in Shays's command, also pilfered weapons, specifically, "arms and a powder horn." When not with the insurgents, Rose taught school in Massachusetts and New York. Nearing execution day, Rose found it preposterous that his "Taking Guns . . . would have been Judged a Robbery, or that by any Law Robbery Could be Esteemed worse than Treason." Preposterous as it seemed, for stealing weapons Bly and Rose found themselves surrounded by a preacher, the militia, and a "numerous concourse of spectators."[14]

Stephen West, pastor of the Church at Stockbridge delivered a sermon in which he interpreted the spectacle for the crowd. The "affecting and melancholy occasion" for which they had gathered, he declared, was designed to fix "our attention to the nature and importance of civil government and lead us to prize and revere it as a divine institution." The pastor explained that God provided civil authorities with the power to avenge "sins against society"; indeed, without that right the ends of government could not be achieved, nor "the good and safety of society secured." West informed Bly and Rose that since they set themselves against the community, "so the community now set themselves against you." He concluded by reminding the assembly that the execution served as a "solemn warning against breaking the bonds of civil society."[15]

The last words and dying speeches of Bly and Rose were constructed as an address to "the Good People of Massachusetts, more especially to Daniel Shays and other officers of the Militia, and the Selectmen of Towns who have been instrumental in raising the Opposition to the Government of this Commonwealth." It is unlikely that Bly and Rose spoke these precise words at the gallows or at the prison. Whoever wrote the last words of these criminals felt little need for subtlety. The condemned men admitted, "Our fate is a loud and solemn lesson to you who have excited the people to rise against the Government," and they pleaded with the people of Massachusetts to "remember that Government is absolutely necessary to restrain the corrupt passions of men; obey your honest Governors;—be not allured by designing men—pay your honest debts and your reasonable taxes—use your utmost endeavors to give peace to your divided, distracted country."[16]

A piece in the *Worcester Magazine* restated the message of civil order. According to this witness of the execution, the "fate of Bly and Rose is full of instruction and must force conviction upon the minds of all those who have arisen up in an open rebellion against the laws, that their crimes will not go long unpunished; and however much they defy the powers of government, they shall soon meet with their due rewards." The state had transformed the grievances of frontier debtors, grievances not unlike those the colonists had levied against Great Britain, into the crimes of corrupt passion and treasonous rebellion.[17]

Bly petitioned the Governor to "Pardon a poor guilty Wrech." He claimed to have been "Actuated by the heat of Passion . . . and the Advice and Instigation of men older in years and more Wicked than himself." Bly declared, "I . . . most heartily and truly repent for my Conduct." "With Trembling, with Fear, and with Anxiety," Rose too petitioned for clemency. "Foreign born and a stranger in America," Rose pleaded that he was swept up with discussions of "Grievances of Taxes, of Salaries, & of Oppressions . . . the universal Topic of Conversation." He confessed to joining in with Shays and, as a penitent "honest, peacible, and Faithfull Subject," begged for mercy. The Governor rejected both petitions.[18]

Curiously, the earliest historians of Shays's Rebellion viewed it as a demonstration that civil authorities could meet any challenge to the newly established order without use of excessive force. George Minot, a Boston-trained lawyer writing in 1788, applauded the state which "governs its subjects without oppression, and reclaims them without severity." The rebels, according to Minot, swallowed a lesson in the authority of the state, and the government displayed mercy by reprieving those sentenced to death. James Sullivan's biographer concurred: "The government, by its wise and moderate measure, aided by the support of an enlightened community, was enabled to crush a dangerous rebellion, and to reclaim its disaffected citizens, without recourse to capital punishment." Minot's interpretation must be viewed as a part of the myth of a virtuous, humane national character. He wanted desperately to believe that the American Republic, in contrast to the British monarchy, did not need to hang its citizens. Minot did not mention that the final act in the suppression of the rebellion was the execution of John Bly and Charles Rose.[19]

II

Shays' Rebellion posed a direct challenge to the political order of Massachusetts, and this explains the clarity and severity of the language used at the execution of Bly and Rose. But the ritual enacted at Lenox was not an aberration prompted by an unusual event; the execution spectacle throughout America repeatedly addressed the theme of civil and public order. The sermon presented the view of the social leaders of the community. The minister's sermon, however, constituted but one of several aspects of the execution day ritual devoted to inculcating "good order, holiness, and virtue." The lives, last words, and dying confessions of prisoners elaborated on the problem of disorder, examined the origins of crime, and directed a warning to spectators gathered at the gallows.

The pamphlets and broadsides that contained the lives, last words, and dying confessions of a criminal were sold on execution day and circulated throughout the community. Some care must be exercised, however, in using this literary genre as an historical source. The content of these gallows speeches was formulaic; each printed confession utilized familiar terms and addressed similar issues. Someone other than the prisoner edited, if not completely fabricated, the last words of criminals. A narrator of the life and confession of one doomed convict admitted that the text "is penned from the criminal's mouth, though not always exactly in his own words. Some moral reflections are interspersed." In another confession the "editor" noted that "many tautologies and superfluous repetitions are expurged; bad orthography, and other parts of grammar corrected; and instances of stile improved." A manual for ministers attending doomed criminals even included a suggested form for the confession: "Prostrate on this earth, which is soon to receive my wretched and sinful body . . . I present myself before thee . . . to confess and bewail my sinfulness in general, and particularly my horrible crime of bloodguiltiness, in violently taking away the life of (*here name the person murdered*)."[20]

Who was responsible for revising and rectifying the criminal's thought in gallows literature? We know that in one case David Daggett anonymously edited *Sketches of the Life of Joseph Mountain,* a widely circulated pamphlet that sold for six pence. Daggett graduated from Yale College in 1783. He practiced law in New Haven and in October 1791, a year after Mountain's execution, was chosen to be a representative of New Haven in the General Assembly. Daggett also served as United States

Senator (1813–19) and mayor of New Haven (1828–30). In other cases as well a combination of clergymen and civil authorities molded the outline of a prisoner's tale into a moral lesson for the public. Ministers attended the prisoner in jail, and the sheriff held responsibility for the criminal from day of conviction to day of execution, sometimes a period of several months. One burglar's confession even thanked the gaoler for his "good advice and counsel." Although these sources cannot reveal the actual thoughts and feelings of the prisoner, the printed last words and dying confessions demonstrate the uses to which authorities put the condemned.[21]

The last words and dying confessions hinged on the warning typically given toward the close of the ceremony. The warning extended the moral lessons offered on execution day. The minister's lengthy sermon rebuked behavior that defiled republican government and disordered social relations; the prisoner's terse warnings catalogued vices and absolved society of responsibility for criminal behavior. Typical of these admonitions were the last words of two burglars executed at Worcester, Massachusetts, on June 19, 1783: "We pray that our unhappy fate may be a solemn *Warning* to *Youth* and induce them to forsake the paths of vice and immortality, and seek the road of virtue and happiness." Similarly, another criminal bequeathed the world a history of his "vicious Practices, hoping that all people will take warning by my evil example and shun vice and follow virtue." The vices which led to an "immature and ignominious death" included "bad company, excessive drinking, prophane cursing, swearing, shameful debauchness, disobedience to parents, [and] the profanation of the Lord's Day." One teenager, executed at Dedham, warned with his "dying breath and last words . . . Do not CHEAT—Do not STEAL—Do not LIE—Do not commit ADULTERY—Especially, do not destroy VIRGIN INNOCENCE—and, above all, do not KILL."[22]

Gallows literature treated the crimes for which the state executed convicts, ranging from robbery to murder, as symptoms of a disease that began when an individual veered off the path of righteousness and virtue. According to the warnings, such a deviation occurred early in life. Many fell on the "slippery paths of youth," and authorities made certain that the message contained in gallows speeches encouraged segments of society, especially youth, to behave appropriately. "We warn all, especially young people, that they would avoid the vices we have been addicted to," advised four criminals who were executed on July 2, 1778. One woman, aged twenty-nine, who was executed at Boston for highway robbery, hoped "my awful and untimely fate will be a solemn warning and caution to every one, but more particularly to the Youth, especially those of my own sex." A black man hanged for burglary prayed that "my un-happy fate will be a warning to all, especially to the youth, and those of my color, to abstain from the least appearance of evil." And a nineteen-year-old criminal hoped his "unhappy Fate . . . will be a Warning to all young Men to abstain from excess of Liquor, bad company, and lewd women, which have brought me to this untimely end."[23]

The condemned who directed their warnings to the youth were them-selves young. In the last quarter of the eighteenth century, of a sample of thirty-seven executions for which the age of the criminal is known, the median age of the person executed was twenty-five years. In their warnings, these criminals not only alerted the young to the dangers of vice but advised children to obey their parents. In this way authorities hoped the execution would steer a younger generation away from what an older one viewed as immoral, while also binding children to their rulers and the examples of their elders. At the same time, these warnings exculpated the parents from the sins of their children.[24]

"We earnestly entreat you to be obedient to your parents, and hearken to their good advice" served as the moral credo enshrined by the crimi-nal's last words. Criminal behavior, the dying confessions foretold, began at an early age, and the pattern that led to the gallows seldom varied—swearing by age nine, stealing a small item like gingerbread or green corn by age twelve, joining in bad company, drinking, and, inevitably, committing a crime for which one would hang. This pattern of small malefactions "leading to the most dreadful enormities" meant that parents could not neglect "family Instruction and Government." Yet, according to gallows literature alone, parents almost never failed in their respon-sibility to their children.[25]

Nearly every account of the life of a criminal sentenced to hang ex-tolled the virtue of the prisoner's parents. Doomed convicts repeatedly described parents as "good, reputable" or "sober and honest." The mes-sage nearly always was that, if the condemned "had followed their good advice [they] should never have come to this untimely fate." Criminals portrayed parents and masters as "industrious to instruct" and "impress [the prisoner's] mind with sentiments of virtue." Whenever children dis-obeyed and became "speedily initiated in practices disgraceful to human nature and destructive of every moral virtue," it was despite the best efforts of parents. Criminals confessed they were "naturally too much inclined to vice, to profit by [a parent's] precepts or example."[26]

By constructing the message of the dying confession in this manner, civil and religious leaders hoped to strengthen familial order, which they believed to be the basis of a stable social order. In a sermon delivered the morning of the execution of Hannah Ocuish, "a mulatto girl twleve years and nine months," Henry Channing, pastor of the Congregational Church at New London, prayed that "every spectator of this day's painful scene, learn the importance of faithfulness in the relations of Parent and Master. . . . Dutiful and obedient children are an heritage of the Lord." Another minister invoked traditional phrases when he addressed the "younger generation" at an execution in 1796 and explained why obedient children were essential: "Your fathers are dropping away, one after another, and if you live in the world, you must be their successors in the great affairs of church and state."[27]

Aaron Bancroft, pastor of the Second Church of Worcester, linked the question of morals and youth to the prospects of the new nation. "Moral virtues," he insisted, "are of the highest importance to the interests of civil society. We are told that they are more especially necessary to the support of a government like ours. . . . The prospects of the next generation, the success of those liberal measures in government and religion, which we have adopted, and in which every good man feels himself interested, depend in a great degree on the general practices of the youth of the present day." In the 1790s, Bancroft had reason to be concerned because students throughout the country, perhaps re-enacting a Revolutionary rite that occurred just before their time, began rebelling against the authority of their teachers. Bancroft, who in his twenties had marched with the Minutemen, now feared what the youth of the 1790s might provoke.[28]

The homilies to parents and warnings to youth that pervaded the gallows literature of the late eighteenth century must be understood in the context of what one scholar has labeled a "revolt against patriarchal authority." According to this view, a generation of children, the patriot generation, rebelled against both their real and their metaphorical parents. In the process, they reshaped family life, politics, and culture in America. At the gallows, however, we find evidence of a reaction to the rebellion of youth, and the persistence of a more traditional understanding of family relations. On execution day, elders punished youthful offenders who portrayed themselves as disobedient and rebellious; the doomed prisoners, in turn, warned children to beware and, at the same time, released their parents from responsibility for the actions or fate of the younger generation. In this way, standard language employed in the Puritan assault on declension in the seventeenth century was now invoked to combat what some social leaders, former youthful rebels themselves, feared as a revolution by youth in the late eighteenth century.[29]

If parents were not responsible or accountable for the "wickedness" and "ungodliness" of their children, how did authorities explain the licentious, sinful behavior they imagined as enveloping the new Republic, a country they believed to be especially dependent on public virtue for its survival? For the most part, the understanding of the causes of crime contained within gallows literature focused on the individual and seldom on the environment. Ministers depicted criminals as "naturally vicious" agents who embraced iniquity despite the best efforts of pious parents and benevolent rulers; prisoners described themselves as "naturally inclined to vice." It was up to the individual whether or not to "indulge in vicious passions," claimed James Dana, and the responsibility of society to punish those who did.[30]

Only occasionally did a minister in an execution sermon argue that parents and society shared responsibility in producing deviant behavior. Two ministers who advocated this position, Aaron Bancroft and Noah Worcester, helped forge the rise of Unitarianism in New England, a liberal religious denomination linked with an opposition to capital punishment. Neither Bancroft nor Worcester, as far as we know, opposed the death penalty, but both posited a relationship between social environment and criminality. At the execution of Samuel Frost on October 31, 1793, Bancroft described the prisoner's father as "greatly deficient" and alleged that he set an "impious, cruel, and barbaric" example for his son. "It is easier to *prevent* than to *cure* habits of vice," proclaimed Bancroft, who believed that "early impressions are deep, they are influential." Noah Worcester, pastor of the Church at Thornton, asserted that "we all must plead guilty before the bar of conscience as having had some share in corrupting the morals of the community, and levelling the highway to the gallows." "Is it not evident," he inquired, "that parents, in general, have become too negligent with regard to the morals of their children?"[31]

Both ministers emphasized the responsibility of "rulers, public teachers, professors of religion, and heads of families" in the "suppression of vice" and "reformation of morals." In this way they departed from the beliefs of most other ministers. If a psychology that emphasized the educability of the individual and the impressionability of the senses prevailed in the late eighteenth century, it was hardly evident in the ritual of execution day. Even Bancroft and Worcester viewed public executions as indispensable in checking further profligacy. Uzal Ogden, minister at the New Presbyterian Church in Newark, New Jersey, summed up the intent of capital punishment this way: "For the honor . . . of our country and its laws, for the good and safety of the commonwealth, and to avoid the frowns of a righteous and holy God, the awful sentence is executed." Not to hang the prisoner, he argued, implied that the community tacitly approved the crime and therefore shared in the guilt. In the final evaluation, as far as Ogden was concerned, neither civil and religious leaders nor parents and teachers could be held accountable for criminal behavior.[32]

While the emphasis on individual responsibility for deviant behavior might have relieved many a delinquent parent, the "natural viciousness" of a criminal could explain only so much. How could one distinguish the vicious from the virtuous? Who, despite proper upbringing, was most likely to fall? Who behaved criminally? Profiles of gallows victims help provide answers to some of these questions. Former soldiers, foreigners, and other "outsiders" were most likely to be hanged. Town leaders perceived and presented members of these groups as invaders who infested and corrupted otherwise virtuous communities.

In the last quarter of the eighteenth century, many of the men executed by civil authorities had belonged to the army. Typical of the confessions made by ex-soldiers at the gallows was one criminal's statement that, after joining the military, "I gave myself up to all manner of debauchery." Another convicted soldier revealed, "During my short stay in the army, I became acquainted with many vices that I had not to follow into before." One deserter warned others at his execution not to follow his example, "lest they incur the vengeance of Heaven, and of their injured Country." The worst fears of those who had witnessed the British occupation of Boston and invasion of America, and who shared in a Whig ideology that dreaded standing armies, were confirmed in the accounts by former soldiers. A military presence, of whatever nationality, could act only as a corrosive force in the Republic.[33]

By executing soldiers in civil ceremonies, authorities also wished to prevent desertion at a time when the revolutionary cause was far from secure. Moreover, some Americans hoped that the example of soldiers hanged for highway robbery, counterfeiting, rape, and murder would help assure an orderly transition from military to civilian life. The number of former soldiers executed after the Revolution indicated, in part, that the military had not simply melted peaceably into the countryside. This provided an easy, available explanation for why virtue seemed to have lapsed. By pinning the perceived expansion of vice in the 1780s and 1790s on those who once belonged to the military, and on other outsiders, civic and religious leaders could maintain the strained belief that most Americans actively upheld virtue.

In addition to soldiers, foreign-born convicts accounted for a significant percentage of persons executed in America. Charles Rose had called himself a stranger and a foreigner; many other victims of the gallows began life in places other than where they were hanged. Of the nine people executed in Worcester County in the last quarter of the eighteenth century, for example, none was a native of Worcester. Biographical information on criminals executed in America between 1776 and 1812 reveals that at least half were not born in the United States. Of twenty-five men and women for whom place of birth is known, thirteen had immigrated to the United States. Of these thirteen, eight arrived from Ireland. Of the twelve born in the United States, six were black and one was an Indian. Only two of the twelve were executed in the same state in which they were born and one of these two, a man named Johnson Green, had a black father, and Indian mother, and had joined the army against his mother's "good advice."[34]

Juries most likely found it easier to convict outsiders—defined as foreigners, minorities, and those literally not from the immediate community—of capital crimes, and governors felt less pressure to commute the death sentence of those with few ties to the community. Those executed were people for whom spectators might feel the least sympathy, and, as a result, authorities hoped, the assembled would unite against the condemned to defend social stability. In an execution sermon delivered in 1784, one minister admitted, "Our gallows have rarely been occupied, except by natives of foreign countries, or neighbouring States." The danger here was that witnesses to the execution would identify so little with the criminal that they would become indifferent to the lessons of the day. To insure against complacency, ministers reminded spectators to "think not that crimes are peculiar to the *complexion* of the prisoner." Anyone "esteemed at having a virtuous character" might in a short span of time degenerate. As a civil ritual, a spectacle for man, executions could teach a stern lesson about civic responsibility and try to fashion a uniform model for republican behavior without suggesting that the community was eroding from within. Still, there was the problem of allowing those who did not fit the gallows profile to relax in a false certainty that they would not be the ones to repudiate republican ideals; there was a risk that spectators would blame all deviance on contaminated outsiders. As a religious spectacle, a spectacle for angels, however, the culture of execution day made it clear that everyone within the community was suspect.[35]

III

While the civil component of execution day shifted to accommodate the republican concerns and terms of the Revolutionary era, many aspects of the ritual changed little throughout the seventeenth and eighteenth centuries. In the last quarter of the eighteenth century, the vocabulary of execution day contained new idioms that carried special meaning in the American Republic and conventional phrases that resonated across time. Increase and Cotton Mather would have felt at ease with the sermons and confessions delivered at the gallows in the last quarter of the eighteenth century. Both Mathers had in their time admonished children against rebelling, warned them to heed the advice of parents, and alerted them to the dangers of Sabbath breaking, drinking, and lying. Both men blamed deviance on "criminal propensities," not the social environment. The content of execution sermons had become so formulaic that, in 1791, William Smith, rector of Trinity Church in Newport, published a guide for ministers "Consisting of Prayers, Lessons, and Meditations, with Suitable Devotions Before, and at the Time of Execution." In particular, the religious dimension of the hanging spectacle expressed the conventions of Christian eschatology. Increase Mather had exhorted the prisoner not to exclude himself from salvation by "Impenitency." Rector Smith's guide emphasized penitence and conversion. In the religious component of execution day, no issue transcended in importance the problem of true and sincere penitence and salvation.[36]

Civil and religious authorities could scrutinize and attempt to control external behavior, but, try as they might, they could only hope that outward behavior reflected accurately the innermost beliefs of the populace. Execution day summoned the inhabitants of numerous towns to bear witness to the fate of those whose actions, social leaders claimed, undermined the order and virtue of the Republic; the state demonstrated that those who were caught would hang. But how could authorities know whether spectators internalized the civil message of obedience to government? What if behind blank stares lurked contemptuous criminals? What of those who were not discovered? Stephen West's sermon at the execution of Bly and Rose addressed the problem. "Human laws," he informed those assembled, "extend no further than to the external actions and conduct of men; or rather to the tempers and exercises of the heart, only as they *appear*." "No human tribunal," reminded another minister, "can investigate the secret emotions of the heart." Only "the knowledge of God extends to the secret motions and exercises of the heart," concluded Reverend West, who midway shifted the focus of his sermon from the issue of civic responsibility to the question of religious devotion.[37]

Most ministers had always been content to focus on appearance only, believing with West that God both determined and had full knowledge of the internal state of man. Others in the seventeenth and eighteenth centuries also considered outward appearance of greater importance than internal reality. Benjamin Franklin's memoir, for example, reminded the reader of the significance of maintaining appearances, whatever the reality. In the early nineteenth century this relationship of outer to inner, public to private, would be reversed. The true inner self, not appearance, now mattered; it was no longer sufficient that God had knowledge of the private self: man wanted it too. Uncertain, however, as to the best means for prying beneath appearances, and content to leave the private self to God, ministers in the early Republic continued to rely on the doomed criminal's sincere public performance of true penitence as a sign of salvation.

On execution day, ministers expected the prisoner to enact the drama of penitence and redemption. Condemned to die by civil authorities who believed they acted in accordance with divine precepts, criminals were encouraged and manipulated to recant publicly their sins and plead for the mercy of God. Clergy offered the "true penitence" of the prisoner as proof of the saving grace of God; the execution spectacle dangled before spectators eyes the journey "from the gallows to glory." In this way the ritual of execution served multiple purposes. The idea that the criminal "would this day be in heaven" made the hanging more palatable to some. Preachers also provided explicit lessons as to the characteristics of true repentance, characteristics that required citizens to adhere to a behavioral model not at all unlike the one demanded of them by the civil component of execution day. As a religious ceremony, the execution spectacle reminded spectators that they too must die. By likening the innocent spectator to the doomed criminal, ministers encouraged observers to begin repenting their own crimes against God and society.[38]

The ritual of execution day required that condemned prisoners demonstrate publicly that they were penitent, and execution sermons repeatedly pounded the chord of penitence. One minister excoriated the criminal: "We deplore your wretchedness! —Nothing consoles us but your penitence!" Spectators were drilled on the characteristics of true repentance and sincere conversion. Perez Fobes instructed those assembled to witness the hanging of John Dixon for burglary that the true penitent believed that he deserved to die, that he "had a painful and affecting sense of the intrinsic evil and baseness of his crime, as committed against God," and that the "pardoning mercy" of God would save him. Fobes warned that a "true repentance is never too late . . . but a late repentance is seldom true." He encouraged spectators to get on with the business of repudiating their own sins.[39]

In a sermon delivered at Haverhill, New Hampshire, prior to the hanging of Thomas Powers for rape, Noah Worcester summarized the religious meaning of the event:

We are convened this day to be spectators of a most solemn and affecting event, the launching of a moral vessel from the land of probation into the boundless ocean of eternity, and endless retribution *never to return*. And whether it will depart, freighted with the love of God, penitence, faith, and the joys of pardoning grace, as a vessel of mercy . . . or freighted with pride, impenitence, unbelief, and the guilt of unpardoned sin, as a vessel of wrath fitted to destruction, is, to us, a matter of dreadful uncertainty.[40]

If the civil component of execution day highlighted the temporal death of the criminal, the religious meaning of the event shifted the focus to the eternal life of the condemned. In this way the State presented itself as both punitive and benevolent, strictly punishing for the immediate benefit of society and even the everlasting welfare of the prisoner. So that the spectators might grasp this message completely, ministers urged the criminal to perform the role of the true penitent at the gallows. For observers, this was perhaps the most dramatic episode in the theater of executions. How would the prisoner act at the gallows? What sort of moral vessel would the criminal become?

In their "walk over the gloomy stage" of execution day, most prisoners seemed to have expressed their concern with true penitence. Bly and Rose warned that "in the high court of Heaven . . . pardons are not there granted to unrepenting sinners." Thomas Mount, hanged for burglary in Rhode Island, was possessed by a "desire to be truly penitent for [his] crimes, both against the law of God and the law of men." Robert Young's last words extended the drama of penitence to the crowd. He warned spectators "to forsake their evil way and seek the Lord . . . and not persist in those pernicious courses that will inevitably end in the destruction of their bodies and endanger their precious souls."[41]

Clergy who offered "some account of the prisoners in their Last Stage" usually confirmed for the crowd that a criminal's rhetoric matched reality. Ministers often described the successful conversion experience of the criminal in prison, sometimes with a boast that perhaps reflects a ministerial desire for recognition as much as concern over the prisoner's spiritual welfare. One criminal expressed his "thanks to all the ministers of this Town, who haved favored me with their assistance, in opening my blind Eyes, *as to a Future State*." These accounts attempted to convince spectators that the condemned "prayed . . . till they were turned off" and "spent all their time in reading the Bible." Several criminals were alleged to have been hanged "with a countenance that bespoke . . . inward peace." If, as some historians have argued, the position and authority of the clergy was slipping in the last half of the eighteenth century, execution day presented ministers with an opportunity to rekindle their reputations and re-establish their influence.[42]

On execution day, the prisoner was packaged as truly penitent, and in some cases the condemned undoubtedly behaved that way; most often, written sources ascribed to the prisoner the role of the sincere penitent. Of great interest are the few instances in which we find evidence that criminals failed to conform to the behavior expected of them. James Dana reminded Joseph Mountain that "since your confinement you have by no means given the best evidence of true contrition," and "your indifference to your state . . . hath astonished us." Similarly, Samuel Frost "showed few or no signs of penitence" at the gallows, despite the minister's warning to "be not then insensible, stupid, and hardened while the realities of eternity are . . . before you."[43]

Tantalizing as these fragments are, evidence of criminals refusing to act as they were expected to act is rare. And even when they did, the prisoner's dissent did not disrupt the proceedings. Ministers used the unremorseful criminal as an opportunity to fulminate on the dangers of impenitence. Some evidence suggests that, even when the criminal did not perform as desired, spectators who wanted to witness the apparent effects of grace interpreted the criminal's behavior as penitent. At the execution of Isaac Combs, an Indian, Joshua Spalding warned the convict that he did not seem "to be a true penitent," and yet another minister who observed the affair reported dutifully and formulaically in his diary that Combs appeared "sober & devout."[44]

Lest the drama of penitence be lost on the multitude assembled to witness the execution spectacle, ministers clarified the relationship of the criminal to the populace-at-large. Expressing the tension between public appearance and private reality, Perez Fobes warned that "the difference [between the criminal and the crowd] may consist only in this, that he is detected and condemned, but they as yet are concealed from human eye." Another minister asserted that "it is possible, yea probable, that there are some in this audience who are even more guilty than the prisoner; but their crimes are not yet detected . . . all *hope* to escape the hand of justice. But this hope is in vain; whether your crimes are known and punished on earth, or not: God knows every secret. . . . The day of Judgment will undeceive you." One minister put it most succinctly. "You are all sinners," he told the gathering at one execution. If sin belonged in common to the criminal and the crowd, then so too did the promise of salvation for the truly penitent. Ministers urged those assembled not

to delay until it was too late and they found themselves condemned to
die upon the gallows.[45]

By explicitly linking the crowds with the criminal, preachers tried to
persuade the spectators at executions to see themselves as participants in
the ceremony who were required to alter their ways. In this context authorities used hanging day as an opportunity to induce spectators to "be
afraid of sin, and a life of ungodliness." Ministers accomplished this by
emphasizing the imminence and horror of death, by transforming the execution spectacle into a civil day of judgment. Religious figures made it
clear that, while the state served as hangman, such action was taken with
the direct authority of God. If "the counsel of heaven determined that
such a prodigy of vice should no longer infest society," then what was
to prevent God, through the agency of the state, from reaching in and
taking the life of any of the spectators, each of whom was sinful?[46]

At a prescribed time and in a public manner, spectators at executions
knew they would witness ritualized death, and ministers warned them
what to expect. "Before this sun goes down," predicted one clergyman,
"his body, now vigorous and active, will be a lifeless ghastly corps[e],
coffined and buried, deep down among the sheeted dead." "Death is the
King of terrors," warned Joshua Spalding, "though viewed in his most
frequent and common forms, but to see one in health cut down in the
midst of life by the hand of justice, O how shocking! this fills the mind
with ideas that cannot be expressed. . . . He that is to suffer this day is
not the only one in the assembly under the sentence of death; for death
hath passed upon all, for all have sinned." Nathan Strong expressed it
even more tersely to the assembled: "Unless we repent, we shall all like-
wise perish."[47]

The icon of the truly penitent prisoner and the emphasis on mortality
meant that religious values could be placed alongside civic ones at the
core of the cultural order as conceived by community elites; ministerial
function and authority could be reaffirmed and reinforced; the focus of
execution day could be expanded from the pure temporality of civic concerns to the eternal realm of religious matters. Ministers claimed that,
the sooner citizens "realize their dependence on God," the less likely they
were to perish at the gallows or die at home, impenitent and doomed.
"The present occasion suggests a powerful motive to engage persons to
maintain family order and government, and to instill the principles of
religion and virtue into the minds of children . . . ," summarized one
minister, who went on to ask rhetorically, "if due restraint, instruction,
and government be neglected, what are we to expect but a general pro-

fligacy of manners and a rapid increase in *Publick Executions*?" At the
execution of Joseph Mountain, James Dana also dicussed the problem of
"incalculating morality": "It would be well, could we . . . prevail with
all by representing the reasonableness, excellence, and advantages of virtue, the turpitude and misery of vice. But we are compelled to persuade
men by the terror of future judgment, and future wrath."[48]

Ministers such as James Dana, who demanded obedience, terrorized
listeners, and preached as a spokesman for "the God of Order," marked
the persistence of seventeenth-century cultural forms. Employing traditional Puritan language, many Presbyterian and Congregationalist ministers in post-Revolutionary America seemed uninfluenced by the intellectual currents of their day. Even as Dana preached, some jurists and
philosophers advanced a new mode of inculcating morality, one based
not on the terror of death but on the reformation of life, not dependent
on public vengeance but instead intent on shaping private morality. Yet
execution sermons remind us that the cultural style of the early American
Republic was forged out of diverse materials. As a type, ministers like
Dana may have been at their height in the seventeenth century, but at
least on execution day, in the late eighteenth and early nineteenth century,
they recycled and refashioned phrases and arguments that still held enormous currency.

IV

Themes of civil and religious order permeated the ritual of execution day
in the early American Republic. But how did spectators receive the messages pitched at them in oral, printed, and dramatic form on hanging day?
The crowds at executions left faint tracks for the historian to follow. What
we can ascertain about spectator behavior emerges from sources provided
by self-interested parties. Eager for the execution to function as a celebration of order, local authorities reported that "the spectators who were
present at the gallows were silent and attentive," or that "all was solemn
and still and evinced that affectionate sympathy which so eminently char-
acterises the American people."[49]

Within these glossed accounts, however, lurk hints that the behavior
of those assembled at executions occasionally made authorities skittish.
A letter on the hanging of Bly and Rose reported that the crowd "behaved
with a *seeming* sensibility, *scarcely* a threat was uttered, or a murmur
heard, against government." At another execution one commentator reported overt dissent on the part of the assembly, a "considerable" number

of whom "manifested their doubts and dissatisfactions concerning the lawfulness of the intended execution." Unfortunately, the record is mute as to what these dissents entailed.[50]

Civil authorities may have anticipated resistance, but as far as we can tell, there were no attempts to rescue criminals at the gallows, no riots, no popular refusal to comply with the rites of execution day. If the message conveyed at the gallows violated the beliefs of the spectators, we have no evidence of it. Indeed, one of the few instances of recorded conflict between the community and authorities demonstrates that some citizens were insulted by what they viewed as the State's overzealous preparation for an execution. At the hanging of John Young for murder, an irate editor of a New York newspaper reported that "the order of the Executive for a large military force, to attend on this occasion, has given rise to a variety of reflections. It has been said that the city is disgraced by the supposition that any of its inhabitants could wish to [save] a murderer from punishment." To the editor, some of the people of New York believed that they shared the concern of the executive with civil obligations and religious duties; an excessive display of force violated republican tenets and might only provoke resistance where none was planned.[51]

The absence of conflict between spectators and the State might be explained by the biographical profile of gallows victims. Since the condemned was typically an outsider, a marginal, transient suspect, there was little basis for social ties and mutual obligations between the prisoner and any one segment of the population. There was no obvious constituency to challenge the probity of the hanging. Threats issued by Shaysites against the government should any of their men hang for high treason was the exception. The crowd at the execution of Bly and Rose behaved as it did precisely because of a large constituency of united dissenters, many of whom knew each other personally. Without such a context, the hanging of most prisoners provoked little conflict.

Shards of evidence indicate that spectators shared in the proceedings well enough to recapitulate the vocabulary of execution day in their diaries. William Bentley, Unitarian clergyman of the East Church at Salem, witnessed several executions, and all his accounts emphasize the behavior of the criminal. Bentley was a social leader, an established and influential minister who thought in terms similar to those expressed by his colleagues in execution sermons. At the hanging of Henry Blackburn on January 14, 1796, Bentley noted that the prisoner "behaved . . . with his usual insensibility but not with indecency." But another diary, written by an unknown Salem resident, recorded something quite different. The entry reads in part that "the Criminal behav'd at Church with the greatest seriousness and propriety, with his hands & Eyes lifted towards heaven—& when addressed by the Revd Mr. Fisher, he paid the strictest attention—on his way to the gallows—he express'd his firm hope & belief of his future happiness through the Redeemer . . . he died, a Sincere Penitent."[52]

The discrepancy between the two accounts reveals the differences between a privileged minister and a religious parishioner. Bentley knew that Blackburn was hardly penitent, that the criminal failed to fulfill one of the key expectations of the condemned. But the spectator, probably a respected member of Saint Peter's Church, interpreted the prisoner's not indecent attitude as sincere, penitential behavior. This was the thrust of Fisher's sermon on the morning of the execution, and this religious lesson about sin and salvation impressed itself on one spectator at the hanging. Many others undoubtedly carried with them different understandings and feelings about the event. Some must have expressed sympathy for the culprit. Others probably gave not a peep for magistrates, ministers, or criminals, choosing instead to enjoy a full day's outing.

Whatever the reaction of spectators, social authorities hoped the carefully designed ritual of execution day would effectively transmit those values they deemed necessary to the preservation of social order. A woodcut of the execution scene used to illustrate a broadside printed in 1788 contained all the components of the ceremony (Figure 1). The woodcut depicts church, state, criminal, and crowd. Atop the hill, toward town, the drawing portrays the church, symbolically and often geographically the center of the community. At the execution itself, the figure of an official on horseback dominates the scene. With a sword in his left hand he has just given the signal and the prisoner has been "turned off." A cart containing a coffin and hitched to a white horse stands ready to remove the body once it is cut down. Hooded and clothed in white robes trimmed with black, the prisoner's body has been enlisted in the spectacle of order. His dress demonstrated the power of the state and church to expose outwardly those who were judged inwardly evil. The crowd is portrayed as vast and orderly, the faces all sober and respectful. They have just been warned to fulfill their civil and religious obligations. They have just witnessed public justice, death, and what they believed to be redemption. Only the spectators are presented as full figures. The artist has them peer out from the woodcut, a reminder that the public execution is for the crowd, an image of a community united, a model of how the viewer is expected to behave.

Social authorities relied on the ritual of execution day to promote civil and religious order. But what if rather than encouraging virtue, hanging

FIGURE 1. Woodcut illustration of an execution scene from *The Last Words and Dying Speech of Elisha Thomas* (1788). (*Courtesy, American Antiquarian Society, Worcester, Mass.*)

day spread vice? What if rather than securing the republic and advancing morality, executions actually undermined government and retarded religion? What if criminals could be reformed? These questions emerged from the Revolutionary era and were posed throughout the 1780s and 1790s. Answers to them would help initiate nothing less than a transformation in the rites of punishment.

3

The Opposition to Capital Punishment in Post-Revolutionary America

> I am indeed surprised that capital punishment has not yet been totally abolished in this country. . . . Is there any need for such terrible punishments?
>
> BRISSOT DE WARVILLE, *New Travels in the United States* (1791)

In January 1793, Benjamin Rush joined a crowd of thousands near the Walnut Street Jail in Philadelphia to witness a public spectacle, the first balloon ascension in America. In a letter to a friend Rush described the affair as "truly sublime," and he marveled at how "every faculty of the mind was seized, expanded, and captivated. . . . 40,000 people concentrating their eyes and thoughts at the *same* instant, upon the *same* object, and all deriving nearly the *same* degrees of pleasure from it." The experience fulfilled for Rush the highest promise of public gatherings. Such spectacles educated, stimulated, and united a disparate group of people in social harmony and common interest. Such spectacles symbolized the progress and enlightenment of mankind. By comparison, public hangings posed the antithesis to the affair he had just witnessed. Executions polluted the sensibilities of spectators, destroyed social order, and violated republican and Christian values. Capital punishment, he believed, had no place in a new nation seeking the glory and destiny that was its due.[1]

Rush was one of many essayists who, following the American Revolution, launched an unprecedented assault on the death penalty. Through lectures, pamphlets, and personal correspondence these advocates of the revision of the criminal law commented repeatedly on the problem of punishment; others defended the death penalty with equal ardor. This was not the first time capital punishment had come under attack. Numerous Enlightenment figures had addressed themselves to the problem of severe punishments, and Americans undoubtedly participated in this transatlantic revolt against harsh penalties. The Enlightenment spirit alone, however, is too broad a concept to account for the opposition to capital punishment in America. The timing and content of the movement against the death penalty in the early Republic must be examined as a product of a social context shaped by the Revolution and an intellectual context governed by republican ideology and liberal theology.

I

Whatever the Enlightenment entailed, it certainly promoted the belief that man could change society and that societies were badly in need of alteration and amelioration. In the eighteenth century, reason seemed to illuminate more than revelation, and discoverable laws loomed more natural than inherited superstition. Philosophers tinkered with the machinery of society in the belief that they could get it to run better; the part having to do with crimes and punishments seemed to them especially decrepit.

It was Montesquieu who set the standard for an Enlightenment critique of the criminal law. In his *Persian Letters* (1721) and especially *The Spirit of Laws* (1748), Montesquieu argued against the severity of punishments. Extreme terror, he thought, violated the liberty of citizens. Since such severity characterized despotic governments, he thought excessive punishments especially unsuitable for republics. To Montesquieu, the distinction between crimes and their corresponding punishments should be "drawn from nature." He argued that to punish a thief as one would a murderer was to destroy any just proportion between crimes and punishments and encourage commission of the greater rather than lesser offense.[2]

Following Montesquieu's lead, philosophers everywhere condemned the abuses and irregularities of the penal law. The *Encyclopédie* (1751–65) included a plea for reform. Voltaire, incensed over the torture of Jean Calas, whom authorities accused of having murdered his own son, cast his formidable fame on the side of humanity. And in Milan, Cesare Beccaria, cribbing from Montesquieu, Diderot, D'Alembert, Helvetius, and Hume produced the consumate Enlightenment tract on the subject, *An Essay on Crimes and Punishments*.[3]

A marquis's son, and a descendent of prominent religious and civil figures, Beccaria had undoubtedly been expected to make something of his life. His early training at a Jesuit College in Parma, however, left him passionless for learning. He returned to Milan in his early twenties, and there, the story has it, he read Montesquieu's *Persian Letters* and embraced the social philosophy of the Enlightenment. Beccaria studied law and joined a group that gathered regularly to discuss philosophy, literature, and society. Beccaria's *An Essay on Crimes and Punishments* grew out of these meetings. The work served as Beccaria's introduction to the world of continental intellectuals, and it quickly became the most frequently cited text in discussions of the need for criminal reform.[4]

Dei Delitti e delle Pene was first published in 1764, and translations of Beccaria's essay circulated soon thereafter. The first English edition appeared in London in 1767, and additional editions were advertised in New York in 1773, published in Charlestown in 1777, and in Philadelphia in 1778. In the 1780s most catalogues of books for sale in America included an edition of Beccaria's essay, and newspapers such as the *New-Haven Gazette and Connecticut Magazine* serialized Beccaria for their readers.[5]

The availability of Beccaria's essay in America made it a useful source in discussions about crimes and punishments. For example, commencement day exercises at Yale in 1788 included a forensic disputation on "whether capital punishment was in any case lawful." Jeremiah Mason, one of the participants in that debate, later confessed to his diary, "I stole most of my arguments from the treatise of Marquis Beccaria, then little known in this country." Had the student realized that just two years earlier a local newspaper had serialized Beccaria's essay he might have been less zealous in his plagiarism. Familiar or not, Mason felt his oration succeeded because the argument "was new, and consequently well received by the audience; indeed, its novelty excited considerable notice."[6]

Although the Yale undergraduate probably exaggerated the reaction of his audience to Beccaria's ideas, *An Essay on Crimes and Punishments* did provide a forceful summary statement of one school of eighteenth-century penal theory. At the center of Beccaria's treatise was an analysis of the objects of punishment and a discussion of how best to achieve them. Beccaria argued that punishment must preserve the bond of society and deter crime. "The end of punishment is no other," he asserted, "than to prevent the criminal from doing further injury to society, and to prevent others from committing the like offense." In one stroke, Beccaria had tried to eliminate justifications of punishments based on vengeance, and instead install deterrence at the core of penal philosophy. The jurist insisted that only a system of rational punishment based on certainty rather than severity, one which rendered punishments proportional to crimes, could accomplish these goals. Beccaria opposed excessive punishments such as torture because he believed that no punishment could undo a crime already committed, and that severity alone failed to serve for long as a deterrent.[7]

While several eighteenth-century jurists and philosophers would readily have concurred with these principles, Beccaria's critique of capital punishment separated him from the likes of Rousseau or Montesquieu. To begin with, the death penalty, according to Beccaria, violated the terms of the social contract. Although citizens relinquished a portion of their liberty in forming the contract, Beccaria asserted that no one ever gave to any other the right to take away life. Furthermore, capital punishment undermined the objects of punishment as he saw them. The jurist declared the death penalty did not act as a deterrent; public executions, he argued, provided only a "momentary spectacle" and were therefore a "less efficacious method of deterring others than the continued example of a man deprived of his liberty." If the purpose of punishment was to prevent crime, then the severity needed to accomplish this end, and that much alone, could be justified. For Beccaria, the death penalty was an excessive and yet inadequate shield to society. He proposed "perpetual slavery"—lifetime imprisonment—as a more effective deterrent because it was a more horrifying punishment than death for the spectator to contemplate.[8]

Beccaria's essay served as an extremely important and influential application of certain Enlightenment principles—balance, proportion, benevolence—to the problem of criminal jurisprudence. When in 1789 Leopold, the Grand Duke of Tuscany, created a penal code that abolished capital punishment entirely, he took his lead from Beccaria. In the United States as well, essayists paraphrased the jurist's principle of certainty rather than severity in punishments.[9] No less a figure than Thomas Jefferson credited Beccaria with awakening the world to the unnecessary severity of capital punishment. In 1807 a correspondent solicited from Jefferson a list of works essential to an understanding of the "organization of society into civil government." For a man whose library exceeded 6500 volumes and who shared in the creation of a new political order, the President most likely found the request amusing. He responded that "the subject . . . would require time and space for even moderate development. My occupations limit me to a very short notice of them." Jefferson mentioned Locke, Sidney, Priestley, Chipman, and the *Federalist Papers*. The only other name he included was Cesare Beccaria on crimes and punishments "because of the demonstrative manner in which he had treated that branch of the subject." Fourteen years later, in writing his memoir, Jefferson again had occasion to recall Beccaria who "had satisfied the reasonable world of the unrightfulness and inefficiency of the punishment of crimes by death." In issuing this encomium for Beccaria, Jefferson must have thought back nearly fifty years to when Beccaria's essay first became popular, and when Jefferson, as a member of the committee to revise the laws of Virginia, prepared a bill for proportioning crimes and punishments.[10]

Jefferson's opinion of Beccaria was a sincere one, but his recollections in 1821, coming at a time when many of the reforms first proposed in the 1780s had been realized, undoubtedly inflated the influence of the dead jurist. Beccaria's essay alone did not induce educated elites in America to oppose capital punishment following the Revolution. When, in the 1780s, colleges such as Yale and Princeton began for the first time to debate the place of capital punishment in society, they were not led to do so because of any single Enlightenment tract. No matter how powerful, books do not create their audience; readers create books. Essayists already concerned with the problem of punishment in America used Beccaria's treatise in the same manner as Jeremiah Mason had, as a sourcebook for arguments against the death penalty. More important, a republican, religious language unlike anything in Beccaria permeated discussions of crime and punishment in America. For theorists in the United States, the reformation of the criminal, and not vengeance or deterrence, served as the principal end of punishment. Although some colonists expressed their dismay with excessive punishments prior to the break from Great Britain, Americans became acutely sensitized to the issue of the gallows in the context of the Revolution and the opportunity it provided to design a new polity. Only after the Revolution did a debate over capital punishment emerge; only after the Revolution did legislatures revise the criminal law and authorize construction of new penal institutions. The experience of the Revolution and the problem of how to make punishments consistent with the objects of republican, Christian institutions sparked the initial opposition to the death penalty in the early Republic.

II

The decision to fight for independence meant treason, and most colonists knew it. The rebels, according to some British officers, would at last earn one of the rights of Englishmen—death by hanging. General Gage's proclamation of June 12, 1775, offered pardon to those who would lay down their arms; those who would not, especially patriot leaders such as John Hancock and Sam Adams, would face the gallows. One widely published poem lampooning "Tom Gage's Proclamation" summarized the document as "threatening devastation,/ And speedy jugulation,/ of the New England nation."[11]

Patriots did not accept the potential consequences of treason lightly. One diarist noted that in 1775 his friends offered him little encouragement to oppose Great Britain. "As this is a civil war," they forewarned, "if I should fall into the hands of the British the gallows will be my fate. The terrors of the gallows are not to be conquered, but I must indulge the hope that I may escape it." James Thacher did escape the gallows, and his military journal is one of the most complete to survive the Revolutionary War. In it he recounts an event which he is "credibly informed" occurred on the day the Declaration was signed: "Mr. Harrison, a delegate from Virginia, is a large portly man—Mr. Gerry of Massachusetts is slender and spare. A little time after the solemn transaction of signing the instrument, Mr. Harrison said smilingly to Mr. Gerry, 'When the hanging scene comes to be exhibited I shall have the advantage over you on account of my size. All will be over with me in a moment, but you will be kicking in the air a half hour after I am gone.' "[12]

Thacher's two anecdotes suggest a relationship between the Revolution and a rising preoccupation with executions. This concern over the gallows should not be mistaken for an opposition to the death penalty; such a critique would not emerge until after the war. But the anxiety over executions and the perception of British behavior during the Revolutionary conflict sensitized Americans to the issue of capital punishment.

Throughout the Revolutionary War, patriots condemned the British for barbaric behavior. In part this was an expression of the rhetoric evident in any conflict; the patriots were no less savage according to the British. But many Americans believed in "the barbarity of our oppressors" and were horrified at repeated examples of "inhuman and worse than savage cruelty" by the British. By comparison, Americans viewed themselves as benevolent and humane in war and, by extension, in peace. These perceptions thrived well into the post-Revolutionary decades and resonated in the debate over the place of the gallows in American society.[13]

In the summer of 1777, Abigail Adams summarized her feelings about the British in a letter to Mercy Otis Warren. "The history and the Events of the present day," Adams lamented, "must fill every Human Breast with Horrour. Every week produces some Horrid Scene perpetrated by our Barbarous foes. Not content with a uniform Series of cruelties practised by their own Hands, but they must let loose the infernal savages, those 'dogs of warr,' and cry Havock to them." As Americans such as Adams viewed it, there were many examples of British barbarity from which to choose. As early as April 1777 a committee appointed by Congress reported its findings on the conduct of British soldiers and found "wanton and oppressive devastation of the country, and destruction of property . . . the inhuman treatment of those who were so unfortunate as to become prisoners . . . the savage butchery of those who had submitted and were incapable of resistance, . . . the lust and brutality of the soldiers in abusing women." In particular, one episode late in the war outraged many Americans and injected the issue of the death penalty into public discourse: the hanging of Joshua Huddy in New Jersey on April 12, 1782.[14]

Throughout the war, the exploits of the Associated Loyalists terrorized patriots in New Jersey. The Board of Directors of Associated Loyalists, founded in 1780 and headed by William Franklin, authorized guerrilla warfare throughout the Mid-Atlantic States. Patriots had formed their own group, the Monmouth Retaliators, and the war within a war that ensued became particularly ferocious. Over one hundred residents from Essex County, New Jersey, petitioned the General Assembly for relief from Loyalist raids. The language they used demonstrates that they had learned the rhetorical code well. They pleaded for liberation from "the power of the most Inhuman and more than Savage Barbarity, practised by our Enemies."[15]

A group of these refugees, as the loyalists were also known, captured Joshua Huddy, an artillery captain in the militia, during an attack on the blockhead located on Toms River. Huddy was imprisoned on a sloop in New York Harbor when he learned that loyalists planned to execute him in retaliation for the murder of Phillip White, a refugee. Little is known about White except that patriots captured him in Monmouth the same week loyalists grabbed Huddy, and that, on the way to Freehold, patriot retaliators brutally executed their prisoner. Sometime on April 12, 1782, a party of loyalists headed by Captain Richard Lippincott took Huddy to Sandy Hook in Monmouth County, where they hanged him in vengeance for the "Cruel murders of our Brethren."[16]

The reactions to the Huddy execution reveal a disgust with what some Americans perceived as the cruel and inhuman actions of the British. One of Thomas Paine's Crisis Letters, addressed to Sir Guy Carleton, claimed that "as far as our knowledge goes there is not a more detestable character, nor a meaner or more barbarous enemy than the present British one. . . . [The execution] is an original in the history of civilized barbarians, and is truly British." The words "truly British" in this context illuminate one of the ways by which some patriots began to distinguish themselves from their enemies. The British, defined as those who did not join the Revolution, were portrayed as debased and barbarous. Americans, however, viewed themselves as the virtuous and humane citizens of a new nation.[17]

The events that followed the Huddy execution confirmed this belief for Americans. Washington asked the general and field officers, "Is retaliation justifiable and expedient?" Washington himself believed that "this instance of Barbarity . . . calls loudly for Retaliation," and he labeled Huddy's execution "the most wanton, unprecedented and unhuman Murder that ever disgraced the arms of a civilized people." The officers decided to retaliate and chose by lot a British officer of equal rank for execution. General Hazen reported that Captain Charles Asgill was selected and described him as "a young Gentleman of seventeen Years of Age; a most amiable character; the only Sone of Sir Charles Asgill, Baronet; Heir to an extensive Fortune; an honourable Title; and of course he has great interest in the British Court and Armies."[18]

For a time it looked as if Asgill would suffer death. When a British court-martial acquitted Captain Richard Lippincott, who actually hanged Huddy, patriot tempers boiled over. If patriots executed Asgill, Americans believed they would not bear responsibility for his death; this too, they rationalized, would result from British inhumanity. Paine's letter to Carleton made the point clearly. "Captain Asgill, in the present case, is not the guilty man," explained Common Sense. "The villain and the victim are here separated characters. You hold the one and we hold the other. You disown or effect to disown and reprobate the conduct of Lippincott, yet you give him sanctuary; and by so doing you as effectually become the executioner of Asgill, as if you put the rope round his neck and dismissed him from this world."[19]

The selection of Asgill, however, created a number of problems. Not only was he descended from a well-connected gentry family, but the articles of surrender signed at Yorktown, where he was captured, protected him against reprisal. The negotiations over Asgill continued throughout the summer and into the fall of 1782, when Congress, at the recommendation of Washington, decided finally to release him.

In a Crisis Letter published in 1778, Common Sense observed that "the humanity of America hath hitherto restrained her from acts of retaliation." Asgill's liberation pleased some Americans, for it demonstrated to them that this principle still operated. They interpreted his release as illustrating the "benevolent and humane" nature of Washington and, by extension, of Americans. One soldier regretted the failure to avenge Huddy's execution, but accepted Washington's "benevolent feelings" as the reason why.[20]

A remarkable exchange of letters between Alexander Hamilton and Henry Knox in the midst of the Asgill affair encapsulated many of the issues raised by the contemplated execution. Hamilton wrote that the proceedings against Asgill "if persisted in will be derogatory to the national character . . .":

> A sacrifice of this sort is entirely repugnant to the genius of the age we live in and is without example in modern history nor can it fail to be considered in Europe as wanton and unnecessary. . . . [S]o Solemn and deliberate a sacrifice of the innocent for the guilty must be condemned on the present received notions of humanity, and encourage an opinion that we are in a certain degree in a state or barbarism. . . .[21]

"My sentiments on frequent executions at this or any other period," Knox responded, "are very similar to yours. I am persuaded that after reflexions will convince dispassionate and enlightened minds that executions have been too frequent, under the color of the Laws of the different states and they hereafter will be recited to sully the purity of our cause."[22]

Both Hamilton and Knox tried as they could to justify the many executions committed by American forces, a feat that became increasingly difficult, but not impossible, while also maintaining a faith in the "purity" of the patriot cause. In actuality, patriots executed offenders as frequently and as barbarously as their enemies. Washington believed firmly in the death penalty as a deterrent and a means necessary to preserve order and discipline. An "unnatural war," he claimed, often resulted in excessive acts. Under Washington's orders scores of men from both the continental and British armies faced the gallows. Although the general expressed his regret at authorizing a retaliatory execution, he released Asgill ultimately not as a result of American humanity but because the French intervened on behalf of his "rank, fortune, and connection."[23]

Neither Hamilton nor Knox, for that matter, condemned capital punishment in principle. In the Asgill case they opposed the execution of an innocent person which, if realized, would stain Washington's reputation and disturb their sense of a humane national character. A critique of the death penalty per se did not arise during the revolution. But events such as the Huddy and Asgill affair helped inject a set of dichotomous terms into national discourse—patriot humanity versus loyalist barbarity, American benevolence versus British cruelty—which fused with a republican preoccupation over the moral constitution of Americans and helped shape the argument against the excessive use of capital punishment.

The portrayal of American humanity was but one of the ways the war molded attitudes toward the death penalty. The Revolution directed attention to the problems of crime and punishment in another, more direct way as well. It is a truism that wars are generally accompanied by an increase in criminal activity. Courts, as traditional mechanisms for preserving order and prosecuting criminals, break down amidst armed conflict; soldiers, notorious for stretching the limits of military necessity, plunder as they can. It was no coincidence, troubled legislators remarked, that a majority of those executed after the war had served as soldiers previously. Authorities believed that following the Revolution they faced not only the task of forming a republic but also an unprecedented crime wave that the legal system could not control.[24]

There is some evidence to suggest that legislators confronted an actual crisis in the criminal justice system that hampered their ability to contain crime. In post-Revolutionary Virginia, for example, one-third of those prisoners examined at the county level for felony were discharged, and one-third of those tried were acquitted. Also, through downgraded indictments many defendants managed to escape the ultimate penalty of the law. It is difficult to establish with complete certainty whether there was indeed an actual rise in criminal activity and a simultaneous decline in the efficiency of the criminal justice system. But whatever the social reality, Americans in post-Revolutionary America believed that criminal activity raged out of control. In 1784, one observer offered his impression that "scarce a morning arrives, but we hear of some house or store having been broken open the past night. . . . It must give every man of fealing the most sensible pain, when he observes how insufficient our penal laws are to answer the end [for which] they were designed." This social perception of crime on the loose intensified the desire to restructure the criminal justice system.[25]

The notoriety of bandits such as Thomas Mount heightened the concern with crime. Mount belonged to the Flash Company, an organized band of highwaymen who spoke in slang—the Flash language—and swore allegiance only to one another. In 1791, one minister warned that this "gang of plunderers has infested the United States ever since the late-war." Although not much is known about the Flash Company as organized bandits, Thomas Mount's confession sheds light on the activities of one member. Mount was born in East Jersey in 1764. In 1775, with war breaking out, he left his parents to enlist in the patriot cause. During the war, Mount served with various militia companies and with the Continental army. He deserted at Valley Forge and joined the British only to return to the American army after he broke open a supply store. He traveled about, cheating captains of advanced enlistment pay and, while staying with one regiment, stealing watches, leather, corduroy, stockings, linen, and whatever else he could get his hands on. Tried for desertion, a military court sentenced him to receive five hundred lashes, but he escaped from the guard house before execution of sentence.[26]

After the war, Mount devoted himself to stealing. He criss-crossed the northeastern United States, traveling from Philadelphia to New York to Boston and back again. At one point, he was caught and given "100 lashes for theft and 25 for giving the court saucy answers." Sometimes with companions and sometimes alone, Mount preyed on citizens of the Republic for years, until he one day found himself in Newport. He broke into a store, stole $700 worth of goods, and was captured and sentenced to death. As he had so easily managed numerous times before, he tried to escape twice and failed narrowly both times. Newspapers described Mount as "the most hardened villain that ever disgraced a gaol." Admonished to reform his ways, Mount was reported to reply, "No, no that is impossible. Tommy Mount must be hung for a thief." On May 27, 1791, authorities in Little Rest granted Mount his wish and sent him dangling to a desired death. In Flash Company language he was "topped for cracking a ken" (hanged for robbing a house). One newspaper suggested that "an excessive and ungovernable levity of mind" characterized the prisoner even in his final days, but the formulized last speech and dying words portrayed him as truly penitent and sorrowful.[27]

The actions of the Flash Company, seemingly undiminished by the fate of some of its members, reinforced fears that the fragile but glorious experiment in republican government might be destroyed not by foreign powers but by domestic crimes. The apparent rise in criminal prosecutions, according to one minister, "evidences a corruption of morals, and growth in wickedness, and gives reason to fear that capital punishment will be multiplied." This nervousness over what seemed like rampant criminal activity lent additional urgency to discussions of the problem of crime and punishment in post-Revolutionary America. Perhaps executions did not prevent crime after all. Perhaps public hangings would only hasten the downfall of the Republic. If so, the salvation of the Republic hinged on implementing punishments alternative to death.[28]

The necessity of creating republican institutions, one of the central issues confronting Americans in the last quarter of the eighteenth century, also forced a reconsideration of the place of capital punishment in society. Patriot leaders feared the frailty of republican governments, and the social perception of crime on the loose only deepened these anxieties. Republican political forms decentralized power while maximizing liberty. As a result, the threat of destruction from within, through faction, or without, by invasion, was great. Republics, theorists believed, became prone to disorder and licentiousness. Their survival seemed to depend upon the people, who were expected to display a particular set of moral and social values. These centered on the idea of virtue, the linchpin of republicanism.[29] "Public virtue," John Adams declared, "is the only Foundation of Republics." By public virtue Adams meant the sacrifice of private interests for the common good. Virtue entailed combating vice, licentiousness, and extravagance, corrosive forces in a republic, by a "firm adherence to justice, moderation, temperance, industry, and frugality."[30]

The language of a republican moral code could be found everywhere in post-Revolutionary America. Republican ideology did not originate with Americans. It had its roots in Florentine civic humanism and English Commonwealth ideology before eager colonists transformed it and used it to help fashion a new political universe. Nor did everyone share the republican vision. Early national ideology was a diverse lot, filled with arguments the terms of which were not always agreed upon. At the very moment some Americans earnestly invoked republican ideals, others offered inchoate defenses of self-interest and ambition, traits antithetical to a republican world view. Cracks in the republican edifice, however, served only to intensify the desire to create institutions consistent with republican values.

Americans who attempted to reconcile republican ideology with the problem of punishment faced some difficult questions. How could they venerate virtue and dread vice, yet cope with crime? How could they, as members of a supposedly benevolent and humane Republic, punish criminals? How could those labeled vicious be transformed into the virtuous without violating republican ideals? One issue seemed clear: if severe and excessive punishments marked monarchies, mild and benevolent ones would have to characterize republics. The logic of republicanism forced some Americans to reconsider the problem of deviance and to oppose capital punishment as unrepublican. In the mid-eighteenth century, a transatlantic reformulation of ideas about the purposes of punishment had already initiated a re-evaluation of the place of the gallows in society. But the experience of the Revolution and the dilemma of republicanism created an urgency in America that structured the timing and content of that debate as it took shape following the war.

III

In the Revolutionary era, a diverse group of Americans considered the death penalty morally and politically repugnant. Radicals such as George Logan, the Jeffersonian Republican congressman from Philadelphia, and conservatives such as William Bradford, the Federalist attorney general under Washington, opposed capital punishment. Other prominent Americans, although not initially desiring the total abolition of the death penalty, favored some revision of the laws for which prisoners could be executed. Thomas Jefferson, early in the Revolutionary struggle, drafted a bill for the Virginia legislature that eliminated the death penalty for all crimes except murder and treason. Benjamin Franklin asked, "Is it not murder . . . to put a man to death for an offence which does not deserve death?" As Governor of New York, John Jay urged the legislature to revise the penal laws of the state. James Madison also supported reform. When in 1790 Rush sent Madison a pamphlet that advocated the abandonment of the gallows in favor of new punishments that reformed criminals, Madison responded that he had been "for a considerable time a firm believer" in such a doctrine. Above all others, it was Rush, the most influential physician in America, a signer of the Declaration, and a prolific essayist, who devoted the largest portion of his enormous energies to what had become the problem of capital punishment. Primarily through his writings we can track the contours of the argument against the death penalty in the early Republic.[31]

In the 1780s and 1790s Benjamin Rush ignited public debate over capital punishment and sparked agitation for the amelioration of Pennsylvania's penal code. Despite these achievements, in his own time, his reputation suffered. A zealous patriot who happened to suggest the title for Thomas Paine's *Common Sense,* Rush also alienated many by his opposition to Pennsylvania's Constitution and his criticism of Washington's capabilities as a military commander. Rush was also at the center of a bitter, vituperative controversy over the origins and treatment of yellow fever. The causes of the epidemic, the physician insisted, were domestic, and the best treatment, he argued, consisted of bloodletting and purging. In 1793, and again in 1797, while those who could afford to flee to the healthier environment of the countryside did so, Rush remained in Philadelphia to care for the dying. He lost a great many patients and was reviled publicly for his views. Although he won a lawsuit against William Cobbett, his most notorious antagonist, Rush felt the need to defend his actions for the rest of his life.

In 1800, Rush began to write an autobiography for his family in order to exculpate himself from the accusations of the previous decade. He titled it "Travels Through Life," and by that he meant more the journey of the mind than the wanderings of the body. Unlike other major figures of the Revolutionary period who skitted about America and Europe, Rush lived in Philadelphia from 1769 until his death in 1813. He had seen

Edinburgh, London, and Paris as a medical student and was thereafter quite content to devote himself to his patients, students, and writings. But rather than the serene career of a respected professor and eminent physician, Rush led the turbulent life of an activist who had a vision of an ordered, moral society which he was determined to help secure for the new American Republic.[32]

Rush's non-medical writings included essays on temperance, slave-holding, insanity, public schools, and female education. Along with the death penalty, these topics constituted, for him, the most important social and moral questions of the day. As a prominent citizen of Philadelphia, Rush had little difficulty in gaining a hearing for his ideas. His thoughts on public punishments and the death penalty were delivered orally before the Society for Promoting Political Enquiries, published in the *American Museum,* and printed separately as pamphlets. Articles on this topic by other writers, many of them published anonymously, appeared as well in the literary magazines of the day.[33]

Rush's ideas on capital punishment were familiar to many Americans. As a synthesizer, Rush gathered every argument against capital punishment he could unearth, and this certainly included Beccaria's axiom that certainty, not severity, should characterize punishments. Rush cited Beccaria as an authority to support the connection between the abolition of capital punishment and the "order and happiness" of society. Like Beccaria, Rush insisted that capital punishment did not serve as a deterrent. But whereas Beccaria reasoned from utilitarian concerns, Rush based his arguments on political and moral grounds. Deterrence mattered far less to him than the reformation of the criminal. For Rush, republican ideology and liberal theology served as the essential starting points in developing an incontrovertible argument for the abolition of the death penalty.[34]

Rush's introduction to classical republicanism and Commonwealth ideology came early in life. His studies as a medical student in Edinburgh between 1766 and 1768 exposed him to the ideas and philosophers of the Scottish Enlightenment. On a tour of the continent in 1769, the young physician befriended Catherine Macauley, James Burgh, and other prominent Whigs. His experience in Scotland, Rush recalled in his autobiography, led him to adopt republican principles. The evolution of the "republican ferment" in America inspired him to challenge errors not only in government but in "medicine, . . . education, penal laws, and capital punishments."[35]

"When I speak of a republic," Rush informed John Adams, "I mean a government consisting *of three* branches, and each derived at different

times and for different periods from the PEOPLE." Once the structure of
government has been altered, once monarchy was abolished, other changes
would necessarily ensue. This was the meaning of Rush's often quoted
observation that "we have changed our forms of government, but it remains yet to effect a revolution in our principles, opinions, and manners
so as to accommodate them to the forms of government we have adopted."[36]
Republicanism was defined in opposition to monarchy, but the differences were far greater than simply between modes of government. A new
political structure necessitated the creation of a parallel cultural frame-
work; a revolution in American social institutions would follow the one
in political organization. "Our republican forms of government," Rush
predicted in the midst of the Revolutionary conflict, "will in time beget
republican opinions and manners."[37]

If government and culture were related, American must purify society
of foreign influence. The preface to the laws for the Society for Promoting Political Enquiries, a group that gathered at Franklin's house in
Philadelphia and before which Rush delivered his assault on public punishments, observed, "We have grafted on an Infant Commonwealth, the
Manners of ancient and corrupted Monarchies." Rush, like many other
patriots, associated monarchy and aristocracy with the disintegration of
ideas, affections, manners, morals, and language in America. "Monarchy
is a public and practical Lye," Rush delcared, "Republicanism is the re-
verse of this." For this reason there would be no medium between pure
republicanism and absolute monarchy, for one contained "the *living* principle of liberty" and the other "the *deadly* principle of tyranny."[38]

Monarchies relish titles, Rush observed, whereas republics reject them;
monarchies sustain servile relationships, but republics establish egalitarian ones; monarchies rely on capital punishment to preserve order while
republics must abolish the death penalty or face disorder. Every execution
undermined the vitality and security of America by drawing the Republic
back toward monarchical institutions and away from republican virtue.
To Rush, humanity was the foundation of virtue; in its inhumanity the
death penalty eroded virtue without which the American Republic would
fall.[39]

In Rush's mind there was reason for concern about the virtue of the
people. The defeats suffered early in the war suggested to him in 1776
that "we have overrated the public virtue of our country." Twelve years
later, in defending the newly drafted Constitution, Rush lamented that the
"present moral character" of Americans demonstrated "too plainly that
the people are as much disposed to vice as their rulers." What was needed
was a "vigorous and efficient government . . . that establishes justice,

insures order, cherishes virtue, secures property, and protects from every species of violence." But this experiment in government and society, frightfully tenuous as it was, could never succeed as long as it retained the gallows, a device antithetical to the principles and goals of a republican nation.[40]

In a single passage first published in 1792, Rush brought together his ideas about the origins of capital punishment:

> Capital punishments are the natural offspring of monarchical governments. Kings believe that they possess their crowns by a *divine* right; no wonder, therefore, they assume the divine power of taking away human life. Kings consider their subjects as their property; no wonder, therefore, they shed their blood with as little emotion as men shed the blood of their sheep or cattle. But the principles of republican governments speak a very different language. They teach us the absurdity of the divine origin of kingly power. . . . They appreciate human life, and increase public and private obligations to preserve it. They consider human sacrifices as no less offensive to the sovereignty of the people, than they are to the majesty of heaven. . . . The united states have adopted these peaceful and benevolent forms of government. It becomes them therefore to adopt their mild and benevolent principles. An execution in a republic is like a human sacrifice in religion. It is an offering to monarchy, and to that malignant being, who has been stiled a murderer from the beginning, and who delights equally in murder, whether it be perpetrated by the cold, but vindictive arm of the law, or by the angry hand of private revenge.[41]

To cleanse America of the polluting influence of its colonial experience, and to perfect the republican experiment, every state would have to abolish the death penalty and create a system of punishment consistent with republican values.

Anxiety over the fragility of the American Republic was exacerbated by the French Revolution, which also illustrated the relationship between forms of government and punishment, but carried the connection a dramatic step further. In his rejoinder to Edmund Burke's denunciation of the French Revolution, Thomas Paine felt compelled to explain why citizens severed the heads of government officials, stuck them through spikes, and paraded with them through Paris. "They learn it from the governments they live under," observed Paine, "and retaliate the punishments they have been accustomed to behold. . . . It may perhaps be said, that it signifies nothing to a man what is done to him after he is dead; but it signifies much to the living. It either tortures their feelings, or it hardens their hearts; and in either case, it instructs them how to punish when power falls into their hands. Lay then the axe at the root, and teach gov-

ernments humanity. It is their sanguinary punishments which corrupt
mankind." The lesson was clear; when the people arose they would punish as they had been punished. Paine's argument warned rulers what to
expect should the people rebel and emphasized that public executions
taught behavior that was antithetical to republican morality.[42]

Republican ideals raised questions about capital punishment that could
lead to the abolition of the gallows. Indeed, the opposition to capital punishment would have stood no chance at all if it could not be justified on
republican grounds. Yet however compelling the republican logic to abolish the death penalty, republican ideals could also justify preserving the
gallows. Recall Sam Adams's edict that "the man who dares to rebel
against the laws of a republic ought to suffer death." Adams undoubtedly
had in mind the traditional frailty and instability of republican politics, a
volatile situation that he thought necessitated the death penalty if order
were to be maintained. Both Rush and Adams feared a crisis of social
order in the early Republic. But in each case, republican beliefs led to
different conclusions on the subject of the necessity of capital punishment.

IV

Republican ideology provided some of the key moral phrases spoken by
Americans in the last half of the eighteenth century. Equally influential
was the vocabulary furnished by religious beliefs. However secular we
sometimes imagine Revolutionary Americans to have been, many patriots
believed that a liberal theology would help to sustain the Republic. The
new institutions of punishment would have to be consonant not only with
republican ideals but with Christian precepts as well.

Americans extolled the connection between republican ideology and
Christian theology. Indeed, one of the virtues of republican government
was that it appeared "more calculated to promote Christianity than monarchies." Rush declared that "all *monarchy* is *antichristian.*" But "republican forms of government are the best repositories of the Gospel,"
he told one Universalist minister. "I have always considered Christianity
as the *strong ground* of republicanism," Rush informed Jefferson, "the
spirit is opposed, not only to the splendor, but even to the very forms of
monarchy, and many of its precepts have for their objects republican liberty and equality as well as simplicity, integrity, and economy in government. It is only necessary for republicanism to ally itself with the
Christian religion to overturn all the corrupted political and religious institutions in the world."[43]

The application of the gospel would perfect republican institutions and complete the Revolution initiated by rebellion from Great Britain. Rush believed it was the "Spirit of the Gospel (though unacknowledged) which is now rooting monarchy out of the world." If the obligation of Christianity was to "promote repentance, forgive injuries, and discharge the duties of universal benevolence," then capital punishment, which contradicted these precepts, must be eradicated. "A belief in God's universal love to all his creatures, and that he will finally restore all those of them that are miserable to happiness," Rush insisted, "is a *polar* truth . . . it establishes the *equality* of mankind—it abolishes the punishment of death for any crime—and converts jails into houses of repentance and reformation." In an attempt to awaken Americans to this "truth," Rush and the other writers who opposed capital punishment for all crimes including murder assailed the scriptural interpretation adduced in defense of the death penalty.[44]

Rush argued that "a religion which commands us to forgive and even to do good to our enemies, can never authorise the punishment of murder by death," and he offered an interpretation of divine revelation in order to prove his claim. The precept given to Noah in Genesis 9:6 posed the greatest challenge to the opponents of capital punishment. "Whoso sheddeth man's blood, by man shall his blood be shed" was a familiar verse invoked frequently on execution day. For most ministers it offered irrefutable evidence that divine law provided civil law with the authority to execute criminals; that only by hanging the murderer was God's will obeyed.[45]

Rush assaulted the logic of this position. Noah's command was no more an authority for capital punishment than "drinking is a precedent for drunkenness." To begin with, the meaning of Genesis 9:6 hinged on a question of interpretation. Rush argued that "it is rather a *prediction,* than a law." Rush insisted that the precept was not a command to be followed by humans but an expression of what would occur, in the same mode as "He that taketh up the sword, shall perish by the sword." Furthermore, it was sacrilegious for legislators to elevate human institutions by believing that they shared with God the right to punish by death. Such a usurpation of God's prerogative, Rush thought, must cease. Rush declared that any solitary scriptural text could be used to support any opinion, no matter how absurd. He prayed that, instead, man be governed by the whole spirit of the gospel. That spirit was encapsulated by the declaration "The Son of Man came not to *destroy* men's lives, but to *save* them." "I will not believe an angel from heaven," Rush asserted, "should he declare that the punishment of death for any crime was inculcated, or permitted by the spirit of the gospel."[46]

The writers who opposed capital punishment also had to contend with the Mosaic code, which advanced the principle of retaliation and authorized the death penalty for numerous offenses. Rush rebuked the Mosaic laws as designed for an ignorant, wicked people and looked toward the "triumph of truth and Christianity over ignorance and Judaism." He further argued that if a portion of the Mosaic law applied to American society, all of it did. It followed then that adultery, blasphemy, idolatry, Sabbath-breaking, and the abuse of parents must be punished by death. But all of these were no longer capital crimes because the gospel dispensation repudiated them. The Mosaic code, opponents of capital punishment argued, belonged to a specific set of circumstances in a certain era; enlightened America bore no similarity to either those conditions or that time.[47]

The only part of the Old Testament accepted by Rush as a dictate concerning capital punishment was the commandment "Thou shalt not kill." It is "murder to punish murder by death," Rush declared. The lesson of the case of Cain, in which God himself acted as judge, dictated against the death penalty. Not only was Cain not executed for murder, Rush noted, but he was marked so that he would never be put to death. Mankind, then, should follow Divine example, conceive of punishments other than death, and learn to conduct affairs with a "gentle and forgiving spirit."[48]

Theologically, Rush grounded his rejection of capital punishment in a repudiation of Calvinist dogma. With its emphasis on a stern and judgmental God, human depravity, limited atonement, and eternal punishment, Calvinism seemed to him anti-republican, anti-Christian, and inhumane. Instead, Rush and many other members of the pre- and post-Revolutionary generations were moving toward a more liberal theological position. Few journeyed as far as Thomas Paine or Ethan Allen toward Deism, but many imbibed the principles of Arminianism and converted to Unitarianism or Universalism. In general these rising denominations advanced a faith in a benevolent and forgiving deity. They emphasized human choice in the struggle for righteousness and the battle against sin, and believed in the salvation of all men. According to liberal theological tenets, God did not punish eternally for this prevented reformation; the sinful should be punished for the purposes of discipline, not retribution. Religious liberals transformed the meaning of the crucifixion of Christ from a display of God's punitive anger at the sins of mankind into his concern for man's welfare. Many of these concepts had evolved over the eighteenth century in England and especially in New England, where, by the nineteenth century, Unitarianism would become a potent intellectual force. In Philadelphia, Joseph Priestley's Unitarianism, with its Socinian emphasis on the humanity of Christ, posed the greatest challenge to orthodox Calvinist principles. Rush himself renounced his connection with Presbyterianism and embraced the Universalist belief in the salvation of all men.[49]

With its emphasis on benevolence, humanity, reformation, and universal salvation, a liberal creed could help sustain an opposition to capital punishment. The fear of eternal punishment, Rush argued, did not deter many people from immoral behavior. Rather, it was a "belief in God's Universal Love," according to Rush, that would reform the criminals and necessitate the abolition of the gallows.[50]

If liberal theology bolstered the argument against capital punishment, Calvinist dogma did just the opposite.[51] Robert Annan, an orthodox minister and pastor of the Scot's Presbyterian Church in Philadelphia, replied to Rush's essay on the injustice of capital punishment. Annan called Rush a Socinian skeptic and a Deist. Rush wanted to eliminate God from governing the world, Annan claimed, by removing from magistrates the authority to execute criminals, a power granted directly by God. It was customary for such people to "undervalue the Old Testament." Annan defended Genesis 9:6 by arguing that even if it was a prediction it carried an "infallible mark of divine approbation." As for the first murder, Annan argued that Cain was not executed because society then was more savage; with "civilization, justice, and equity" rose the gallows. Christ, according to the minister, did not appear as an "earthly prince," and Annan accused Rush of confusing "the spiritual kingdom of Christ with the kingdoms of this world." Christ did not tamper with civil laws and while it was "contrary to the spirit of Christianity, to commit murder," it was "perfectly agreeable to it, to put the murderer to death." "Liberality, in religious sentiments, is become a popular and common cry," lamented Annan, but the gospel cannot be manipulated to oppose the gallows. Rather, capital punishment "is really the means of divine appointments to support humanity."[52]

Rush labeled Annan's arguments "flimsy" and thought they "would apply better to the 15th rather than 18th century." "They all appear to flow from his severe Calvinistical principles," observed the Universalist physician. "It is impossible to advance human happiness," Rush exhorted, "while we believe the Supreme Being to possess the passions of weak or wicked men and govern our conduct with such opinions. 'The Son of Man came not to destroy men's *lives,* but to *save* them' is a passage that at once refutes all the arguments that ever were offered in favor of slavery, war, and capital punishments." Rush's belief in the doctrines of universal salvation and final restitution bound him "to the whole human race: these are the principles which animate me in all my labors for the interests of my fellow creatures."[53]

The insistence on salvation and reformation, however, could lead one to support the death penalty as well as to oppose it. At the gallows, ministers too claimed that the souls of prisoners were their greatest concern and that the executed but truly penitent criminal was saved whereas the imprisoned convict was not. Preachers declared that eternal reformation, the ascent from the gallows to glory, was far more important than farfetched schemes for temporal reform.

Rush would have none of this. The realization of his vision of a virtuous, Christian Republic necessitated the abolition of capital punishment for all crimes. This was one consequence of a war fought to reject monarchical institutions. It was one lesson of a war that swelled criminal activity in America and made social authorities nervous over disorder. To Rush's mind, republican ideology and liberal theology demanded the abolition of the death penalty and the creation of punishments that not only prevented crime but also healed, saved, and reformed criminals.

4

The Dream of Reformation and the Limits of Reform

> It is possible we may not live to witness the approaching regeneration of our world, but the more active we are bringing it about, the more fitted we shall be for that world where justice and benevolence eternally prevail.
>
> BENJAMIN RUSH to JEREMY BELKNAP (1792)

In 1796, the duc de Rochefoucauld-Liancourt, a French aristocrat exiled by the Revolution to Philadelphia, commented that "the attempt at an almost entire abolition of the punishment of death, and the substitution of a system of reason and justice, to that of bonds, ill-treatment, and arbitrary punishment, was never made but in America."[1] Liancourt's omission of several European experiments in criminal reform perhaps suggests his desire to compliment American readers. But Liancourt, like many other European observers and activists, had reason to marvel at events in America. Whereas before and during the Revolution authorities often executed thieves, robbers, counterfeiters, and rapists, in the 1780s and 1790s legislatures approved revised penal codes and authorized construction of a new institution of punishment, the penitentiary. Pennsylvania led the way in 1786 by eliminating the death penalty for robbery, burglary, and sodomy. By 1794, only those convicted of first-degree murder could be executed. In 1796, New York, New Jersey, and Virginia also voted to reduce the number of capital crimes. Even Congress, in one of the first attempts to create a national penal law, appointed a committee to investigate alterations in the penal laws of the United States that would provide "milder punishments for certain crimes for which infamous and capital punishments are now inflicted."[2]

In some ways, the post-Revolutionary revision of the criminal law away from reliance on the death penalty realized the wish expressed by several of the new state constitutions framed in 1776. Many of these documents included articles opposing excessive punishments and vague penal laws. Maryland's Declaration of Rights affirmed that "sanguinary laws ought to be avoided." Pennsylvania's Constitution directed that "punishments [be] made in some cases less sanguinary, and in general more proportionate to the crimes." The Virginia Bill of Rights declared against "cruel and unusual punishments," and, in 1776, legislators there embarked on a campaign to revise the laws of the state. When the people of New Hampshire finally approved a constitution in 1784, the Bill of Rights asserted that "a multitude of sanguinary laws is both impolitic and unjust. The true design of all punishments being to reform, not to exterminate, mankind." In expressing these beliefs, Americans drew on what had become conventional phrases in eighteenth-century political and legal philosophy.[3]

Yet the initial desire to reform the penal laws resulted in few immediate changes. In Virginia, for example, Thomas Jefferson, who extracted lengthy passages from Montesquieu and Beccaria in his Commonplace Book, prepared a bill for "Proportioning Crimes and Punishments in Cases Heretofore Capital." Jefferson's code proposed the death penalty only for treason and murder. Moreover, he adopted the *lex talionis,* the law of retaliation, for the punishment of crimes. Thus, a murderer who poisoned his victim would be poisoned by the state; a rapist would face castration. Crimes such as robbery, burglary, and counterfeiting, capital offenses in every other state in 1776, would be punished by a certain number of years at public labor.[4]

Jefferson's desire to devise a "gradation of punishments" was sparked by the Enlightenment wish to simplify and order the universe according to fundamental principles, and aided by the Revolution which necessitated the implementation of laws consistent with republicanism. But the legal revision did not get very far in the 1770s. Not until after the Revolution would the opposition to capital punishment and revision of the criminal law be accelerated, and even then in terms quite different from Jefferson's. Edmund Pendleton, also a member of the Virginia committee to alter the laws, expressed one reason why he believed the legislature did not accept the new penal code in 1776. He wrote Jefferson:

> I don't know how far you may extend your reformation as to Our Criminal System of Laws. That it has hitherto been too Sanguinary, punishing too many crimes with death, I confess, and could wish to see that changed for some other mode of Punishment in most cases, but if you mean to relax all Punishments and rely on Virtue and the Public good as sufficient to prompt Obedience of the Laws, you must find a new race of men to be the Subjects of it.[5]

Pendleton's comment was a revealing one. In the minds of men such as Jefferson, Enlightenment philosophy and Revolutionary ideology might have dictated the overhaul of the criminal code and penal practices, but these belief systems did not provide a blueprint from which to work. Pendleton worried about how far the changes should go. Virtue sounded fine in theory, but if the gallows were eliminated, what would the state do to those who acted against the public good, to those who relied solely on self-interest to govern their actions? Implicit in his letter was a concern over how these changes should be implemented and what effect they would have on the chances for the Republic to survive. Since no philosopher had opposed capital punishment entirely, dare the state? No philosopher knew what to substitute for the death penalty and, at first, neither did the legislators in America. The Virginia house did not revise the penal code until 1796. By then, the argument against capital punishment, the reform of the penal code, and the experiment with the penitentiary in Pennsylvania provided a model for the resolution of some of Pendleton's concerns.

I

On September 15, 1786, the Pennsylvania Assembly responded to the desire expressed in the state constitution ten years earlier and revised the criminal laws of the state. With respect to capital crimes, the act made robbery, burglary, and sodomy punishable by up to ten years at hard labor instead of death. As for non-capital crimes, the act provided for a scale of punishments based on fines and years of imprisonment. Punishments such as "burning in the hand" and "cutting off the ears" were replaced with prison terms, but most punishments were still to be "publicly . . . imposed."[6]

The reform of the criminal law in Pennsylvania, as well as in other states following the Revolution, was not a simple matter of statutory revision, of bringing the law into conformity with practice. To be sure, legal practices such as benefit of clergy, the return of partial verdicts, and the discretionary power of prosecutors often served to mitigate the harshness of the law and save the condemned from the gallows. Yet at the time legislatures eliminated certain capital statutes, the application of the criminal law in America was, if anything, turning more severe than lenient. During and immediately following the Revolution, hangings increased dramatically. Between 1777 and 1787, Pennsylvania authorities executed 86 prisoners of whom approximately 40 were hanged for robbery or burglary. Clearly, an explanation for the elimination of the death penalty for offenses other than first-degree murder must go beyond the internal workings of the legal system and encompass broader social and cultural currents.[7]

That Pennsylvania was the first state to revise its criminal laws did not surprise many activists in the late eighteenth century. After all, the original Quaker criminal code enacted by the Great Law of 1682 had made only murder and treason a capital crime; in 1718, the English criminal code was reimposed. Revolutionaries who believed the laws must be brought into conformity with republican beliefs were overjoyed to find in the history of Pennsylvania's criminal codes evidence that severity and barbarity never belonged naturally to the colony, that "our criminal law is an exotic plant and not a native growth of Pennsylvania."[8]

The severe and excessive punishments of English law may not have been viewed as indigenous to Pennsylvania, but the Quaker philosophy of benevolence and pacifism certainly was. On both sides of the Atlantic, many of those who worked for the revision of the penal laws and abolition of capital punishment were Quakers: John Fothergill and John Coakley Lettsom in England, Caleb Lownes in Philadelphia, Thomas Eddy in New York. Quakers constitued at least half of the members of the Philadelphia Society for Alleviating the Miseries of Public Prisons founded in 1787.

A tradition of Quaker concern and involvement with prison reform dated to the founder, George Fox, and especially to the activities of John Bellers in England. In 1699, Bellers argued against the death penalty, declaring it a "Stain . . . to Religion," and he called for the regulation of prisons. This sensitivity to the need for penal reform stemmed, in part, from the incarceration and persecution of many Quakers. During his imprisonment at Derby, for example, George Fox was appalled by the conditions he observed. More important was the Quaker belief that the reformation of any individual was possible. "If you would reform your lives," Bellers advised criminals in prison, "you will find . . . Peace and Joy. . . ." If all mankind was "capable by a thor' Reformation to become Saints on Earth," then the death penalty was not only unnecessary, but it also violated a fundamental religious precept.[9]

The Quaker commitment to pacifism also led logically to an opposition to capital punishment. The Quaker declaration of 1661 stated, "All bloody Principles and Practices we . . . do utterly deny." For many Quakers this came to mean not only war but the death penalty and duelling as well. In sending Lettsom a copy of his *Inquiry into the Justice and Policy of Punishing Murder by Death,* Rush presumed his friends would "have no objections to my principles upon that subject, for they evidently lead to the tenet of your society with respect to the lawfulness of war."[10]

The Criminal Code of 1682, a legacy of involvement in prison reform, a faith in individual reformation, and a belief in non-violence all contributed to the willingness of many Quakers in Pennsylvania to support the abolition of the death penalty and reform of the penal code in the 1780s. Predisposed as they were by philosophy and heritage to oppose severe penal measures, some Delaware Valley Quakers were further provoked by their experience during the Revolutionary War.

Most Quakers suffered during the American Revolution. As a group they abjured war and violence; for their refusal to fight for the patriot cause, authorities in Pennsylvania imprisoned many Quakers and even executed those who apparently supported the loyalists. The cases of Abraham Carlisle and John Roberts, in particular, stirred the passions of Philadelphia citizens. In 1778, Carlisle, a carpenter, and Roberts, a miller, were tried and convicted of treason. Carlisle, the prosecution alleged, had accepted a commission from General Howe to guard the gates of the city. Patriots accused Roberts of acting as a guide for Howe's invading army. The court sentenced both men to death.[11]

Quaker and non-Quaker residents of Philadelphia appealed to the Supreme Executive Council for the pardon of Carlisle and Roberts. One petition reminded the Council that the "characteristick of the True Americans shall be Humanity, mercy, charity & forgiveness." A memorial from ministers of the gospel prayed that the "Foundation of our civil Liberty may be firmly established without the Blood of our Fellow-citizens." Another petition, signed by more than one hundred citizens, insisted that a "Pardon sometimes conduces more than Punishment, to the interest of the Public as well as that of the Individual." In the 1780s, these arguments would appear among those that activists used against capital punishment in general.[12]

Despite the numerous petitions, the state executed Abraham Carlisle and John Roberts on the commons in Philadelphia. One Quaker woman expressed her disbelief that "they have actually put to Death, Han'd on the Commons, John Roberts and Abraham Carlisle this morning, or about noon—an awful solemn day it has been." Undoubtedly, many of the petitioners on behalf of the two Quaker artisans shared this distress. Although we cannot directly connect the execution of Carlisle and Roberts with the agitation against the death penalty and the revision of the penal laws less then a decade later, it is suggestive that the hundreds of petitioners included Benjamin Rush and dozens of members of the Philadelphia Society for Alleviating the Miseries of Public Prisons. Twenty-nine-year-old Thomas Eddy, who later would lead the movement to reform the criminal laws of New York, also witnessed the persecution of Carlisle and Roberts and recalled the event as an adult. Once the war ended, new ideas of punishment that emphasized the public good and especially the reformation of the criminal meant that hangings such as Carlisle's and Roberts's should never again occur.[13]

II

The preamble to the Pennsylvania law of 1786 that repealed the death penalty for certain crimes asserted that "it is the wish of every good government to reclaim rather than destory," and that "punishments directed by the laws now in force . . . do not answer the principal ends of society in inflicting them, to wit, to correct and reform the offenders" and to act as a deterrent. This emphasis on reformation galvanized both the opposition to capital punishment and the creation of the penitentiary. The faith that individuals could be reformed transcended state and national boundaries. But in post-Revolutionary America, particularly in Pennsylvania, the goals of reformation and perfection seemed palpable, almost inevitable.[14]

The belief that the individual could indeed effect his own reformation erupted over the course of the seventeenth and eighteenth centuries. The sprouting of liberal religious creeds in the cracks of Calvinism meant that human effort might now matter in the business of salvation. With its rejection of the Calvinist emphasis on human depravity, eternal punishment, and a punitive God, liberal creeds allowed for universal salvation, opposed strictly retributive punishments, and advanced a belief in a benevolent deity. Quaker theology in particular, with its faith in the presence of God within the individual, affirmed that mankind was not entirely polluted. Man's duty to benevolence, the possibility of salvation in life, and the withdrawal from coercive discipline led penal theorists to reject the death penalty and seek alternative punishments.

Lockean theories of education, which stressed the malleability of the individual, also contributed to the reformative ideal. John Locke rejected innate ideas, emphasized the impressionability of the senses, and, in so doing, propounded an environmentalist approach to character formation. To Locke, the mind was pliable; the creation of the rational, self-sufficient, industrious man he so desired depended merely on manipulating the impressions that shaped both mind and character. Lockean pedagogy called for cultivating affective, non-violent relationships in order to raise children and reform those whose earliest experiences had led them off the path of virtue. As Americans labored self-consciously to revise systems of punishment in the early Republic, Lockean ideals contributed to a revolution in attitudes toward discipline. In an oration to the Tammany Society, one speaker declared that "the doctrine of *innate ideas* has long since been exploded by the immortal Locke." Instead, man is viewed as "the creature of education and the child of habitude." If the environment, and not predetermined principles, shaped individual character, then human agents played the determinative role in generating virtue and eliminating vice. By these lights, the state should not execute criminals. Such spectacles not only impressed immorality and violence upon the crowd, they also failed entirely to reform the condemned into republican citizens.[15]

In addition to Lockean epistemology, the common-sense school of Scottish philosophy could also be harnessed in opposition to capital punishment and in favor of reformation. According to the Scots and their American followers, the moral sense served as the means by which man discerned moral good from evil. Humanity's revulsion at the sight of the gallows, common-sense disciples argued, indicated that the moral sense disapproved of the death penalty. Faculty psychology, embedded in Scottish moral philosophy, maintained that the faculties or capacities of the mind, divided traditionally into reason, emotion, and will, could be stimulated and strengthened under the proper regimen. Along with associationist psychology, which held the promise of creating a perfectly virtuous, Christian society merely if one generated morally correct and natural associations of ideas, these beliefs helped popularize a social environmentalist psychology in the late eighteenth century.[16]

The faith in the reformability and perfectability of man contributed to a redefinition of the causes of criminality, supported a reconsideration of the death penalty, and elevated the reformation of the criminal into the principal end of punishment. No longer wicked agents given over to evil, criminals, in the late eighteenth century, seemed to suffer a disordering of the faculties which prevented them from choosing correctly between good and evil. If the environment disordered one's senses, then the environment could reorder them as well. One opponent of capital punishment put it most succinctly: "Let every criminal, then, be considered as a person laboring under an infectious disorder. Mental disease is, indeed, the cause of all crimes."[17]

The most troubling question for activists in the 1780s and 1790s centered not on whether reformation was or ought to be the primary object of punishment, but rather on how to achieve the reformation of the individual. Capital punishment certainly was not the answer. As one death penalty opponent asserted, "the ideas of reforming a criminal by the virtues of the halter, is too ludicrous to dwell on." Another proponent of penal reform commented that "the punishment of death precludes the possibility of the amendment of the criminal by any human means. Every hope of reformation is at once cut off without a single effort to accomplish so just and benevolent a purpose." Some writers suggested hard labor; others proposed a "hospital for the reformation of criminals." The problem of what punishment to substitute for the death penalty was still unresolved when Pennsylvania's legislature revised the state penal code.[18]

In order to reform the criminal and prevent others from committing crimes, the Act of 1786 provided for punishment by "continued hard labor, publicly and disgracefully imposed . . . in streets of cities and towns, and upon the highways of the open country" as well as in prisons. The faith in hard labor as a corrective measure originated in sixteenth-century Holland, where the state opened workhouses for men and women. Of course, the importance of industry over idleness was bound up in what is commonly called the Protestant work ethic. In 1786, most almanacs in Philadelphia and elsewhere included the proverb that industry promoted virtue. Under the new law those criminals sentenced to public labor, who prior to the reduction of capital offenses might have been executed, became known as the wheelbarrow men. Ironed and chained, with shaved heads and coarse uniforms lettered to indicate the crime committed, they cleaned and repaired the streets of Philadelphia and the surrounding towns. Their reformation, authorities believed, would come through public humiliation, industry, and temperance. Deterrence would be achieved, legislators hoped, by a public display of marked, if not doomed, offenders.[19]

It became readily apparent, however, that the "wheelbarrow law" neither reformed the prisoners nor prevented vice. Indeed, it seemed to many that the convicts became even more licentious and that unprecedented amounts of criminal activity infested the community. In his *Account of the Alteration and Present State of the Penal Laws of Pennsylvania*, Caleb Lownes recalled that the law was "productive of the *greatest evils* . . . the disorders of society, the robberies, burglaries, breaches of prison, alarms in town and country—the drunkenness, profanity and indecencies of the prisoners in the streets, must be in the memory of most." The wheelbarrow men begged for aid and plotted to escape. Citizens who felt sorry for the convicts provided them with liquor, tobacco, and food. Thomas Jefferson recalled that "exhibited as a public spectacle, with shaved heads and mean clothing, working on the high roads, produced in the criminals such a prostration of character, such an abandonment of self-respect, as, instead of reforming, plunged them into the most desperate and hardened depravity of morals and character." One contemporary summarized the problem with public punishments in gang labor this way: "the greatest object of punishment, viz. the reformation of criminals, was completely defeated."[20]

Disturbed by the consequences of the wheelbarrow law, Rush delivered his *Enquiry into the Effects of Public Punishments upon Criminals, and upon Society* in March 1787, six months after passage of the new law. Reasoning from the principles of environmentalist psychology, he argued that "the reformation of a criminal can never be effected by a public punishment" because it destroys any sense of shame in the criminal, it annihilates character, and it does not last long enough to produce changes "in body or mind" which are needed "to reform obstinate habits of vice." Public punishments, Rush declared, produced crimes rather than prevented them because regardless of how spectators viewed the scene, public punishment stimulated a range of responses, all of which damaged society. Prisoners who appear distressed, he noted, seemed to elicit sympathy from spectators. This sympathy, or sensibility, Rush viewed as one of the essential components of the moral faculty. But since spectators could not relieve their profound sense of sympathy on a criminal, Rush feared the destruction of sensibility altogether and an increase in social disorder—because "while we pity, we secretely condemn the law which inflicts the punishment." Even when such punishments failed to generate sympathy for the criminal, they served only to "excite . . . terror in the minds of spectators," thereby polluting their moral constitution.[21]

Rush also claimed that the wheelbarrow law undermined the value of labor. Comparing the law with Southern slave labor, he wondered whether it was not true that, where blacks were forced to work, whites were reluctant to labor? He feared that the spectacle of criminals working in the streets would lure citizens away from their business and, as a result, promote general idleness. Rush concluded that "if public punishments are injurious to criminals and to society, it follows, that crimes should be punished in private, or not punished at all."[22]

A belief in the capacity of the individual to reform, fueled by republican ideology, liberal theology, and environmentalist psychology, propelled Rush in his denunciation of capital and public punishments. But if neither the death penalty nor public labor provided the solution, how could the state punish and, at the same time, reform criminals? For Rush, the answer rested in the creation of a "house of repentance" that punished offenders in privacy. The opposition to the death penalty and the first attempts at revision of the criminal code, efforts grounded in changing concepts of punishment, gave rise to the first penitentiary system in America.[23]

Rush did not initially propose a specific plan of treatment for his "house of repentance." He thought that the most effective punishments probably consisted of "BODILY PAIN, LABOUR, WATCHFULNESS, SOLITUDE, and SI-

LENCE . . . joined with CLEANLINESS and SIMPLE DIET." In suggesting these punishments Rush summarized the wisdom of penal reformers on both sides of the Atlantic who, fortified with copies of John Howard's *The State of the Prisons* (1777), had begun an assault on abhorrent prison conditions. The more important point Rush thought he was making was that all punishments should be private. Such punishments, both the type and the duration of which would be kept from the prisoner and the community, Rush believed to be "of the utmost importance in reforming criminals." He reasoned that "crimes produce a stain, which may be washed out by reformation . . . but public punishments leave scars, which disfigure the whole character." The physician claimed to have "no more doubt of every crime having its cure in moral and physical influence than . . . of the efficacy of the Peruvian bark in curing the intermitting fever." It was merely a matter, in an age of wondrous machines and enlightened ideas, of discovering the appropriate remedy for the particular vice.[24]

The new experiment in private punishment was hurried along by the drastic consequences of the wheelbarrow law. The legislature had passed the law on September 15, 1786. A year later Rush wrote Lettsom that because of its "bad effects" the law would be repealed. In January 1788, the Philadelphia Society for Alleviating the Miseries of Public Prisons petitioned the legislature against punishments "publickly and disgracefully Imposed." Nearly a year passed when one night, in October 1788, over thirty wheelbarrow men escaped. Newspapers reported that the escaped convicts "resumed their former practices of depredation upon persons and property." Apparently, some of the "Gang of armed villains" fled to New York where they "committed divers[e] street-robberies and Burglaries," much to the chagrin of authorities there. The escape of these convicts provoked a new chorus in favor of altering the penal laws. One correspondent averred that "the ravages . . . which are committed every day upon the property, limbs and even lives of our citizens by the wheelbarrow men, who have lately excaped from the gaol, lead us to wish for some other more effectual mode of punishing criminals." By Acts passed on March 27, 1789, and, especially, April 5, 1790, the legislature repealed the wheelbarrow law, restructured the prison system, and adopted "unremitted solitude" as the punishment thought best suited to reform the criminal. An Act of April 22, 1794, reduced capital crimes to first-degree murder only.[25]

Activists in Pennsylvania did not invent the idea of solitude as punishment; it belonged more to the age rather than to any individual. References to solitude appeared in the first decades of the eighteenth century, when several English pamphleteers suggested the separation of convicts prior to sentencing. In 1753, Henry Fielding, a London magistrate, recommended solitude and fasting as the most "effectual means of bringing the most Abandoned Profligates to Reason and Order." By the 1770s and 1780s, nearly everyone was abuzz with the possibility of solitary confinement. The Maison de Force at Ghent, a prison which separated convicts at night, was completed in 1775; in England, Jonas Hanway published *Solitude in Imprisonment* (1776) and called for the creation of a prison that would isolate inmates completely; activists in Philadelphia familiarized themselves with Sir Thomas Beevor's attempt in 1785 to remodel the bridewell at Wymondham on Hanway's principles.[26]

If others were alerted to the idea of solitude as punishment, however, nowhere did it seem as important nor was it pursued with greater devotion than in Pennsylvania in the 1780s and 1790s. Visionaries like Rush saw no limitations to the experiment of reforming the individual in America. A republican nation, baptized in Revolution, the United States appeared to Rush on the verge of fulfilling the greatest hopes of the Enlightenment. And if the death penalty violated the principles of the republican gospel on which the nation was supposedly based, and if public punishments were a fiasco, then solitude alone, it seemed, promised to reform criminals. A look at the discussion of how solitude would accomplish this goal—by rearranging deranged moral faculties and promoting penitence—helps to illuminate further the psychology of reformation in the eighteenth century.

III

Physicians, scientists, and moral philosophers stressed that solitude would reorder an individual's faculties. One proponent of penal reform argued that "solitude and darkness are known to have a powerful influence on the mind. When the avenue of external sense is shut, and every accession of ideas from without precluded—the soul becomes an object to herself, her agitations subside: and her faculties tend to the natural equipoise." Rush claimed that "by removing men out of the reach of the exciting cause, they are often reformed."[27]

Implicit in these comments was more than just a medical approach to what activists viewed as a mental disease. Solitude seemed to offer a cure for the disordering of faculties and unleashing of passions because it was society itself that acted as the "exciting cause." In attacking the wheelbarrow law Rush had argued that prisoners must be secluded from one another and from the public because of the likelihood of corruption. But they also had to be isolated for a time from the disorienting and disturbing effects of society. "Company, conversation, and even business are the opiates of the Spirit of God . . .," Rush declared. "Too much cannot be said in favor of SOLITUDE as a means of reformation," because the heat of conscience, released in seclusion, thawed the soul numbed by social interaction.[28]

Robert Turnbull, a South Carolina lawyer and writer who visited the Philadelphia prison, offered a similar perspective. "It is in this state of seclusion from the world," he observed, "that the mind can be brought to contemplate itself—to judge of its powers—and thence to acquire the resolution and energy necessary to protect its avenues from the intrusion of vicious thoughts." Turnbull's analysis of the virtue of solitude portrayed society as a force of dissolution rather than sustenance, as something that deranged one's inner gyroscope rather than balanced it. To offset this, the prison was transformed into an institution where the individual could be secluded from the dizzying effects of a society in motion—secluded that he might return to it better prepared to resist temptations and cope with pressures.[29]

That the prison was now called the "penitentiary" illuminates another reason for solitude as punishment. Solitude figured in the calculus of faculties, but it especially mattered in the promotion of penitence. If true penitence, unlike the "counterfeit contrition" evident in ritual recantations at the gallows, came from within the individual, then prisons need only provide an environment for the "calm contemplation of mind which brings on penitance."[30] In providing solitude to its inmates, the prison was to function as a church. Prison, Rush asserted, "out-preaches the preacher in conveying useful instruction to the heart." The word "penitentiary" itself, which was not used consistently until the turn of the century, embodies this original meaning of the new prison as a place designed to produce penitence and promote salvation. Reformers called this new facility a "house of repentance," "a house of amendment," or even a "school of reformation." Caleb Lownes, one of the inspectors of the Philadelphia prison, used the term "solitary cell" synonymously with "penitentiary house." Committed to the dream of reformation, some reformers thought they had found in solitude the mechanism for conversion. By curtailing the passions and fostering penitance, solitude promised to turn vicious criminals into virtuous citizens.[31]

In the adapted Walnut Street facility in Philadelphia, circa 1790, the solitary cell stood eight feet by six feet by nine feet. It contained a small window and a mattress. The prisoner ate once a day and after a certain amount of time was granted permission to read only the Bible. All those convicted of crimes previously capital could spend as much as one-half their sentence in solitary confinement. One observer likened the system of solitude, with its emphasis on an abstemious, almost monastic life-style, to that of many of the religious sects. Founded as it was on religious and scientific principles, and designed to induce penitence and virtue through solitude and introspection, solitary confinement appealed to many individuals who opposed capital punishment as cruel, barbarous, and inhumane. Yet one of the reasons for its widespread and near instantaneous acceptance was that solitary confinement also attracted those who generally supported the death penalty, thought deterrence the main goal in punishment, and thought terror both the most effective deterrent and the best reformative agent.[32]

Whereas Turnbull did not specify how solitude necessarily led to penitance, another correspondent expressed what he saw as the central mechanism in reformation—terror:

> Conscience cannot long sleep in *solitude*. The worst of men, when left for a while to themselves, are made prisoners by their own reflections. These reflections are the messengers of Heaven to bring them to repentance, and a sense of their duty. . . . To be delivered to a merciless overseer of a public work of any kind, or to be delivered to a sheriff for execution, are both light punishments compared with a wicked man being delivered by *solitude* and *confinement* to his own reflections.[33]

In this scheme solitude succeeded because no prisoner could long endure the maelstrom unleashed by confinement. The convict would become truly penitent and converted from evil ways or he would remain, life-long if necessary, a prisoner to his own contemplation.

Others concurred with this view of solitude as something to be feared. William Paley, whose *Principles of Moral and Political Philosophy* (1785) circulated widely in America as well as England, thought the virtue of solitary imprisonment was that it "would augment the terror of the punishment." Enoch Edwards, president of the Philadelphia Court of Quarter-Sessions, informed one grand jury that solitude replaced both public and capital punishment because it was considered a "greater evil than certain death." Newspapers in America and England reported that prisoners in solitary "beg, with the greatest earnestness, that they may be hanged out of their misery."[34] At times the opponents of capital punishment also offered the argument that solitude succeeded as a punishment because it was so terrible to contemplate. Defenders of the gallows enjoyed nothing more than to point out the apparent contradiction between the anti-gallows activists' vaunted claims of humanity and Christianity and yet their willingness to impose a punishment more feared by some than death.[35]

This ambiguity in what constituted "humanity" speaks more to the complex meaning of solitude as a punishment than to an inconsistency in the position of most opponents of the death penalty. To be sure, opponents of capital punishment tried to appeal to as wide an audience as possible; some citizens favored solitude because it was more humane than public hanging, others because it was in some ways less so. The idea of the penitentiary could unite people with different agendas—those who sought to liberate the individual through reformation and those who desired to control him through incarceration. In the 1780s and 1790s, the Pennsylvania legislature adopted solitary imprisonment to replace certain capital crimes precisely because such a penalty could absorb antagonistic views of punishment and society. Advocates peddled solitude as both less and more horrifying than public executions; it promised to produce a penitent convict both through "calm contemplation" and by unleashing terrible reflections; it permitted the convict's withdrawal from society so that he could be reimmersed in it, while it also suggested that to be severed from institutional connections entirely was to be lost. A supple concept, solitude as punishment united theorists with dissimilar agendas and conflicting ideologies.

Whatever ambiguity existed in the meaning of solitude, the transition from public punishments to solitary confinement implied a significant shift in the assumptions underlying how punishment worked. The principle behind public punishments was to shame prisoners enough that they would conform rather than again face communal contempt, but not so much that prisoners lost all sense of shame, as Rush feared happened to the wheelbarrow men. When one contemporary reported that the wheelbarrow men were so "adverse to this shameful exposure . . . [they] preferred death to it," she was commenting on the failure of the central mechanism in public, non-capital punishment—shame. By comparison, solitude operated on the principle that the prisoner, secluded and isolated, in time would feel guilty for his actions and repent. The penitentiary would help reform the prisoner by leading him to internalize certain values—piety, industry, sobriety—and authorities hoped that the inmate's guilt over violating these newly discovered standards would induce penitence and reformation.[36]

IV

Perhaps because the penitentiary emerged quickly and with little opposition, it is difficult to pinpoint precisely who supported it. Promoters of the scheme to substitute solitary confinement for the death penalty never tired of claiming that the revision of penal laws reflected "the general and ardent desire of the people." If by "the people" this essayist had in mind mostly everyone, or a particular social group, or an intellectual community, he did not specify. Certainly, if most citizens of the Republic shared an opposition to capital punishment, as anti-gallows writers claimed, one might expect the expression of popular opposition to the gallows on execution day. Such dissent, however, did not take place.[37]

By attributing the desire to revise systems of punishment to "the people," writers revealed their belief that the reasons for the elimination of the gallows were so fundamental, so linked to republican and Christian values, that only eccentrics, traitors, or atheists dare oppose them. To say, however, that "the people" did not demand changes in the criminal law and modes of punishment is not to claim that the topic of penal reform was not a popular one. For a literate, well-educated, eastern elite, at least, the problem of the death penalty demanded attention. It received it in a variety of places. In commencement exercises students at Princeton, Columbia, and Yale began to debate whether the criminal laws in America were too harsh. Literary and philosophical society members also discussed the issue. And newspapers from Boston to Baltimore included essays and letters on the problem of punishment. Even Alexander Hamilton, who was no radical, recognized that "the idea of cruelty inspires disgust. . . . The temper of our country is not a little opposed to the frequency of capital punishment."[38]

The temperament to which Hamilton referred certainly belonged to a distinct but interrelated and influential group of activists who, in the 1790s, promoted and guided alterations in the criminal law. For the most part, these men participated in politics and understood well the mechanics of legislative maneuvering. By the standards of the day they were learned, professional, and highly successful. In Philadelphia, for example, Benjamin Rush was no isolated crank. Signer of the Declaration, prominent physician, friend to Adams and Jefferson, Rush not only articulated a program of reform but served as lobbyist for his ideas as well. Before the Society for Promoting Political Enquiries, in the pages of the *American Museum* (whose editor, Mathew Carey, also supported penal reform), in pamphlets, and through correspondence Rush campaigned for alterations in the penal law. He was supported in his efforts by William Bradford, attorney-general of Pennsylvania and a future attorney-general of the United States, and Caleb Lownes, a Quaker merchant who became one of the inspectors of the Walnut Street Prison. The Philadelphia Society for Alleviating the Miseries of Public Prisons served as a pressure group, organizing meetings and petitioning the legislature. In addition to Rush and Lownes, prominent members of the Society included William White, the episcopal bishop of Philadelphia; Zachariah Poulson, a publisher; and Tench Coxe, a financier and manufacturer.

The social position of the proponents of reform was no different elsewhere. In 1795, following Pennsylvania's lead, the Governor of New York, George Clinton, requested that the legislature address the problem of a "criminal law . . . so repugnant to the genius of our constitution." Governor John Jay reiterated the message a year later. In 1796, Thomas Eddy and Philip Schuyler journeyed to Philadelphia to inspect the Walnut Street Prison. Eddy was on his way to earning the appellation "Howard of America." A successful Quaker merchant, raised in Philadelphia, Eddy helped navigate the revision of the criminal law through the New York legislature and served as inspector of the newly constructed Newgate Prison. He had support from Philip Schuyler, general of the northern theatre during the Revolutionary War, influential member of the state senate, and Alexander Hamilton's father-in-law. Schuyler may have been one of the most powerful men in the New York legislature but Ambrose Spencer was the most articulate. Spencer, who went on to serve as Chief Justice of the state of New York, introduced the bill that became law in 1796. Dr. Samuel Latham Mitchill, professor of natural history and chemistry at Columbia and Rush's counterpart in New York, supported the measure.[39]

Elsewhere, the scenario was the same. In each case a combination of legislators, prominent professional and commercial men, and religious figures, mostly Quaker and Universalist, directed a campaign to reduce the number of capital crimes and construct a penitentiary. Although differing at times in emphasis (Rush held a minority view in desiring the total abolition of capital punishment) and philosophy (that is, the most effective means of achieving reformation) these activists shared a sense of common endeavor. Thus, having successfully delivered a new criminal code first, Pennsylvania served as midwife to the experiment elsewhere. The pamphlets of Rush, Bradford, and Lownes circulated among members of various legislatures, including Massachusetts and South Carolina. In Virginia, George K. Taylor implored the house to "imitate and adopt" Pennsylvania's criminal system. Jefferson, in his memoir, offered his understanding of why the reform succeeded in 1796 and not 1776: "Public opinion was ripening by time, by reflection, and by the example of Pennsylvania." By 1805, New York, New Jersey, Connecticut, Virginia, and Massachusetts each claimed penitentiaries constructed in part upon the principle of solitude.[40]

Just as English and European works helped shape the ideas expressed by American essayists, the reduction in the number of capital crimes and invention of a penitentiary system in the United States had a profound impact across the Atlantic. The duc de Rochefoucauld-Liancourt's pamphlet, *Des Prisons de Philadelphia, par un european* (1796) influenced a generation of reformers in France. In England as well, Romilly, Bentham, Colquhoun, and Roscoe studied Pennsylvania's attempt to eradicate capital punishment and reform the individual through solitude.[41]

There was, of course, conflict and dissent over the penal reform project, but, if an organized opposition existed, it is as difficult a group to isolate and identify as "the people." Certain individuals, such as the Presbyterian minister Robert Annan of Philadelphia, publicly defended capital punishment and retributive punishments. A number of legislators also made their opposition to reform known. In New York, for example, Senator Samuel Jones, a conservative attorney, attempted to substitute a bill that authorized the construction of a penitentiary *without* reducing the number of capital crimes. The assembly defeated his effort, and one newspaper criticized Jones's attachment to "antiquated maxims and forms" such as capital punishment. It is revealing that, even in opposition to the revision of the criminal code, Jones proposed and supported the building of a penitentiary.[42]

Perhaps the most pointed critique of incarceration came not from any legislator or jurist but from a convict. In the 1780s, Stephen Burroughs, a preacher's son, was sentenced to three years' imprisonment for counterfeiting. He served part of his sentence at the newly authorized Castle Island facility in Boston Harbor, one of the first experiments at incarceration with hard labor. In his *Memoirs* (1798), Burroughs reflected back on his shock and horror at learning that, instead of being confined in some common county jail, from which even a partly lame prisoner could easily escape, he had been sentenced to three years in a state of "close confinement." What most surprised him was how, in authorizing this new form of punishment, legislators had forsaken a central principle of the Revolution—liberty. "How is this," he wondered, "that a country which has stood the foremost in asserting the cause of liberty, that those who have tasted the bitter cup of slavery, and have known from hence the value of liberty, should so soon after obtaining that blessing themselves, deprive others of it?" If life without liberty was not worth living, as so many patriots declared, how then could the state trifle with first principles by substituting "slavery for death upon revision of the criminal code."[43]

Burroughs's rhetorical question went unanswered. If Americans fought the Revolution on republican principles, especially for liberty and independence, then in the abstract the penitentiary signified a repudiation of some of those principles. The prisoner, Burroughs observed, was reduced to a state of dependency. Cut off from society, his liberty circumscribed, his independence excised, the inmate had before him only "one continual scene of gloomy horrors." It is perhaps one of the ironies of the penitentiary system that the method believed best to reform common criminals into representative republicans was itself unrepublican. Over thirty years before Tocqueville and Beaumont's visit to America, Burroughs had anticipated their insight that "whilst society in the United States gives the example of the most extended liberty, the prisons of the same country offer the spectacle of the most complete despotism."[44]

V

In the last decade of the eighteenth century, nearly every state legislature in America adopted the idea of the penitentiary as a substitute for sanguinary punishments and an institution for reformation. So convinced were they in the principle of reformation and the efficacy of solitude as a means of amending and reclaiming criminals that, as early as 1791, the Board of Inspectors in Philadelphia proclaimed: "The prison is no longer a scene of debauchery, idleness, and profanity . . . but a school of reformation."[45]

The faith in reformation, however, barely survived the century. Problems with the new penitentiary system rapidly eclipsed all earlier enthusiasm. By 1822, a commission appointed to investigate the penitentiaries of America asked, "Has the system answered the expectations of its founders and advocates?" and answered, "It has not." Prison boards in Pennsylvania, New York, and Massachusetts discovered that the principle of reformation, while sound, did not convert easily into practice. Walnut Street Prison, for example, became overcrowded, and officials there could not enforce solitude. Inspectors considered the failure to prevent "the constant intercourse of criminals" the "fundamental error" in the new state prisons. Some legislators also grew increasingly uncomfortable with the rising expense of maintaining a penitentiary. The directors of the Massachusetts State Prison expressed their dismay with the costs of "this new mode of punishing criminals" but added quickly that "benevolent institutions are always expensive" and that, if "the cause of humanity has been promoted, if scenes of barbarity . . . have been removed from the public eye, if a few instances only of repentance and reformation have been wrought by this mild and salutary correction; surely these are blessings worth purchasing, even at a greater price."[46]

Structural problems and mounting expenses could be dealt with, it seemed, provided penitentiaries delivered on the promise of reformation. Within a decade, however, it became clear that reformation—returning the prisoner to "moral order, rectitude, and self-respect"—was not to be easily achieved. In 1817, Philadelphia authorities reported that, of 451 convicts in the penitentiary, 162 had been previously convicted. The story was no different in Massachusetts where, of some 300 convicts, 90 were "under commitment for a second, third, or fourth time." Officials began to fret that prisoners, having figured out what was expected of them, "put on the exterior of penitence" in order to gain release. At least one convict confirmed the worst fears of authorities when he reported that, although "a reformation of those who are disorderly through a vicious disposition" was the primary object of punishment, prisons such as Castle Island served instead as a "perfect school of vice." "Instead of becoming good members of society," he warned, "the convicts have generally taken to a course of the most atrocious transgressions after their liberation." No one could any longer endorse the penitentiary as a means of reformation without some qualification. The principle of reformation itself, as the primary object in punishment, lost much of its shimmer.[47]

By the second decade of the nineteenth century, these problems of the penitentiary system—overcrowding, mounting expenses, excessive pardoning, and the failure of reformation—were evident. When in 1818 legislators in Massachusetts stood ready to abandon "the beautiful and brilliant theory of reclaiming the unprincipled" as "vain and illusory," they merely certified what many had come to expect years earlier. In 1801, Thomas Eddy observed that the citizens had "become impatient that the alteration of the penal code has not yet produced greater and more decided effects. . . . They sometimes even express a regret at the change which has been wrought in our laws, and returning to a system of accumulated severity and terror, wish to see every offense against life and property punished with death." The citizens Eddy referred to were most likely disturbed by the failure of the penitentiary to reform criminals and prevent crime.[48]

Even before the flood of reports in the 1810s, the project in penal reform halted. No state abolished capital punishment entirely, and only Pennsylvania eliminated the death penalty for all crimes except first-degree murder. Having remodeled some old prisons, as at Walnut Street, and constructed some new facilities, as Newgate Prison in New York, activists sat back to observe the remarkable effects of their endeavors. But as it became clear that the practice did not live up to the ideal, the ideals themselves tarnished in the twilight of the eighteenth century. Perhaps some of the Revolutionary excitement and enlightenment fervor seemed suddenly faded and uncompelling. By the first years of the nineteenth century, the promise of the perfectable American Republic was unrealized, and those who had united for different reasons to support and help push through changes in the penal system ran out of energy and imagination.

For Rush, this retreat from reform and apparent repudiation of humanity came as a bitter disappointment; he too withdrew from social concerns and readjusted his sense of the desirable and the possible. "Tired out and distressed with the unsuccessful issue of all my public labors," Rush informed Eddy in 1803 that he was limiting his involvement to the medical world. He feared the "restoration of our old laws for whipping, cropping, burning in the hand, and taking away life," but recognized that "many . . . citizens wish for it" and that problems with Pennsylvania's mild penal code had created cause for concern. Rush gave up hope that he would live to witness the moral regeneration of the world and the perfection of the American Republic. "All systems of political order and happiness," he wrote John Adams, "seem of late years to have disappointed their founders and advocates. Civilization, science, and commerce have long ago failed in their attempts to improve the condition of mankind, and even liberty itself, from which more was expected than from all other human means, has lately appeared to be insufficient for that purpose."[49]

Rush consoled himself "by recollecting that the seeds of all the great changes for the better in the condition of mankind, have been sowed years and centuries before they came to pass." Truth, he thought, resembled trees: "Some ripen in a short time, while others require half a century or more to bring them to perfection." As long as somebody planted the seeds, he thought, they would one day germinate. Still, it irked him that later generations would probably credit Bradford and Franklin for proposing alterations in the penal code, this despite one's "good-humored ridicule" of the project at first and the other's general indifference to the issue altogether. Rumbling beneath these mixed feelings of hope, regret, and insecurity, however, was a gnawing concern that perhaps the entire experiment in reformation, be it for criminals and alcoholics, the sick and the insane, was misplaced and idealistic.[50]

In a remarkable letter, Rush offered an account of one of his dreams.[51] He had been elected President of the United States and as his first act he persuaded Congress to pass a law prohibiting the importation and consumption of "ardent spirits." Much to his astonishment citizens violently opposed the law. One day a "venerable but plain-looking man" arrived to remonstrate against the prohibition. This petitioner argued that, without ardent spirits, farmers and artisans did not have the strength to work, ministers and lawyers lost the ability to preach and plead, and women became "peevish and quarrelsome" from lack of brandy in their tea. In general, the abolition of ardent spirits did "violence to the physical and commercial habits of our citizens."

In response, the President chastised the old man for not having faith that Americans would "submit to the empire of Reason." Reason, he insisted, would convince citizens of the importance of sobriety and morality. But "you forget that it was Reason . . . that produced all the crimes and calamities of the French Revolution," chortled the old man, and that a book called *The Age of Reason* "demoralized half the Christian world." The petitioner suggested another empire to which all men yielded, the "EMPIRE OF HABIT." "You might as well arrest the orbs of heaven in their course as *suddenly* change the habits of a whole people," exclaimed the visitor. The President had the man thrown out; the dreamer, Benjamin Rush, awoke weeping.

Rush's dream embodied the central tension in reformation. Nearly everyone could agree that it was desirable to reform criminals and rid society of their depredations. But where did one draw the line in who was a fit subject for reformation? If criminals, how about the poor? If the poor, what of those who spoke a different language, wore unusual clothes, or advocated heretical ideas? Moreover, how should they be reformed? Was not solitude as coercive as torture? Why, if man truly was morally self-governing and improvable, should the state attempt authoritatively to alter people? Rush and the members of his class wanted to remake the world into a species of man that was a mirror of their own self-perception: disciplined, industrious, frugal, temperate, faithful. Other citizens in the new Republic, including criminals, had a different idea as to what characteristics people should display. The tension between the desire to homogenize society according to a single model and the desire to permit, indeed encourage, diversity would continue to trouble "reformers" long after Rush stopped dreaming.

The waning of reform in the first decade of the nineteenth century did not herald the end of efforts to abolish capital punishment, revise the penal laws, or construct an effective penitentiary. In the 1820s and 1830s penal theorists offered new arguments and different strategies. By then, Rush's idea that criminality, like a fever, could be cured seemed naive at best. Rush had thought of all criminals as the same, each suffering from a disease that a unitary treatment could relieve. But in the collapse of the first penitentiary system observers now viewed the matter differently. No two criminals had a similar constitution, no two were deviant because of the exact same interaction with their environment, and, therefore, no single regimen of punishment, such as solitude, could succeed with all inmates. In theory, this necessitated classifying prisoners by their crimes and constitutions and punishing each variant differently. But so cumbersome and expensive would this be to administer, and without guaranteeing a resolution to the problem of reforming the criminal, that the faith in reformation itself diminished. In 1831, Elam Lynds, warden at Sing Sing in New York, flatly declared, "I do not believe in a *complete* reform" of the prisoner. Rush would not have understood this. For him, the perfectability of man was possible in the temporal world as well as the eternal universe, and he clung desperately to the dream of reformation until the bitter end.[52]

5

The Origins of Private Executions in America

The prison-yard . . . has been the scene of terrible performances. Into this narrow, grave-like place, men are brought out to die. The wretched creature stands beneath the gibbet on the ground; the rope about his neck; and when the sign is given, a weight at its other end comes running down, and swings him up into the air—a corpse.

The law requires that there be present at this dismal spectacle, the judge, the jury, and citizens to the amount of twenty-five. From the community it is hidden. To the dissolute and bad, the thing remains a frightful mystery. Between the criminal and them, the prison-wall is interposed as a thick gloomy veil. It is the curtain to his bed of death, his winding sheet, and grave. From him it shuts out life, and all the motives to unrepenting hardihood in that last hour, which its mere sight and presence is often all-sufficient to sustain. There are no bold eyes to make him bold; no ruffians to uphold a ruffian's name before. All beyond the pitiless stone wall is unknown space.

CHARLES DICKENS, *American Notes* (1842)

On April 18, 1845, the state of Pennsylvania executed twenty-six-year-old Samuel Zepphon. A short time after noon, the prisoner departed his cell accompanied by clergymen and guarded by officers of the law. He trudged toward the gallows with a rope around his neck and his arms pinioned behind him. According to one account, "The mournful *cortege*, with solemn tread, slowly proceeded to the place of execution, the preachers and pious consolers singing appropriate hymns." On reaching the gallows the minister offered a prayer as the prisoner wept. Zepphon did not deliver any last words, choosing instead to bid goodbye quietly to the crowd around him and saying only, "I did not kill Cuffee Todd." The sheriff pulled a white cap over the prisoner's eyes and the drop fell. Through the "carelessness of the executioner," however, too much rope had been allowed and, rather than his neck being broken, Zepphon crashed to the ground. "Groaning from mental and physical suffering," Zepphon was raised to the scaffold once more and, with the rope readjusted and noose secured, again plunged into "the awful realities of death upon the gallows." Thirty-seven minutes later authorities cut him down and delivered his body to his mother for burial.[1]

What distinguished Zepphon's execution from the hundreds of hangings prior to the 1830s was not that it was bungled, but that it took place within the walls of the prison before a group of invited spectators; it was a private, not a public execution. Workmen erected the scaffold in the rear of the Moyamensing Prison Yard, and over one hundred persons attended the execution. Executing prisoners in the quasi-privacy of the prison yard had become standard practice. For Thomas Barrett's hanging at Worcester, the sheriff had the gallows placed in the passageway of the jail. For the execution of John Gordon, Rhode Island authorities constructed the gallows "in the Yard connected with the State Prison and jail, in a corner 25 feet square, and entirely enclosed from any outside view." And in New York, James Eager suffered death in the yard of the Tombs Prison on Centre Street.[2]

By the time of Zepphon's execution, the state of Pennsylvania had been hanging criminals within the confines of prison yards for over ten years. The first private execution took place in 1834, shortly after the legislature passed an act that abolished public hangings. The law required that the punishment "be inflicted . . . within the walls or yard of the jail" in the county in which the criminal was convicted. The sheriff had the discretion to select the witnesses, providing he included at least one physician, the attorney general, and "twelve reputable citizens." The act excluded minors from attending. New Jersey, New York, and Massachusetts followed with similar acts in 1835. By 1845 all the states in New England and the Mid-Atlantic region had eliminated public executions in favor of private hangings.[3]

Despite such a prominent change in so brief a time, contemporaries offered little explanation for the transition from public to private executions. The passage of private execution legislation did not prompt any acute political conflict. At a time when many issues generated rancorous debate, legislators by and large welcomed the idea of eliminating public hangings. In Pennsylvania, for example, the house passed the bill by a vote of 62-13. Generally, those who offered any comment on the proposal favored the move, calling public executions "a spectacle at once revolting and injurious to society." But why did public hangings seem "revolting"? Why was a ritual that had been unchanged in at least one critical aspect, its public design, rather suddenly transformed? What, ultimately, does the new ritual of execution day tell us about America in the 1830s and 1840s?[4]

I

The drift away from public punishments, but not public executions, accelerated in the eighteenth century when activists instituted reformative incarceration as the preferred form of penal discipline. The invention of the penitentiary, with its emphasis of solitude, penitence, and isolation, marked a radical departure in the philosophy of punishment. The penitentiary delved into the prisoner's mind or soul, whereas public punishments operated primarily on the criminal's body. To the extent that deterrence was a desirable end, it would be achieved by making punishment more mysterious and less observable. More important, reformers hoped that in the private space of the penitentiary a prisoner would internalize values consistent with a bourgeois ideal: sobriety, industry, and especially self-restraint.[5]

Proponents of the penitentiary who continued to accept the death penalty for first-degree murder did not suggest that executions should be enacted privately. For them, public executions and capital punishment were synonymous; to eliminate the former was to abolish the latter. If the state continued to execute criminals, it unquestionably must do so in the public arena. When Benjamin Rush advocated a system of private punishments, he had in mind solitude and fasting in the penitentiary as a means of reforming the prisoner, not the gallows. Rush would have found the idea of private executions disturbing—a form of private revenge suitable for monarchy but never a republic. Nor did Robert Annan, the Presbyterian minister who defended capital punishment, conceive of private executions. He feared that, if states abolished public executions entirely, all men would be "exposed to lawless outrage, private assassination, and revenge." He never imagined that the state would assume the role of private executioner.[6]

But by the late 1820s, essayists argued for executions in the privacy of prison as a substitute for public hangings. To at least a certain group of Americans, public executions were becoming increasingly intolerable. Legislators, editors, ministers, and merchants decried public hangings as festivals of disorder that subverted morals, increased crimes, excited sympathy with the criminal, and wasted time. One writer declared that "an hundred persons are made worse, where one is made better by a public execution. Rioting, drunkenness, and every species of disorderly conduct prevail. . . . There is on most occasions that draw people together in large bodies, some attention to decorum, some regard to character, some appearance of feeling; but all these are banished for a time by the thousands who flock together to witness a *public execution.*" Execution day, it was feared, "blunts moral sensibilities . . . and brutalizes people by the barbarity of the example." At the hanging of Horace Carter in 1825, a minister noted that "it is believed that the moral tendency of public punishments is pernicious. The object of public justice would be better secured, if executions took place in the jail yard."[7]

These sentiments reveal a shift in elite perceptions of the execution spectacle. In the first quarter of the nineteenth century the middle and upper classes, increasingly wedded to beliefs and sensibilities that helped make public executions anathema, began to stay away. By doing so, they altered the event itself. Social authorities could no longer depict hanging day as a spectacle of civil and religious order. No longer could it be claimed, as magistrates and ministers had in the eighteenth century, that on execution day the entire community assembled for an effective lesson in morality and piety. In 1816, in discussing one execution, Samuel Breck, heir to a mercantile fortune, wrote in his diary, "The crowd (which however I did not join) to witness his death was excessive." As a member of the Pennsylvania legislature in 1832, Breck supported a bill to abolish the "disgusting exhibition" of public executions. People from the middle and upper classes were beginning to find public hangings revolting; it was becoming a class imperative not to be associated with such disturbing scenes. Disgusted by public executions, but unwilling to advocate the abolition of capital punishment entirely, legislators in the 1820s proposed a new solution to the problem—private executions.[8]

In February 1824, the Pennsylvania senate passed the first legislative resolution to "explore the propriety of executions in the prison yard," and entertained the motion that public executions were "inexpedient, highly demoralizing, and a great and unnecessary waste of public time and labor." The hanging of John Lechler at Lancaster, on October 25, 1822, triggered the legislature's interest in the subject. For opponents of public hangings, the execution of Lechler remained a rallying point long after the elimination of public hangings.[9]

The execution took place on the common, west of the city, between one and two o'clock in the afternoon (see Figure 2 below). Lechler walked from the jail to the gallows guarded by several different companies of volunteer corps and accompanied by four ministers and the City Guard. Estimates of the number of spectators ranged from fifteen thousand to forty thousand. Accounts of the execution reported that no disturbances marred the proceedings. The *Lancaster Gazette*, for example, maintained that "the most perfect order was preserved" and that the "crowd of spectators retired without any of that confusion which too often occurs."[10]

But an editor at one newspaper, the *Yorktown Gazette*, reported the scene differently: "What has taken place at Lancaster would lead one to believe, that the spectacle of public execution produces less reformation than criminal propensity. While an old offense was atoned for, more than a dozen new ones were committed, and some of a capital grade." Here, it seemed, was evidence that public executions not only failed to prevent crime but actually caused it by inciting a portion of the spectators gathered to witness the hanging.[11]

Citing the Lechler case as an example, Jacob Cassat of Adams County, in a report to the Pennsylvania legislature, reviewed the reasons why public executions should be abolished. The spectacle, he feared, "necessarily produces a deleterious effect on the public morals" by diminishing all "sensibility of moral feeling" and indulging the "most debasing passions and appetites." He asserted that only those with reduced moral capacities congregated at public executions and, afterwards, in their revelry, disturbed more "peaceable and well disposed" citizens. By drawing thousands of spectators on a Friday afternoon, public executions also disrupted labor. Since "productive labor is wealth," argued Cassat, public executions, by causing a stoppage of labor, "cannot but materially effect the public interest." Cassat's focus on moral feelings and passions, his depiction of the spectators, and, to a lesser extent, his concern with the effect of the hanging on political economy, summarized the developing argument against public executions. The Pennsylvania legislature tabled Cassat's report, but the idea of "confining capital executions to the limits of the jail yard" continued to engage the imagination of legislators, theorists, professionals, and reformers.[12]

The most prominent commentator on crimes and punishments in the early nineteenth century was Edward Livingston, a Jeffersonian Republican and former congressman and mayor of New York.[13] In his famous report on the penal code to the Louisiana legislature, Livingston elaborated on the psychology of the opposition to public executions, arguing that public executions only aggravated the passions, such as avarice and ambition, that caused crime. Furthermore, public executions stimulated passions in otherwise reasonable people, by familiarizing them with scenes of agony, brutality, and suffering. Livingston reasoned that public executions taught spectators to overcome their natural repugnance to human suffering and led them, eventually, to commit crimes, because the mind "imitates that which has been strongly impressed on the senses." Livingston was not the first to worry about the effects of the execution spectacle on moral faculties, but unlike those before him he placed the psychology of witnessing public executions at the center of his analysis. An understanding of human passions, he thought, provided the key not only to discussion of crime and the ill effects of public executions but to punishment generally. Livingston reasoned that, instead of relying on the death penalty, legislatures should match the punishment to counteract the passion that motivated crime. Thus, if a robber or murderer wished to pass life in "idleness, debauchery, and sensual enjoyment," society must force him to submit to "coarse diet, hard lodging, and incessant labor."[14]

A widespread belief in the plasticity of the human mind and a desire to control deranging human passions helped the idea of substituting private for public executions gain in popularity. It was not in the 1820s, however, but in the 1830s that states began to abolish public hangings. By that time, a new understanding of the mind—phrenology—gripped the imagination of many Americans. This psychological theory explained in scientific terms why and how public executions demoralized spectators.

Developed by two Austrian physicians, Johann Spurzheim and Franz Joseph Gall, and popularized in America by George Combe, phrenology (the term meant discourse on the mind) analyzed behavior by viewing the brain as the mind's organ. Phrenologists divided the mind into two orders, the faculty of feelings and the faculty of intellect. Within the order of feelings were propensities, such as destructiveness, combativeness, and acquisitiveness, and sentiments such as benevolence, firmness, and conscientiousness. The intellectual faculties were divided into four categories that included the senses and the ability to perceive both concrete and abstract qualities. While all were born with a particular constitution, these faculties could be exercised to stimulate the sentiments or harness the propensities. Phrenology elaborated on the environmentalist assumptions in faculty psychology that physicians such as Rush first began to articulate in the last quarter of the eighteenth century. People were not helpless victims of innate, predetermined capacities; they were capable of moral improvement.[15]

Combe himself connected the science of phrenology to capital punishment. Although the death penalty was intended to act as a deterrent, the effect of witnessing an execution depended on the individual's constitution. Combe argued that public executions would effectively deter only "all favorably constituted men," while "it will operate with least effect precisely on those on whom it is most needed, viz., on such as by nature and circumstance are most prone to fall before temptation." As for the murderer, who "possesses the maximum of the brutal propensities which rush headlong to violence," the threat of death does not act as a restraint.

Rather, it "excites the minds" of those who are predisposed to violence. In lieu of capital punishment, Combe insisted that prisons had to provide "moral training" through "religious and intellectual instruction." Such a regimen, Combe felt, offered the "natural means for strengthening the higher and mitigating the vigor of the lower tendencies of the mind." Another means for preventing the reinforcement of the lower tendencies, or propensities, was the abolition of public executions.[16]

If animal propensities led to deviant behavior, phrenology helped to explain precisely how one ritual—the public execution—unleashed the instincts that corroded virtue and stimulated crime. Whereas Combe addressed the question of capital punishment generally, in 1833 one adherent of phrenology offered "Observations on the Curiosity of Those Who Go to Witness Public Executions" under the pseudonym "Humanity." Why, "Humanity" wondered, did thousands travel great distances to witness executions? Certainly it had nothing to do with gaining knowledge, for "all have known from childhood exactly how the whole performance goes on." Rather, "Humanity" argued, it is the propensity of the organ of destructiveness that "draws the gazing multitude." And while that organ was provided for such purposes as hunting, "it is always abused when exercised for no rational purpose; as in the case of witnessing a public execution." The gratification of this propensity, manifested in the "miserable desire of seeing a fellow being hung," strengthens the organ of destructiveness and leads to additional acts of "violence, cruelty, and murder."[17] Charles Caldwell, the foremost American proponent of phrenology and one of Benjamin Rush's students, extended the logic of "Humanity" beyond public hangings to include all executions. "No matter how life is taken away," he declared, "whether publicly or privately; in persons of suitable temperment who either witness the deed or learn it by report, it awakens to action the instinct to destroy human life."[18]

The fascination with phrenology spread rapidly through the United States. In 1822 Combe's *Essays on Phrenology* appeared in an American edition; soon thereafter supporters organized the Central Phrenological Society in Philadelphia. In 1832, Spurzheim himself lectured across the United States, and, upon his death that same year, his followers founded the Boston Phrenological Society. Across America, commercial parlors offered phrenological readings, and journalists published charts depicting the mental constitution of celebrities.

Not everyone embraced the "science of phrenology." Detractors decried phrenology as a "celestial humbug" and a "delusion." Some opposed it as fatalistic, deterministic, and materialistic; others thought it offered a "land of fancy, rather than of fact."[19] But many Americans found in phrenology a convincing and rational explanation for human behavior. Phrenology seemed to disclose why some people behaved the way they did, and it also suggested a program for change. Horace Mann, who as a legislator from Dedham first proposed the abolition of public executions in Massachusetts, was so devoted to phrenology that he named a son after George Combe. Mann once remarked that, should someone tell him "stories of the civilization of the Romans and then inform [him] that 20 or 20,000 of their people could sit a whole day to witness gladiatorial fights, [he] should know that they had not reached true civilisation—i.e. the civilisation when the moral sentiments controlled the animal selfish passions." It is likely that Mann felt similarly about public executions, a ritual that was increasingly understood as threatening, not preserving, social order.[20]

II

In the 1830s phrenology provided a compelling argument against public hangings at a time when social authorities increasingly feared a crisis of public order. Their concern with public order and public space formed another context that, understood in conjunction with the portrait of human psychology provided by phrenology, helps illuminate why legislatures began to abolish public executions in the 1830s.

Social elites never much favored mobs or riots, and in the 1820s and 1830s their fears of public disturbances reached a feverish pitch. With increasing frequency and elevated hyperbole editors addressed what they viewed as "the crisis to which our republican government is already approaching by the fearful and portentious evils of violence, mob-law, and popular commotion . . . ." "Mobs," one editor insisted, "are an open and public violation of the principles of Christianity and of civil freedom; and unless they are soon checked, in a free country, there will be neither law, liberty, nor religion remaining." Another essayist declared in 1835 that "the years 1833 and 1834 will be remarkable in the annals of our country for disregard of the law and illegal violence to persons and property."[21]

Crowds were not always viewed with such hostility. In the Revolutionary period certain urban crowds were tolerated as a legitimate, popular form for the achievement of political and social objectives. If a tax seemed too oppressive, the price of bread excessively high, or an official particularly obnoxious, the actions of the crowd often checked further exploitation. Frequently, these groups also represented the interests of political and social leaders. Although the elite might bristle at certain excesses, they seldom challenged the legitimacy of the crowd.[22]

Yet, by the beginning of the nineteenth century, authorities increasingly feared both urban and rural crowds, whether they assumed a violent or moderate form. With reports of grotesque parades of death from France, with rebellions throughout the near frontier, and with some members of a new nation intent on creating an ordered commercial polity, public disturbances such as mobs were decried as "hostile to the morality, interest, and domestic happiness of a nation." One jurist deprecated riots as "unfriendly to the liberty and existence of society." Social elites came to regard mobs and riots as an outright evil with no legitimate place in a republican society. The mayor of Boston declared that "it is manifestly impossible that any sufficient or justifying cause for popular violence exists in this country, where republican institutions secure to every individual his just share in the government of the whole." A republican nation born of crowds, the greatest threat in America seemed suddenly to be crowds in a republican nation.[23]

Not only had tolerance for the crowd diminished as a desire for public order intensified but also the nature of rioting itself changed. Newspaper accounts of riots increased in frequency for most cities throughout the 1820s, peaking around 1834. Although that may in part have been the consequence of changes in journalistic practices and a decreased tolerance for scenes of public disorder as much as an actual increase in the number of riots, it does indicate the degree to which the middle and upper classes believed social disorder was on the rise. That belief was not wholly an illusion.

Consider the summer of 1834. In New York an anti-abolitionist mob rioted for over a week. Although some newspapers at first supported the mob, as the riot progressed almost all editors called for the use of police to prevent violence and re-establish order. On August 11, near Boston, a mob composed mostly of Protestant laborers burned the Ursuline Convent in Charlestown. Fired by anti-Catholic propaganda and agitated over the burgeoning Irish Catholic presence in and around Boston, these rioters lifted the veil of monastic secrecy. In Philadelphia, August 12 saw the beginning of three nights of race rioting. Urban violence and disorder throughout the Northeast seemed so pervasive that in 1835 Philip Hone, former mayor of New York, thought that "the mob appears to have completely got the ascendency." Following the Charlestown riot one distinguished minister thundered that society has been "shaken to its foundations, all its joints loosened, all its fixtures about to be swept away." In

1835, the same year the legislature abolished public executions, Massachusetts revised its riot act to state clearly that civil commotion would not be tolerated.[24]

Those riots came at a time when everyday urban life was making people nervous about public order. Population explosion, especially from immigration, made cities more dangerous and unhealthy. The population of New York, for example, ballooned from 30,000 in 1790 to 200,000 in 1830. The populations of other northeastern cities tripled and quadrupled. Elites associated the crowding of cities and infusion of peculiar dialects with criminal activity. "Vice," reported one paper in 1827, "is pouring into the city like a torrent." When the cholera epidemic spread through the United States in 1832, many commentators blamed it on the immigrants, the unclean streets, and a general sense of public disarray. With cartloads of bodies drawn through the streets and those who could afford it fleeing for the health of the countryside, the cities appeared literally sick and increasingly disordered.[25]

Public gatherings, whether for executions or riots, parades or festivals, clogged public space and, in a climate of accelerated commercial expansion, threatened the interests of merchants and investors. One legislator insisted that "the loss of time and money, the interruption of business, and the almost total disorganization of almost all pursuits in the immediate neighbourhood of the scene, are serious evils." Some storeowners, especially those who sold liquor and food, may have profited on execution day. But to most legislators, merchants, manufacturers, and professionals, the public life of the streets threatened person, property, and profit. One response to the perception of disorder was legislation that abolished public executions.[26]

III

A belief in the impressionability and plasticity of the mind and the transformation of cities, through population explosion, immigration, epidemics, and rioting deepened middle- and upper-class anxiety over public order. The concern with public assemblies and public space accelerated the shift to a faith in privacy and the creation of an urban environment characterized by class segmentation and social exclusion. Armored with certain sensibilities, the middle and upper classes desired control over passions, authentic private selves, and refuge from public life. The ascendence of these sensibilities, well under way in the 1820s and hastened by social changes, altered attitudes toward public rituals and gatherings and made certain events in the public realm, such as executions, intolerable.

The trend toward privacy for the middle- and upper-class family and the concomitant triumph of a sensibility that led them to loathe the uncouthness of common, public behavior emerged as parts of a broad shift in Western culture spanning several centuries. That transformation was accompanied by a change in attitudes toward death away from a communal, public death and toward an individual, private demise. The germination of Renaissance humanism and Lockean epistemology, the erosion of patriarchal relationships, and the rise of industrial capitalism all played a role in that momentous cultural transformation. But the concern with civility and privacy, with self-control and internal discipline, peaked throughout the West in the nineteenth century.[27]

In the United States, the shift toward privacy manifested itself in specific social and cultural phenomena. Residential segregation along class lines intensified throughout the cities of the Northeast. It was during this period that such diverse locations as the workplace and the theater became more class-stratified. At the same time that classes cut themselves off from one another, middle-class families turned inward to the private realm of the sanctified home. The front parlor became a vehicle to screen out visitors and seclude the personal rooms of the house. The private sphere of domesticity was peddled as the true realm for women; men, corrupted after a day entangled in public affairs, discovered purity only in the home. Families became smaller and parents kept children at home longer. Etiquette books served as primers on how to control one's emotions and avoid public embarrassment. Even mourning for the dead lost its communal fervor and instead became introspective and individualized. In each of these ways the middle and upper classes realized an ideal of privacy and rejected the public, communal sphere as corruptive, disorderly, and even alien.[28]

The reconstitution of community away from diverse public gatherings and toward restricted private assemblies can also be observed in the shifting iconography of gallows broadsides between the eighteenth and nineteenth centuries. Figure 1 (1788) is typical of eighteenth-century depictions of the hanging scene (page 48). In this woodcut only the spectators are presented as full figures; the others are in profile. Assembled as one, the spectators provide a reminder that the public execution is designed for the crowd, an image that the community is united, and a model of how the viewer is expected to behave—sober, respectful, and orderly. The criminal seems hardly to matter at all. In Figure 2 (1822), it is again the crowd and order that matter most, though the unity of the spectators has fractured. Figure 2 is revealing in another respect, for the artist, Lewis Miller, has captured a development in the technology of punishment re-

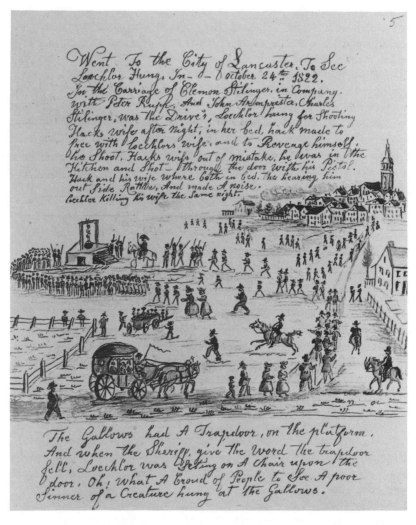

FIGURE 2. Lewis Miller's sketch of the hanging of John Lechler at Lancaster, Pennsylvania in 1822. (*Courtesy, Historical Society of York County*)

lated to the shift in middle-class sensibilities. The gallows constructed for John Lechler's execution had a screened trap door through which the criminal would fall. Such a contraption prevented the public from witnessing the agonizing contortions and expulsions of the body in the minutes after the drop fell. The hanging was still a public one, but the bourgeois ideal that fostered seclusion and restraint manifested itself in the creation of an enclosed trap door, a device designed to insulate spectators from what many viewed as the most revolting part of the ritual.

Figures 3 (1817) and 4 (1825) are characteristic of the redirected focus of the gallows scene. Unlike Miller's drawing, the image is of the doomed criminal alone; the spectators are not represented. The solitary criminal, or the prisoner with attendants, pervaded gallows iconography in the first decades of the nineteenth century. Even before the legislatures abolished public hangings, depictions of the execution scene had already begun to focus away from the assembled and toward the condemned, away from a faith in community and toward an ideal of privacy. Figure 3, which illustrates the bogus *Narrative of the Pious Death of the Penitent Henry Mills*, helps to illuminate another meaning in this shift to private executions. Mills's image suggests two important themes—the penitent criminal and the nervousness nineteenth-century Americans felt about the dichotomy between public roles and private selves.

The performance of the criminal at the gallows constituted a central element in the theater of public executions. Ministers and magistrates fretted that the condemned should enact the role of the truly penitent; even in cases where the penitence of the criminal was suspect, written accounts described the criminal as truly devout. The Thayers (Figure 4), who implicitly defended the murder of their tenant John Love on the grounds that it was better "to run the risk of being hung as to lose [one's] property," were described as appearing "quite humble and penitent" as execution day approached. Ministers might have feared what evil loomed hidden away in the crowd, but few openly questioned the authenticity of the conversion experience at the gallows. In the last decade of the eighteenth century, however, as one of their arguments against capital punishment, opponents of the death penalty assailed gallows conversions as disingenuous. Anti-gallows essayists wondered whether conversion was not a matter of too great importance "to hurry a being into the awful presence of his creator with all his imperfections on his head," especially since the reformation of criminals in penitentiaries now seemed possible. One discussion of the difficulty of conversion in the last hours suggested that those who defer repentance "are crafty deceivers who act fraudulently with God, and pretend to dupe Him with their artifices." Charles Cald-

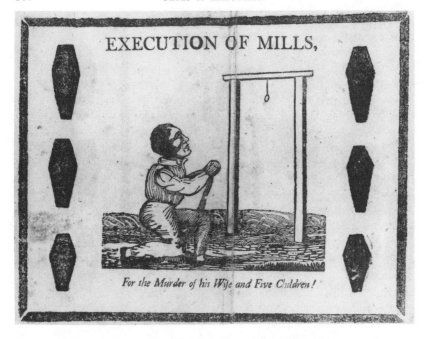

FIGURE 3. Illustration from the *Narrative of the Pious Death of the Penitent Henry Mills* (1817). (*Courtesy, American Antiquarian Society*)

well best summarized the fear that capital punishment encouraged false conversions and, as a result, "fatally interfered" with a prisoner's "higher concerns with Heaven and eternity." "A jail-bred or gibbet-bred repentance and amendment," he warned, "is an event of a character, too improvident and equivocal, to be regarded as a safe guarantee of man's condition beyond the grave." Another essayist, in a *Discourse on Capital Punishment*, lampooned the travesty of a gallows conversion: "If the certainty of suspension on a gallows is the surest and speediest way of preparing man to meet his God . . . everyone should have themselves condemned to the gallows, even for no offense, without delay."[29]

In this atmosphere of deep concern over true penitence, Figure 3 might be viewed as a parody of conversion at the gallows. The title, "The Pious Death of the Penitent Henry Mills," claims too much; his swollen, kneeling body prays too hard. No spectators are present to witness or verify his piety and penitence. Who knew whether those who delayed their conversion to the final moment were truly penitent or merely convincing imposters? How could one determine whether their genuine conversion brought them salvation or their bogus one brought damnation? This di-

FIGURE 4. Broadside depiction accompanying *The Dying Address of the Three Thayers* (1825). (*Courtesy, American Antiquarian Society*)

lemma, always latent in the ritual of public executions and, to a certain extent, a convention in Christian eschatology, seemed especially acute in the early decades of the nineteenth century.

The theme of appearance versus reality, of the public face versus the private self, obsessed Americans. How could people tell that others actually were who they claimed to be? The problem became particularly severe in the highly mobile, well-populated, increasingly commercialized areas of the Mid-Atlantic and Northeast. In the context of a general shift toward an ideal of privacy, the middle classes exalted the private, non-public self as the indicator of truth and authenticity. To be sure, this preoccupation with an authentic self constitutes a major theme in Western literature and thought. But for writers in the first half of the nineteenth century, the humbug, the quack, and the confidence man lurked at every turn.[30]

Herman Melville understood as well as anyone the central reason for the falsity of public performance. In *The Confidence Man: His Masquerade* (1857) he portrayed the pathology of social relations in a capitalist society. Aboard a Mississippi steamer named the *Fidèle* a confidence man assumes multiple personae. Among his disguises, the imposter appears as a salesman, an agent selling stock for a coal company, and a cosmopolitan philanthropist. After gaining the confidence and trust of numerous passengers, he liberates them of their money by telling persuasive stories of woe, peddling a bogus product, or playing on their very lack of confidence in the first place. The story can be read as a meditation upon the products of a society grounded in the marketplace, founded upon contractual relations, and peopled by increasing numbers of highly mobile strangers. If "confidence is the indispensible basis of all sorts of business transactions," then confidence is an inevitable consequence of exchange in a capitalist society. Where there were stock, credit, and profit, there had to be confidence as a lubricant; and where confidence was required, characters profited by posing as the sincere, mannered, and moral person of business.[31]

In this climate of heightened sensitivity to the deceptiveness of appearances and general anxiety over public intercourse, the public performance of the penitent criminal lost much of its former social value. No one could be certain that during the spectacle of public execution the prisoner's conversion was authentic. And even if it were, new sensibilities about the expression of feelings, and the withdrawal of the middle class into privacy, dictated that the last moments of a condemned prisoner's life should occur away from the scrutiny of the general public.

Francis Parkman, Unitarian pastor of the New North Church in Boston and father of the famous historian, united these themes when he reviewed four works on capital punishment for the *Christian Examiner*. Parkman protested "against that loathsome exhibition of religious frenzy, which in the shape of exulting hopes, special assurances of pardon, and of immediate salvation, has been sometimes witness among us." The criminal should not "be encouraged to think," Parkman insisted, "that because his offenses are to be punished by man, he at once becomes a regenerate child of God." Parkman decried the fiction of conversion at the execution which presented "malefactors . . . as if they were martyrs, dying joyfully in Jesus, and ascending from the gallows to glory." Parkman considered such spectacles "as revolting as they are unnecessary." He captured the moral sensibility of the middle and upper classes when he asserted that "the shame, fear, anguish, or even religious frenzy produced in these last stages of earthly misery . . . are not fit spectacles for the public gaze." The solution, Parkman wrote two years prior to the abolition of public executions, was that the religious service, and perhaps the entire hanging, "should be private."[32]

Just as the penitentiary punished criminals privately rather than publicly in hopes of better effecting reformation, private executions, it was felt, might result in genuine rather than bogus conversions. This was the thrust of Thomas Cope's plea for private punishment in 1820. Cope, a Quaker merchant in Philadelphia and activist in the campaign against capital punishment, asked, "If society will persist in the infliction of death for crime, why thus suffer the criminal to be exposed[?] . . . Why not, rather, by seclusion from the world, afford him the opportunity of reflection and repentance?" For merchants such as Cope and ministers such as Parkman, private executions promised to promote the criminal's penitence, protect the public from a "loathsome exhibition," and guard the execution itself from a supposed disorderly public.[33]

A "Report on Punishment by Death," submitted to the Massachusetts legislature in 1831, synthesized the prevalent concerns with public executions. Seeking to restrain "heated, disordered imaginations," desiring to avoid a public gathering of "the daring and profligate," bothered by "the noise of a public execution," and disturbed that citizens came into "communion and fellowship" at this "degrading, disgraceful spectacle," legislators recommended that executions be *"set apart from the public gaze."* Four years later, they would have their way.[34]

The cultural origins of the abolition of public executions, then, can be traced to beliefs about the impressionability of the mind, anxieties over social order and public appearance, and ideals of privacy that made the public realm far less appealing than the private arena. These were the ideas and anxieties around which a middle class coalesced in the early nineteenth century. To be sure, public interactions were not abandoned entirely. At the very moment public executions came under attack, the middle class embraced new forms of ordered, public experience such as schools and revivals. These were desirable, however, because they promoted precisely those values and characteristics that public executions seemed to undermine: restraint, discipline, control, and order. Private hangings precluded the gathering of large groups in congested public spaces; they eliminated a public scene of violent death to which certain citizens, women and children especially, dare not be exposed; they excluded the lower orders from viewing the execution of someone most probably like them; finally, private executions were accessible only to a selected few, and, as a result, they served to reinforce the shared cultural values of the middle and upper levels of American society.

IV

Although the abolition of public executions occurred rapidly and fit with broader cultural trends, some commentators opposed private executions as anti-republican, non-egalitarian, and irrefutable evidence that capital punishment did not deter crime. Andrew Preston Peabody, a Unitarian clergyman and pastor of the South Parish Church in Portsmouth, New Hampshire, reported in the *Christian Examiner* a year before the Pennsylvania legislature abolished public hangings that "it has been proposed to substitute for public, private executions in the criminal's cell, in the presence of none, except the ministers of justice." But, Peabody went on to explain, "this would open the door to the greatest abuses, and, in a community like ours, would never be tolerated; for publicity is the genius of our government and secrecy of operation in every department abhorred by it."[35] Thomas Upham, a Congregationalist minister and professor of moral and mental philosophy at Bowdoin College, considered private executions "a great anomaly . . . in a republican government":

> Our courts of justice must be open to the public; the deliberations of our legislature must be public; not even a poor freemasonry society is to be tolerated because its ceremonies are secret; but when life is to be taken, when a human being is to be smitten down like an ox, when a soul is to be violently hurled into eternity, the most solemn occasion that can be witnessed on earth, then the public must be excluded. But the American public will not long submit to this. If business of this nature is done at all, it must be done in the light of day; if the continuance of capital punishments depends on their being inflicted in private, it may be regarded as certain, that they cannot long exist in this country.[36]

Peabody's and Upham's predictions, grounded as they were in republican and democratic principles, proved inaccurate. The state would deny the general public access to executions. But who was to witness these private hangings? The Pennsylvania law specified that the sheriff should select at least "twelve reputable citizens" in addition to a physician and the attorney general of the county; the New York law was nearly identical. In principle, private executions were supposed to protect the sensibilities of all citizens, eliminate a scene of public chaos and confusion, and permit the prisoner to die quietly penitent; in practice, they became a theatrical event for an assembly of elite men who attended the execution by invitation while the community at large was excluded.

Prison corridors were often jammed on execution day. Approximately 125 persons witnessed Samuel Zepphon's execution at Moyamensing Prison in Philadelphia; about three hundred attended the hanging of James Eager in New York; over one hundred people entered the Leverett Street jail in Boston when the state executed Washington Goode.[37] The scores of people routinely admitted to executions did not represent all groups in society. Rather, the professional and commercial elite of a community gathered at private executions. One account reported that "many of our city authorities" attended the execution of James Eager. "Many merchants" were among the crowd of 250 people at the execution of John White Webster, a Harvard professor. And at the hanging of Ira Stout in Rochester, "the majority of invited guests were professional and public men." Whereas in the eighteenth century the entire community had been summoned to the gallows to affirm common values against outside interference, beginning in the 1830s, an elite segment of society gathered at private executions to celebrate the extinction of vice now viewed as originating from within the community.[38]

The hanging itself was as perturbing behind prison walls as in public. An inspector with the New York Police Department who attended an execution at the Tombs Prison left the affair a critic of capital punishment. He confessed, "It was the most sickening sight that I ever beheld and God grant that I may never have an occasion to witness another execution, and that the death penalty may be abolished and imprisonment for life be substituted."[39]

Some opponents of capital punishment, aware that certain citizens had access to the prison yard, criticized the all-too-public nature of private executions. Francis Lieber, professor of political economy at the University of South Carolina, commented on the misnomer of "private" executions. He preferred to call such hangings the "indoor manner of executing criminals," for "to call them not public is wrong." John L.

O'Sullivan, the editor of the *Democratic Review*, also recognized the class component in private executions. In 1841 he wondered why an execution in New York resembled "a private judicial assassination, which shrinks from the open view of the public, and perpetuates its revolting function only within the guarded precincts of the prison walls in the presence of a small number of officials or privileged spectators." Why, he asked, did it not incorporate the "whole people"? William Lloyd Garrison, who included opposition to the gallows in his litany of reform interests, thought the law permitting private executions "anti-republican" and was disturbed that some people "are not to come in contact with them [executions] anymore than with the Asiatic cholera."[40]

One excluded group was women. At a time when the middle classes exalted women as the embodiment of domesticity and sentimentality, as keepers of morality and virtue, their attendance at executions was denounced as "a matter of surprise and regret, that female curiosity should so far get the better of female delicacy, as to induce their presence at such spectacles." *Niles Weekly Register* reported that only "the lowest order of *prostitutes* attended executions" and suggested that "attending women are fit subjects for the cowhide." Lucy Colman, anti-slavery lecturer and women's rights activist, reported from Rochester that at the execution of Ira Stout "not one of my sex was invited." Some women apparently felt the exclusion unjust. In her *Letters from New York* (1844), Lydia Maria Child, an opponent of capital punishment, commented sarcastically that "*women* deemed themselves not treated with becoming gallantry, because tickets of admittance were denied *them*; and I think it showed unjudicious partiality; for many of them can be taught murder by as short a lesson as any man."[41]

Private executions not only excluded significant portions of the people, they also contradicted the argument that capital punishment acted as a deterrent. Opponents of the gallows zealously highlighted the inconsistency and insisted that the elimination of public executions necessitated the abolition of capital punishment entirely. The *Philadelphia Gazette* editorialized that "the abolition of the former practice of *publicity* on the infliction of the punishment of death is a virtual recognition of the little efficacy attaching to it as a deterrent example; and that the same reason which induces the substitution of *private* executions . . . carried out to its legitimate extension, calls upon us now for the total abolition of the punishment itself." E. H. Chapin, one of the most popular lecturers in antebellum America, asked why "if Capital Punishment is indeed a salutary terror, have some states abolished hanging in public, holding their executions in the prison yard? Plainly, because they produce more evil than good and brutalize instead of softening hearts already prone to crime." And in 1855 Wendell Phillips asked rhetorically, "If this idea of hanging men . . . is correct, then why do you not make your executions as public as possible? Why do you not hang men at the centre of the Commons? Our fathers did it. . . ."[42]

These criticisms of private executions not only raised questions about republican government and the deterrent effect of hangings but also embodied a tension within bourgeois attitudes toward public space and the private realm. Even as the middle class redesigned the public arena and withdrew into privacy, they increasingly attacked selected targets that smacked of secrecy. The explosion of anti-Masonic feeling in the 1820s and the anti-Catholicism expressed in the burning of the Ursuline Convent, to take but two examples, revealed an abhorrence of hidden ritual and "secluded associations." Frederick Marryat, who toured the United States, observed the same phenomenon: "Americans . . . cannot bear anything like a secret." Andrew Peabody and Thomas Upham thought that this repugnance with seclusion and secrecy would apply to private executions as well, but they were mistaken. Those who challenged certain types of private assemblies as too secretive, and as contrary to middle-class Protestant values, promoted private executions as perfectly consonant with those same values. Still, private executions could be construed as obnoxious to the image of an open, egalitarian, democratic society. Indeed, one proponent of private hangings was anxious "to obviate any objections to too great secrecy." The question remains, why did the transition to private hangings not rankle more people?[43]

The opponents of capital punishment might have been expected at the time to challenge private executions, but they never did. Some of them condemned the elitist nature of private executions. Others argued that prison hangings repudiated the logic of a defense of the death penalty. But, generally, they believed that the elimination of public executions would lead to the total abolition of capital punishment. Only in the 1840s did activists begin to realize their error. The abolition of public executions not only left capital punishment intact, it also neutralized the argument that the spectacle of execution disordered society.

As for the spectators, thousands continued to gather outside the prison on hanging day. Depending on the location of the gallows, many of them could glimpse what was going on inside. This was the case of an execution in Belvedere, New Jersey, where the gallows was "raised above the walls of the prison-yard so that spectators without could witness the execution"; it occurred repeatedly at the Leverett Street Jail in Boston where row houses on the west side of the street overlooked the jail yard.

Only a few private executions became "open" to the public in this way, however, and they probably played no significant role in restraining an assault on prison hangings.[44]

Far more significant in deflecting opposition to private executions was a revolution in journalistic practices and printing technology. Prior to the early nineteenth century, newspapers did not furnish lengthy accounts of public executions. A separate genre of gallows literature—broadsides, last words and confessions, ministers' sermons—provided the reading public with details, but newspapers mentioned the hanging only in a terse sentence or two. All this began to change in the 1820s and 1830s. Facilitated by technological inventions such as steam-driven and cylinder presses, a new type of newspaper emerged. It cost one cent rather than six, was pitched to the expanding market of daily buyers rather than a limited number of subscribers, and hawked the "news" (in itself a new concept) to all segments of the community rather than an elite minority interested chiefly in commercial information. Between 1830 and 1840 the number of dailies in America more than doubled. The most influential penny papers emerged at the same time that public executions were eliminated: *New York Sun* in 1833, *New York Herald* in 1835, *Boston Daily Times* in 1836, and the *Philadelphia Public Ledger* in 1836.[45]

When legislators abolished public executions and excluded large segments of the population from witnessing the spectacle, newspaper editors stood ready to provide coverage of the hanging just at the precise moment readers desired accounts of the execution. That the first editors of the penny-press papers came from an artisanal background helps to explain why these publications readily began to report executions. After all, among those excluded from witnessing the hanging spectacle were the working classes. Moreover, these newspaper accounts redirected the information pitched to the public about an execution. Whereas moral and religious messages aimed at the spectator pervaded the gallows literature, factual, descriptive accounts designed for a reader appeared in newspapers. In the eighteenth century, gallows literature seldom depicted the criminal as anything but admitting guilt and truly penitent; in the nineteenth century, newspapers reported the criminal's final actions regardless of the moral implications.[46]

Samuel Zepphon, for example, asserted his innocence with his final words. And readers of both the New York *Sun* and *Herald* learned that Manual Fernandez, alias Richard Jackson, one of the first to be privately executed at Bellevue Prison, spent his final day smoking cigars and drinking brandy provided him by the warden. Only upon sighting the scaffold did his face whiten and lips begin to quiver, and even then his only words were "I am tired, let it go." No mention of penitence, no sermonizing, and no calls to avoid the path he tread disrupted the report of the proceedings. The bulk of one account detailed the post-execution dissection at the Barclay Street Hospital anatomical theater, where surgeons used a galvanic battery to try to stimulate the nerves of Fernandez's stiffened body. Should the final part of the day's event disturb readers, the *Sun* pointed out that the criminal had rendered his victim an "equally lifeless and bloody spectacle." Aside from this incidental justification of the punishment on the grounds of retribution, the account was devoid of any proscriptive messages.[47]

Ironically, what had been thought too corrupting to witness publicly, even with the attendant safeguards of ministers' sermons and formulized moral messages, could now be experienced privately through a printed medium that reported the execution without emphasizing its didactic purpose. Readers were free to construct their own interpretations rather than receive only an official one. But that is not to say that social elites relinquished their desire to forge some kind of cultural consensus. The abolition of public executions and new methods of reportage represented a different approach to the problems of influence and authority. The middle class now preferred private renderings of hangings derived from print rather than public ones viewed and heard collectively. By instituting private executions, legislators eliminated an occasion for public gathering, imposed control over public space, and precluded the open expression of certain passions and emotions. They also fashioned a new illusion of an ordered, consensual society that replaced an earlier depiction of hanging day as a ritual that affirmed communally shared civil and religious values.

The use of newspapers to disseminate information about a private execution was the recommendation of a senate select committee of the New York legislature directed to inquire "into the propriety of abolishing public executions." The committee report summarized what they saw as the most telling defense of public hangings: "that if punishments were privately inflicted, it could not be known whether they were actually, and justly and properly, inflicted upon the persons condemned, or that innocent persons had not become victims." The legislators reasoned that since so few people could obtain "ocular evidence" of the execution, it would be sufficient to protect against any "evasion, perversion, or abuse" by publishing an account of the hanging attested to by "respectable citizens who would attend the execution not as private spectators but as public witnesses."[48]

Herein lies one of the mechanisms of cultural change. The penny-press newspaper permitted the appearance of openness, the illusion that the public had access to events that, in reality, had become shut off to them. Private executions would have been more strenuously opposed without provision for values that still held currency. Only in discovering new means by which to appeal to older cultural forms could those forms themselves be dismantled. That artisans and workingmen, chief among those excluded from private executions, played a central role in the development of these newspapers is one of the ironies of this story. Cultural change, it would seem, required the appearance of stability and tradition, of not tampering with established ways of proceeding, even as the rules were being rewritten.

The New York committee report concluded that "public executions . . . are of a positively injurious and demoralizing tendency." Reasoning from phrenological principles, they asked rhetorically whether those who assemble at executions were "of that class of citizens whose reason is to be convinced, or whose animal feelings are to be excited." And with regard to the criminal the report concluded that, "cut off from the glare and murmurs of the multitude," the solitude of private executions promoted "true contrition and sincere repentance." A month after the report, on May 9, 1835, the New York legislature abolished public executions.[49]

In antebellum America hanging day lost its pedagogical purpose as a public spectacle designed by state authorities and social leaders to deter crime and inculcate a particular set of cultural values. Disgusted by a "loathsome exhibition," anxious over public order, and convinced that public hangings failed to prevent crime, legislatures took execution day away from the general public. The vehicle by which an elite promoted order had changed dramatically. At public executions all members of the community assembled for a lesson in civil and religious order; from the 1830s on, a segment of the urban Northeast—the professional men, the merchants, the city authorities—gathered at the new ritual of execution and had their basest fears of public disorder and convulsion alleviated, their worst nightmares of losing authority and control assuaged, in a private prison spectacle. The rest of the public, skating furiously across a society of opportunity, a boastful democratic society, read about the execution in the morning paper and, for the most part, overlooked this undemocratic swing toward exclusion and privatization. The open, public institutions that so impressed foreign visitors were counterbalanced, perhaps even made possible, by newly formed private mechanisms of order and control such as prison executions—a ritual that used the penny press to peddle the fiction that it was open to public scrutiny while actually revealing itself to only a segment of American society.

6

Anti-Gallows Activists and the Commitment to Moral Reform

It was the times, it is said; yes, but who makes the times?
CHARLES SPEAR, Diary, December 22, 1841

"The subject of capital punishment," insisted the *Pennsylvania Freeman* in 1844, "is claiming much and increasing attention, not only in our own State, but in many other parts of the country." Reformers loved nothing more than to proclaim the popularity of their cause, but even a cursory review of the printed literature of the period indicates that the editor was not exaggerating. During the 1840s, books, pamphlets, and reports by scores of writers flooded the public with arguments against capital punishment. Ministers, editors, and lecturers better known for their devotion to other moral and social causes adopted the anti-gallows movement as their own. When not blasting slavery, Wendell Phillips, Theodore Parker, and William Lloyd Garrison fired salvos at the death penalty. The premier issue of a newspaper devoted entirely to the elimination of the gallows appeared on January 1, 1845. Legislators were swamped with reports and petitions urging the abolition of capital punishment. In 1847, Michigan abolished the death penalty entirely.[1]

It is perhaps ironic that an organized, extended assault on the gallows peaked in the decade following the abolition of public hangings. After all, the elimination of public executions had deprived opponents of capital punishment a critical argument: that such spectacles demoralized the population. Yet, private executions also deprived proponents of a fundamental argument: the contention that hangings served as a deterrent to crime. "Nearly the whole force of this deterrent influence," concluded one legislative report, "is now lost by the almost universal infliction of the death penalty in private. Public opinion, in banishing the gallows from

117

the public gaze, has really abandoned the argument." Hopeful that private executions exposed and neutralized the false concern with deterrence, and energized by a general reform spirit that seemed to pervade the land, anti-gallows activists pressed for the universal abolition of capital punishment.[2]

One manifestation of the wave of reform agitation was the formation of both local and national societies for the abolition of capital punishment. The shift to formal organizations in the 1830s and 1840s transformed the dynamics of social agitation in important ways. No longer were questions such as capital punishment, slavery, and temperance the sole province of an intellectual elite who published their thoughts in pamphlets and, through informal contacts, tried to persuade legislators to take action. Now, under the umbrella of an organization, a formal society, hundreds devoted themselves to a particular cause. Thousands more could express their support through contributions and subscriptions. Reform societies altered the tactics of agitation. As an institutional entity complete with business offices, reform societies lobbied legislatures, organized petition campaigns, sponsored public meetings, and published thousands of inexpensive pamphlets and broadsides. These societies also contributed to the rise of the professional reformer, the individual who chose social activism as a "career."[3]

Reform societies would not have grown so rapidly if not for the social context that sustained them. A revolution in print and communication technology made reform accessible to those who previously could not have read about it in newspapers or heard it debated in the cavernous new lecture halls of antebellum America. The increasing spatial segregation of the urban Northeast also meant that those most likely to join voluntary associations—the middle class—worked and lived in close proximity to one another. Shifts in occupational structure and authority relations further contributed to legitimizing reform as a career. The erosion of ministerial authority in the early nineteenth century not only freed ministers to labor for humanity through voluntary associations rather than church offices but also created a need for new cultural brokers to help exhibit and shape middle-class mores. The professional reformer and reform organization filled that need perfectly.[4]

I

In the 1840s, citizens across the Northeast banded together to oppose capital punishment. In Philadelphia, a committee met in January 1842 and adopted a set of resolutions that denounced the death penalty as an ineffective deterrent, as tending actually to increase crime, as opposed to the "humane feelings and sentiments of the community," and contrary to "that religious regard for human life, without which the peace and welfare of society cannot be maintained." In sum, the participants resolved that capital punishment was "wholly unjust, inexpedient, subversive of the legitimate ends of justice, and contrary to the genius and spirit of Christianity." The New York Society for the Abolition of Capital Punishment grew out of a gathering held in February 1844, and the Massachusetts Society was formed in 1845. All three organizations engaged in similar activities: they raised funds, sponsored petition campaigns, organized lecture circuits, prepared memorials to state legislatures, and circulated literature opposing the death penalty. In addition to collective actions, individual members thundered for reform in their newspapers and from their pulpits.[5]

The three organizations consisted primarily of ministers, lawyers, physicians, journalists, and merchants. In Philadelphia, six members of the standing Committee of Twenty-Five were physicians, including Isaac Parrish, the son of Joseph Parrish, who was also a physician and had participated in a debate over capital punishment decades earlier; Henry S. Patterson, who served as physician-in-chief to both the Philadelphia Dispensary and Almshouse; and John A. Elkinton, who a year earlier had published *A Lecture on Capital Punishment*. Five committeemen were members of the bar, including Richard Vaux, the unsuccessful Democratic candidate for mayor in 1842 and inspector of the state prison; William Darrah Kelley, a Democrat who in 1845 became deputy prosecuting attorney of the state; and Job Tyson, who published *An Essay on the Penal Law of Pennsylvania* in 1827. Thomas Earle, also a member of the bar, was editor of the *Mechanic's Free Press and Reform Advocate*. Three other committeemen also served primarily as editors: Benjamin Matthias of the *Saturday Chronicle*, Robert Morris of the *Pennsylvania Inquirer*, and Joseph C. Neal of the *Pennsylvanian*. The remaining members of the Committee were mostly merchants and artisans. They ranged from the wealthy Quaker merchant Thomas P. Cope, to the apprenticed jeweler turned manufacturer and philanthropist, William Mullen, to John Aston, Jr., a tailor, and Samuel Hart, a druggist.[6]

Given the historical relationship between the Quakers, Philadelphia, and penal reform, it is not surprising that at least one-quarter of the Committee were Quakers. Politically, both Democrats and Whigs joined in opposing capital punishment. The Committee also contained a mixture of young and old. In 1842 Enoch Taylor, a Whig lawyer, was 24, William D. Kelley was 28, and Richard Vaux only 26; Cope was 75, and Elkinton was Taylor's grandfather. This combination of liberal religious views, bipartisan political beliefs, and youthfulness characterized the other reform societies as well.

The founders of the New York association included Horace Greeley, John L. O'Sullivan, William S. Balch, Jacob Harsen, and Josiah Hopper. Greeley, editor of the influential *Tribune*, was at the beginning of a long career in politics and reform. O'Sullivan edited the *United States Magazine and Democratic Review* and served as a state legislator. Balch acted as pastor at the Third Universalist Church in the city. Harsen was a physician, as was Hopper, grandson of the Quaker reformer Isaac T. Hopper. On that night in 1844 these men formed the American Society for the Collection and Diffusion of Information in Relation to the Punishment of Death. The following year they changed the name to the New York Society for the Abolition of Capital Punishment.[7]

The officers of the Society represented a segment of the editorial, political, and legal elite of the city. William Cullen Bryant, editor of the Democratic *Evening Post* and a Unitarian, served as president. O'Sullivan served as corresponding secretary. The Steering Committee of Five consisted of Greeley and Harsen, Parke Godwin (William Bryant's son-in-law and also an editor), William H. Channing (nephew of William Ellery Channing and a Unitarian minister), and Samuel H. Tilden (a Democrat and at the time corporation counsel of New York City). In 1845, William T. McCoun, justice of the state supreme court, succeeded Bryant as president. The key members of the Society were relatively young: O'Sullivan at 29, Greeley at 31, Godwin at 26, and Tilden at 28 suggest that, at least in part, a youthful idealism guided the actions of these men. Moreover, as of 1842, these "reformers" were just entering the political and social world of New York. They would, for the most part, go on to have long, influential careers, and their early involvement in the anti-gallows movement served as much to introduce them to one another and the avenues to power as to fulfill their desire for social reform.

O'Sullivan, a prominent New York Democrat, and Greeley, an influential Whig editor, worked together for the abolition of capital punishment. Since Democrats and Whigs are often depicted as hopelessly divided in their ideas about society, their collaboration may seem surprising. To be sure, these political parties fought bitterly over such issues as banks, tariffs, railroads, and westward expansion. But whatever their differences in attitudes toward the use of government and the virtue of the people, both Democrats and Whigs found in their respective party ideologies reason to oppose capital punishment. For Democrats such as O'Sullivan, the constitutional doctrine of self-government was easily applied to the social realm. Capital punishment not only exceeded the power of the state; it also deprived individuals of the opportunity to learn how to govern their own lives. Since so many of those executed by the state were poor, Democrats viewed the death penalty as an embodiment of inequality and privilege. Whigs such as Greeley differed fundamentally with the Democratic insistence that the government that governed least governed best, but other aspects of Whig social philosophy led some Whigs to oppose capital punishment. Whigs may not have had as much faith as Democrats in democratic government, but they cherished the ideals of self-restraint and moral improvement. Many Whigs saw the gallows as an impediment to the development of the kind of society they dreamed of fashioning: industrious, disciplined, and culturally homogeneous. The execution of a citizen was a confession that the Whig ideal did not always work. Democrats and Whigs battled over the shape that American society should take, but individuals from both parties could agree that the gallows had no place in either model.[8]

The Massachusetts Society for the Abolition of Capital Punishment also contained an amalgam of professionals. The delegates to a meeting in New York for the purposes of forming a national society included Robert Rantoul, Jr., Democratic legislator; Amasa Walker, economist; Charles Spear, E. H. Chapin, Samuel May, and John Pierpont, two Universalist and two Unitarian ministers respectively; and Walter Channing, a physician. On the whole, these activists were older than their New York and Philadelphia colleagues. In addition to lobbying for the commutation of death sentences, circulating petitions, and holding public meetings, the Massachusetts Society sponsored the publication of *The Hangman*, a periodical devoted to the anti-gallows cause.[9]

Members of the New York, Philadelphia, and Massachusetts societies for the abolition of capital punishment met in 1845 and formed a national organization, the Society for the Abolition of the Punishment of Death. The presidents of each state society acted as vice presidents of the national group. George Mifflin Dallas, Philadelphia Democrat and Vice President of the United States at the time, accepted appointment as president of the society. The national society never became as influential as other national organizations such as the American Anti-Slavery Society, but especially with the Vice President of the country at its head, it did serve to legitimize further the opposition to capital punishment as a reform led not by utopians, anarchists, and social visionaries, although many radicals supported the cause, but by middle-class professionals and well-heeled citizens.

As a consequence of their respectability, reform societies such as these often worked at cross purposes. Associations helped legitimize reform as an acceptable, institutional means of effecting change. When well-known social and political figures lent their names to various boards of officers, they helped make these organizations official, expert commentators on any given social question. But often the result was to encourage associations to take fairly conservative positions. Arguments over aims and means within organizations would often be resolved only if societies found an agreeable middle ground. Otherwise, they risked disruption and fragmentation. The splitting of reform societies, which occurred almost as rapidly as groups were formed, decentralized the authority of any single association and, consequently, undermined the effectiveness of social agitation generally. Organizations for reform, then, cut two ways. They publicized, organized, and helped legitimize opposition to certain social problems, but they also tended either to sanitize issues or to splinter into so many factions that effecting change became, if anything, more unlikely.

While the members of the Philadelphia, New York, and Massachusetts societies were men, women also assumed an active but separate role in the campaign against capital punishment. Some women in New York formed a Female Anti-Capital Punishment Society. Lydia Maria Child, author of the extremely popular *Letter from New York* and an anti-slavery advocate, also opposed capital punishment. Child, however, refused to join formally any association because she despised the bickering and infighting and thought that the "tendency to *co-erce* individual freedom," evident at one extreme in slavery, was also a problem with reform organizations. Instead, Child labored on her own and at personal expense for the abolition of capital punishment. It is likely that one of her published letters, read by thousands, had a greater effect on public sentiment than the numerous resolutions passed by all the anti-gallows societies combined. After John C. Colt committed suicide on the day of his scheduled execution and the crowd surrounding the Tombs Prison reacted with disappointment, Child lamented, "To-day, I cannot write of beauty; for I am sad and troubled. Heart, head, and conscience are all in battle-array against the savage customs of my time. . . . Executions always excite a universal shudder among the innocent, the humane, and the wise-hearted. It is the voice of God, crying aloud within us against the savageness of this wicked custom."[10]

In Philadelphia women met and petitioned the legislature to abolish capital punishment. One petition in 1847 contained 1,777 names to be added to the 10,000 that had been collected earlier. The female petitioners recapitulated the most familiar arguments against capital punishment and emphasized one point neglected by most other writers: it is the "*poor*" who are executed, "while the more wealthy universally escape the penalty." In recognizing inequality in the administration of the death penalty, these middle-class women testified to those class tensions that permeated the 1840s, tensions that would lead the middle class further into seclusion and, as a consequence, exacerbate those very divisions they feared and deplored.[11]

The young activists who opposed capital punishment came of age in a palpably changing social environment. The world inhabited by sons and daughters always differs from that of fathers and mothers, but never more so than in the first decades of the nineteenth century. Population exploded throughout the Northeast as those who no longer had the opportunity to inherit land or work for themselves joined other strangers in towns and cities. These people were among those who constituted part of a reformulation in social relations in America. Whereas once they were independent producers and artisans, now they were wage-earners, dependent to a certain extent on their employers. Along with shifts in the organization of work came related changes in the design of urban life. Residential areas grew distinct from commercial ones; owners and workers no longer lived near one another or where they worked. This separation of people across economic and residential lines, along with the massive immigration throughout the Northeast, accelerated changes within the middle and upper classes. The middle classes increasingly rejected public life as disorderly and deranging. In doing so, they closed ranks around the ideal of the self-restrained individual and the secluded, domestic family. A consensus on values had never existed in America, but this antebellum generation of urban middle-class families experienced and feared social conflict during peacetime in a way that previous generations had not.[12]

If these transformations made parts of America in the 1830s and 1840s a more impersonal, private, and class-segmented place, they also created a powerful yearning for order, control, and new forms of interaction around which the middle class came to define itself. Participation in moral reform became one of the means by which middle-class Americans engaged and combated an alienating environment. Moral reform societies not only worked to eliminate what its members viewed as social ills but they also served the important task of introducing those from similar backgrounds to one another.

It may seem paradoxical that thousands of middle-class men and women with sensibilities that wedded them to the private arena and made them hostile to public engagement would support and join reform organizations. After all, participation in voluntary associations required that they leave the home, attend open debates, and confront fellow citizens who seemed less concerned with the moral issues of the day than they. Yet these moral reform societies worked precisely toward realizing the middle-class vision of privacy, self-control, and inner restraint; they served as public vehicles to accomplish private ends. Whether the issue was capital punishment, temperance, education, or the abolition of slavery, middle-class Americans launched a public crusade for a more private, controlled social order. The object of reform was to produce citizens who internalized certain values: husbands who tempered their drinking and served as good family men; children who restrained their passions and, on their own initiative, behaved in an adult-like fashion; blacks who, no longer coerced by the master's whip, demonstrated an ability to govern themselves. The members of moral reform organizations envisioned a society where there was no gallows, no war, no intemperance, no slavery, no ignorance, and no poverty. They also believed that to achieve such a place citizens would have to become sober, pious, educated, industrious, and restrained. In these ways, moral reform in the 1840s was simultaneously liberating and restricting, a vision of a thriving utopia and a utopian vision of a consensual, bourgeois society.[13]

II

The career of one reformer, Charles Spear, illuminates the contours of the commitment to reform in antebellum America. Unlike prominent politicans and editors such as Robert Rantoul, Jr., John L. O'Sullivan, and Horace Greeley, for whom the death penalty served as but one of many interests, Spear worked full-time in relative obscurity for the abolition of capital punishment. Compared with reformers such as the patrician Wendell Phillips, the electrifying Theodore Parker, and the inflammatory William Lloyd Garrison, Spear's was a modest career. Indeed, his desire to infiltrate the Boston reform circle and gain the respect of its members constitutes an important part of his story. By 1841, when he published a thin volume, *Names and Titles of the Lord Jesus Christ*, Spear had deserted his role as a parish minister for the peripatetic life of itinerant lecturer and social activist. Several years later, he committed his energies to the question of capital punishment. With the publication of *Essays on the Punishment of Death* in 1844, Spear quickly instituted himself as the foremost proponent of the abolition of capital punishment in New England. In 1845, he published and edited *The Hangman* and helped found the Massachusetts Society for the Abolition of Capital Punishment. He traveled widely, delivered scores of lectures, organized petition campaigns to save the lives of doomed convicts, and even opened his house as an "asylum" for discharged prisoners.

Only the barest outlines of Spear's life are known to us. We do not have enough information to study his upbringing, to understand why he became a printer and then a preacher, or to explain the many moves he made in his lifetime. The central document from which we can begin to understand Spear's devotion to reform is a surviving diary for the period 1841–49. A close analysis of this text and the few additional extant sources for Spear's life suggest that his full-time opposition to capital punishment made possible a career that promised self-improvement, upward mobility, and perhaps even peer recognition. Spear's diary presents an ambitious, religious man, one whose desire to be known, need for money, and deep religious faith guided him to the business of moral reform. That a craving for a successful career motivated Spear and helped him select opposition to capital punishment over the other reforms of the day does not in any way undercut the sincerity and intensity of Spear's commitment to reform. The diary makes it clear, however, that a career in reform offered fame and income, as well as a chance to reshape the world according to religious principles. The diary also illuminates how the personal, moral, and political aspects of reform often worked at cross-purposes and could lead to disappointment, disaffection, and the splintering of reform organizations. All reformers, to be sure, did not replicate the most individualistic aspects of Spear's career. But Spear's ideals and ambitious, his beliefs and desires, undoubtedly were duplicated in the lives of other middle-class activists.[14]

A Thanksgiving Day entry in 1841 contained within it the central themes that structured Spear's involvement in reform: his ambition, his religion, and perhaps even an excessive preoccupation with death. On that day, an exultant Charles Spear counted his blessings. Earlier in the year he had compiled and published *Names and Titles of the Lord Jesus Christ*. Arranged in alphabetical order, the work listed the nomenclature associated through the ages with God. With copies tucked under his arm, Spear called on the ministers of Boston and surrounding areas to gather endorsements, make sales, and gain acquaintances. The "method of selling my own work," as Spear referred to it, was quite common in the antebellum years. The author paid the printer, the binder, and the engraver for copies of the book and assumed the burden of selling it himself. It cost him about thirty-five cents a copy and he sold the volume for around one dollar. Once he deducted expenses such as traveling, a modest profit could be made. Thus, on one week-long trip to Andover, Spear sold about one hundred books and cleared sixty-four dollars, which "was doing great business." More typically, he sold several copies here, a few copies there. Debt was a chronic concern for the forty-year-old married minister with a family. But in his diary entry for November 25, his spirits soared:

> Last year I was all anxiety to finish my book. I have lived to reach this great object of my ambition. And to-day that book is probably in the hands of 8000 readers; for about 3300 have been sold. Yesterday I had the great satisfaction of depositing a copy in the Harvard University!! Here my book will live long after I have left the scenes of the earth. It was a great satisfaction for me to believe that my work will go down to posterity. Say what we may, there are very few who do not want to live after they are dead; not only in a future state of being, but here among our race. And all would like to leave a good name for other generations, whether they deserve one or not. And Oh! what a satisfaction I have when I think that probably a thousand years from now my book will be preaching. . . . And now I begin to have a strong wish to write another work. . . . Two things now seem especially to stand in the way. 1. My present work has not yet been circulated sufficiently. 2. Poverty. But God will open the way in due time. . . . And now I am able to say I have honored my family. I am, in one sense, independent. I can write my own works and then sell them. Indeed I am in new world.[15]

Encapsulated in Spear's thoughts were the sources of his commitment to reform. Most pronounced in this entry is Spear's ambition. He was ambitious to make a name for himself, eager to be considered highly, and anxious to rid himself of debt. Spear's intellectual, social, and financial ambition steered him to the book business and guided his life as an activist. Next, his religious faith led him to choose the subject of his book; throughout his life, the tenets of Universalism sustained Spear's faith in moral reform. Finally, his fear of death, intertwined deeply, of course, with his religious beliefs, also molded his commitment to social activism. Taken together, these concerns structured Spear's calling to a career in reform and shaped his conviction that, with faith in God, man could remake the self, and therefore the world, anew. Each interconnected theme—ambition, religion, and death—merits further discussion.

III

One reason why Spear launched on a "career in authorship" was to use his book as "the medium of an acquaintance with . . . the first men of the age." He sought out the "first men in the country" for stimulating conversation, to introduce Universalist principles, and to win endorsements for his book, thereby enhancing his own reputation in the Boston intellectual community. His "interviews," as he called them, ranged from "the greatest man of the age," William Ellery Channing, to John Quincy Adams, Joseph Story, Thomas Upham, and lesser ministerial and political lights.[16]

His meeting with Channing on December 14, 1841, fulfilled for Spear all the promises of writing and promoting his work. Channing, the most influential Unitarian in America, asked the visitor what sect he belonged to. This initiated a lengthy exchange on the theological differences between the denominations. Since the laboring poor of Boston tended toward Universalism (whereas Unitarianism attracted the professional and mercantile classes) Channing professed a deep interest in the sect. He was worried, however, about rumors of infidelity and want of devotion among Universalists. Spear claimed he heard similar tales told of Unitarians. The two men proceeded to discuss their positions on the doctrine of immortality, future punishment, and endless misery. While both sects reflected the vitality of liberal theology, in the 1840s Unitarians and Universalists regarded one another with as much suspicion as each held for the Calvinist sects. Thus, Channing was relieved to hear that most Universalists did not deny entirely future punishment. The ministers also talked about moral reform. Spear regretted the hesitancy of clergymen to press this subject in the pulpit, and he complimented Channing on his opposition to slavery. And so the afternoon went. Spear brought up the subject of his book and Channing not only bought a copy but gave his name as well. That evening, in reviewing the conversation, Spear wrote, "I felt I had obtained one of the greatest objects of my ambition . . . now what a field lies before me."[17]

One of Spear's ambitions was to encounter great men; another was to extricate himself from debt. If writing books furrowed the eternal soul (by preaching for a millennium) and raked the temporal mind (by meetings with eminent men), selling them fed the mortal body. Anxiety over money was never far from his mind. He realized that selling books and laboring at reform constituted a "world of business," and he speculated that the *Titles* was worth at least five thousand dollars to him. His early success even led him to talk of buying a house in 1843, but several years later he again found himself nearly six hundred dollars in debt and filled with "anxiety about the means of living."[18]

Debt was akin to slavery, and the story of Spear's attempt to aid a freed black named Lunsford Lane illuminates the way in which social agitation could lead to financial as well as spiritual gains. Soliciting money to free his family from slavery, Lane first visited Spear on November 1,

1841. The minister lamented how strange it was "in a land boasting of its free institutions, a man should be unable to have his own wife and children." Spear "wished him success, but could not help him." On January 3, Lane called again. According to the minister, Lane wanted him to use his "influence" to help free his seven children from slavery. Apparently this appeal to Spear's influence worked, for the minister began lecturing on slavery to raise money for Lane. At an anti-slavery meeting on January 10, he helped collect about $126; he exulted over "the luxury of doing good." On the twenty fourth and twenty fifth the minister "gave up myself to Mr. Lane" by traveling to Hanover and Abington and organizing anti-slavery meetings. From this experience Spear found that not only was he helping to liberate Lane's family from slavery but "I was getting myself out also." He returned from the trip having raised "$70 for [himself] and about $125 for Mr. Lane." Spear did not become an activist in order to make money, but, committed to social causes, he tried as he could to extricate himself from debt. Just before Lane left for North Carolina to retrieve his family, Spear confessed that he hated to profit from his services, but why, he asked, "should my family suffer in advancing the interests of others?"[19]

In this way, social reform was a financial as well as an intellectual and moral enterprise. The problem of money pervaded Spear's life; indeed, it was the subject of indebtedness that first led him, at the age of thirty one, to involve himself publicly in an important social question, imprisonment for debt. At that time, in 1833, he labeled imprisonment for debt "one of the most barbarous and disgraceful laws that ever existed" and he depicted its countless "moral, physical, and political evils"—ruining families, impairing credit, and trampling ambition itself. Spear decried imprisonment for debt as revengeful and contrary to Christianity. "Severe laws and loathsome prisons," he declared, have led "us to consider men rather as beasts than human beings." Even worse, the law permitted the creditor to expose a debtor "in the market-place as we do a wild beast." In a capitalist society based on contractual relations, confidence, not coercion, was the lubricant of exchange. The public exposure of a debtor only forced a loss of confidence in the system. The abolition of imprisonment for debt, the activist argued, would induce men to become truly honest and punctual, to "acquire a reputation" if they were to compete successfully in the marketplace.[20]

We do not know whether Spear himself was ever imprisoned for debt. What is certain is that neither his anguish over indebtedness nor his hatred of prisons ever diminished. A decade after he wrote his pamphlet on imprisonment for debt, Spear would develop his arguments further and apply them to an assault on capital punishment and the prison system. In his Thanksgiving Day entry Spear rejoiced that writing books made him "in one sense" independent, because he lived by means of the intellectual capital he carried with him. But he also recorded that poverty would most likely keep him from writing another work soon.[21]

IV

The publication of the *Titles* in 1841 altered Spear's sense of himself. He basked in the meetings with intellectuals of the day; he courted endorsements and coveted reviews of his book; he envisioned an escape from debt. In these ways, the book fulfilled his desire for a successful career. But in the writing, publishing, and selling of the volume, Spear was transformed as well. The total experience of the book, he felt, had converted him to labor for humanity. "My whole intellectual and moral nature," he reflected, "seems to have been cast in a new mould since finishing my book on the Saviour. And the thought occurred to me today that if I had never received any thing for my labour, that I had enriched my moral nature enough to compensate me. I feel . . . a greater interest . . . in all that concerns the human race." The author's sense of being recast to reform society emerged, in part, from discovering an avenue for the fulfillment of his ambitions. "I have become almost another being," he thought. His sense of personal reformation and his faith in the reformability of society reinforced each other. And both beliefs were related inextricably to his religious faith.[22]

Spear's religious beliefs, his Universalism, directed and framed his social activism. Universalism constituted one manifestation of a general withdrawal from Calvinist principles that took place in the last half of the eighteenth century. Although within Universalist circles ministers battled over doctrinal issues, especially the question of Trinitarianism, Universalist theology generally stressed the salvation of mankind, a benevolent, non-coercive God, and the rejection of eternal, everlasting punishment. The idea that all men would be saved, not just the elect, had special appeal on the frontier and to the lower orders of society, who viewed any elite, even an eschatological one, with suspicion. Consistent as it was with rationalist, liberal, and what we would call democratic principles, it was no accident that the popularity of Universalism broadened at the time of the Revolution. John Murray, who left England to escape his debts and in the process shed his Methodism, founded the First Universalist Church in 1779; Charles Chauncy, pastor of the First Church at Boston, finally got up the courage to publish his *Salvation of All Men* in

1784; in 1790, Elhanan Winchester, a former Baptist preacher, led a Universalist convention in Philadelphia that was attended by at least one excited convert from Presbyterianism, Benjamin Rush.[23]

The most influential Universalist preacher in America was Hosea Ballou. Like many Universalists, Ballou had no formal education. The son of a New Hampshire farmer, he came from a Baptist background. Convinced that a benevolent God would not author everlasting damnation, he began to preach universal salvation. In *A Treatise on Atonement* (1805), perhaps the most important statement of Universalist theology, Ballou argued from both reason and faith that there was no trinity, no infinite sin, no eternal punishment, but only a benevolent, just, and loving Deity who provided all with salvation. Between 1790 and 1817, Ballou lived primarily the life of an itinerant preacher, traveling through Vermont, New Hampshire, and Massachusetts, winning converts and forming parishes. After 1817, he settled in Boston where, for thirty-five years, he preached Universalism to parishioners neither as educated nor as affluent as those across town in William Ellery Channing's Unitarian church. One of Ballou's students was Charles Spear.[24]

Spear came under Ballou's influence sometime after 1817; in 1828 Spear accepted a call to the parish at Brewster. He spent nearly ten years as a minister there and at Rockport before settling in Boston. Little is known of these years in Spear's life. Having vacated the role of parish minister, Spear increasingly confessed to dissatisfaction with an "exceedingly corrupt church," and he referred often to the "anxiety attendent on a settled ministry." Not an especially forceful speaker, and often suffering from fatigue and loss of voice as an itinerant lecturer, the toll of weekly sermons might have been too great for him to manage.[25]

There is a suggestion in his diary that perhaps he was dismissed from his parish; if so, that memory undoubtedly shaped his future as a reformer. In 1847 Spear referred to "the great world" as his parish and observed that it was a parish that "may treat roughly, but cannot dismiss me." Given Spear's ambitions and his desire to be well-regarded, it is likely that he found the routines of parish life unfulfilling, a message apparently not lost on his congregation.[26]

While the oral and interpersonal aspects of a settled ministry may not have been to his liking, Spear felt extremely comfortable with the written word. While a minister at Brewster he published his pamphlet on imprisonment for debt. He also wrote essays on temperance and peace for Universalist newspapers. That he apparently maintained a diary for much of his adult life also suggests faith in the power of writing. He began composing the *Titles* before leaving Brewster. Perhaps all along he envisioned the book business as an entrée into a new way of life and his volume as a ticket out of Brewster. And while selling his work fulfilled his intellectual and financial ambitions, his book served a ministerial-like function as well. The *Titles*, Spear believed, would extend his mission to convert the world. Man was mortal, but books could preach for a millennium.

For Spear, the decision to devote himself to "labour for humanity" and strike up "moral lightning and thunder" progressed logically and naturally from Universalist principles. Spear believed in the benevolence of God, freedom of the will, and the salvation of all men. He spurned the Calvinist idea of eternal punishment, arguing that if one admitted endless misery one rejected God's benevolence. In his diary he defined a Universalist as one who believed that all would finally be saved, and he thought it essential to apply the doctrine from the theological to the moral world. These Universalist principles—universal redemption, finite punishment, free will, and God's benevolence—meant that, far from being doomed, mankind would overcome sin and be saved because a just and loving God would tolerate nothing else. Applied to society, these principles, Spear insisted, "will overthrow every existing evil." And so the minister was pleased when at a Washingtonian temperance meeting one man likened the enterprise "to a great sheet let down from heaven, that took in all, and as He raised it, he cried out Steady! Steady! as though he were afraid of losing one." "The future progress of society," Spear claimed, was "connected with the propagation of our [Universalist] sentiments."[27]

Reform, for Spear, was a "moral enterprise," a search for "Moral truth." He believed he was living in the midst of and helping to make a "great moral revolution." He cherished progress and commented frequently on how great events could spring from trifling causes. He used himself as an example of the power of moral persuasion. In June of 1843, Spear attended the Universalist Convention and presented an anti-slavery resolution. He observed "how strange it will seem a few years hence to learn that a Resolution against slavery could hardly pass a Universalist convention. But strange as it may appear, a few years ago and I would have been the very one to oppose the subject." On another occasion, he remembered when "I believed defensive war was right; then I moved and believed only a preparation was right. Now I have given that up. Ought I not then to have charity for those who are yet in the dark." Light and dark, moral truth and corrupt falsehood, regeneration and degeneration—these dichotomies served as the barometers of moral reform. Once people recognized that slavery, war, intemperance and the death penalty were social evils then, led by a faith in universal reformation and the redemption of sin, all would eventually see society in a new light.[28]

Of the many reforms of the day, it was the question of capital punishment that appealed most urgently to Spear, and here the application of his religious beliefs to a specific reform enterprise is evident. Spear argued that "reformation, not severity, should be the true policy of society." All criminals, he thought, could be reformed and prisons should be turned into "moral hospitals," not places of misery and punishment. Rather than returning prisoners to the community, capital punishment cut them off unreformed and unrepentant. The death penalty, Spear argued, was retributive, unreformative, and irremediable; capital punishment contradicted Universalist precepts.[29]

V

Spear's ambition and religion structured his commitment to moral reform. At a more psychological level, his fear of death and preoccupation with health also contributed to his search for a new social arrangement based on Christian principles. The reformer's fixation with mortality was evident in his Thanksgiving Day entry. He referred to departing from earth, and throughout his diary he returned to the question of being "obliged soon to leave the world." He admitted to wanting to live after he was dead and confessed a wish to live a thousand years. Spear's preoccupation with final things was undoubtedly intensified by his religious training. As a minister, he lived daily with questions of salvation, the afterlife, and the millennium. He dreamed of that time when "all would pass forever from beyond the reach of sorrow and death," and he conceived his actions as a reformer to hasten that day.[30]

Spear's preoccupation with mortality assumed a less theological posture as well. Throughout his life he fixated on the subjects of sickness and health and even called himself a hypochondriac at one point. "Sick all day," "quite unwell," "health poor," are frequent refrains in Spear's diary. His anxiety about health usually worsened when he was especially tense about pecuniary affairs. "Disease is upon me," he diagnosed at a time when his newspaper looked as if it would fail and he could not meet his payments. Conversely, at infrequent moments of prosperity he reported his health as "quite good." At times, Spear experienced difficulty speaking in public, and this too he took as an indication of his failing health. Apparently, his concern over his well-being was not entirely psychological. One contemporary believed that Spear's "health was evidently wearing away under excitement and conscientious conflict." But despite his anxiety over illness and the pain of preaching, Spear persevered and at his most martyrlike resigned that he "shall rest in heaven." On his forty-third birthday Spear reflected that "year after year it has seemed as though my health would certainly fail and yet I live on."[31]

Why did a man, preoccupied with eternity, mortality, and sickness, campaign actively for moral reform? Why did he travel widely, lecture frequently, and struggle to earn money when these very activities seemed to exact a severe psychological and physical toll? What was the relationship between Spear's preoccupation with death and his commitment to reform? The Thanksgiving Day entry suggests part of an answer. Much as he would have liked to live a thousand years, Spear knew that was not possible and writing a book seemed to him the closest he could come to immortality. The book served as an extension of self and the printed voice continued its "preaching mission" long after the human voice was silenced.[32]

Spear's belief that a reciprocal relationship existed between physical well-being and moral health provides another link between his bodily concerns and commitment to moral reform. Thus Spear, like so many other middle-class men and women in antebellum America, experimented with regimes of temperate living. "I can live on bread and water," he declared proudly at one juncture. If a healthy body suggested a healthy mind, then moral purity would also contribute to physical well-being. The fewer moral evils, be they intemperance, slavery, or the gallows, the healthier the body-politic and, by extension, even the body. In reforming the world, one was also renewing the self.[33]

The death of his two-year-old son in February 1843 drew Spear deeper into social activism. The minister recorded in his diary, "For the first time I have buried one of my own family. Tonight he lays in the narrow house appointed for all living and his spirit has gone home to a better world. Well, I feel resigned, for I believe I shall see him again. . . . And I shall soon go to meet him, and the, O! the bliss of the bright and beautiful world! God be praised for the promise of my religion. I am surprised at myself. What does it all mean? But to keep up my mind I must constantly be engaged. I find now some advantage in being engaged in the moral reforms." Suppressing his despair over the death of his son, and seeking to occupy his thoughts. Spear embraced the world of moral reform with even greater enthusiasm.[34]

The life of a book, the relationship between physical and moral purity, the death of his son, a preoccupation with eschatological questions, and an overarching faith in the coming of the millennium shaped Spear's commitment to reform. His decision to devote himself to the abolition of capital punishment, the abolition of death, was not unrelated to his own fixation with life.

VI

Spear's intellectual, personal and financial ambitions, his religious beliefs, and his preoccupation with death directed him to the moral reform enterprise, and, once committed, these core values continued to mold his career as an activist. Flushed with the total experience of his first book, Spear redoubled his devotion to social reform. He wanted to "produce something worthy of regard" and by that he meant a book that would make his reputation, contribute to his success, and, not incidentally, help to alter society. As of the day after Thanksgiving 1841, Spear had in mind individual works on slavery, peace, and capital punishment, the Jewish sects and evidences of Christianity, and even a volume of miscellanies. He lamented how much more one could conceive of than accomplish and he promptly began work on another volume altogether, the "Being and Attributes of God."[35]

Having already composed a religious volume, Spear's concentration wandered from his new work. Instead, the author continued to travel, promoting and selling the *Titles*, and attending anti-slavery, temperance, and non-resistance meetings. On August 15, 1842, Spear arrived in Brunswick, Maine, and arranged for a meeting with Thomas Upham, professor at Bowdoin College. In 1836, Upham had published his *Manual of Peace*, an influential work that argued against war and capital punishment on the grounds of the "immutable principle . . . the Inviolability of Human Life." It was Upham's *Manual*, Spear claimed, that convinced him of the truth of the peace principle.[36]

During their conversation, Upham urged Spear to devote his attention to the issues of peace and capital punishment. "Society," Upham observed, "has been employed in making dungeons instead of reforming men," and too many people, he feared, favored the gallows. Spear agreed and added that he disapproved of the idea of imprisonment for life as a substitute for the death penalty. Such a punishment, he thought, was a "living death." Spear argued that, not only must the gallows be razed, but the prisons must also be transformed into moral hospitals. Only then would society commit itself truly to the principle of reformation. Upham ended the conversation by reiterating that Spear's foremost concern should be capital punishment.[37]

Following this meeting, Spear focused intently on the question of the death penalty. He attended gatherings on capital punishment, and when he called on people to sell the *Titles*, he often raised the issue of capital punishment. In his diary, he began to jot down familiar arguments against the death penalty. The abolition of public executions implied something inherently wrong with capital punishment; Genesis 9:6, "Whoso sheddeth man's blood, by man shall his blood be shed," was a prediction, not an imperative; society might "restore property, Liberty, Good name, but not Life." The irremediability of capital punishment in the event of an error was too horrible, he thought, to contemplate. On September 27, 1843, Spear entered that he now intended to write on capital punishment. By November 22, he had finished the first part, and on January 24, 1844, *Essays on Capital Punishment* was published.[38]

As one might expect of a book written and published in under four months, the work was mostly derivative, a simply organized compendium of arguments against capital punishment. Spear drew extensively from Upham's *Manual of Peace* (1836), John L. O'Sullivan's *Report in Favor of the Abolition of the Punishment of Death by Law* (1841), and E. H. Chapin's *Three Discourses on Capital Punishment* (1843). Spear divided the work into two parts, arguments from "history and observation" and arguments from "scripture." In Part I he repeated the position of generations of social contract theorists that no citizen ever consented to relinquish their right to life and added that the right to life was inalienable. Spear emphasized that the death penalty was revengeful and demonstrated society's unwillingness to "heal the moral disorders of the soul by promoting insincere conversions." Finally, Spear decried capital punishment as a danger to liberty: "We look now at the Revolution in our world, at the downfall of republics, yet imagine we are safe; but what was the cause of their destruction? Did they not admit, in all cases, the punishment of death[?]" The scriptural arguments contained in Part II remained the same as those offered by Rush in 1787. The case of Cain demonstrated God's wish to preserve the life of the murderer, the Noachic Covenant was a prediction, the Mosaic code designed only for a particular time, and the gospel intended to save, not destroy, life.[39]

Spear's *Essays on Capital Punishment* pleaded for a "moral revolution." If one admitted the inviolability of human life and transformed prisons into hospitals, society would advance one step closer to "greater purity." It was a straightforward Christian, republican, almost utopian vision of what society could be. Try the experiment, reformers begged, and should it fail there was always time to return to traditional institutions. The personal quest for self-control and well-being and the social quest for reformation and purity reinforced one another. The faith in moral power and a vision of a re-formed society drove scores of activists in the

1840s to attack slavery, intemperance, insanity, and war, in addition to capital punishment, as swarming social evils. Working within the Boston reform community, Spear's specialty after 1844 was the abolition of capital punishment and the welfare of the prison inmate.[40]

Following the publication of *Essays on Capital Punishment*, Spear lectured frequently on the death penalty and peddled copies of his new work. At some point in 1844 he conceived of starting a newspaper devoted to the abolition of the gallows. On January 1, 1845, the premier issue of the *Hangman* appeared, with Charles Spear listed as editor and proprietor. At the same time, the reformer helped found the Massachusetts Society for the Abolition of Capital Punishment and served as recording secretary for the organization.[41]

To the extent his commitment to capital punishment was a calculated decision, Spear could not have chosen better. Anti-slavery had a Garrison and education a Mann, but anti-gallows in Boston still awaited a full-time advocate. After selling 200 copies of the *Essays*, Spear reflected that "it was a good move getting out this work." By May 1845, over 5000 copies circulated and the *Hangman* claimed 2000 subscribers. "The subject of capital punishment," Spear glowed, "is to be one of the most popular of the day."[42]

This is not to suggest that egotistical concerns and financial ambitions alone dictated Spear's involvement. His religious beliefs and preoccupation with death drove his commitment to reform generally and the abolition of capital punishment specifically. The state of society sickened the former minister; he ached for "a new order of things," an order without slavery, war, and capital punishment, without unemployment and inequality, without misery. Spear derived enormous satisfaction from the "blessed work" or "labouring for humanity."[43]

Having invested himself in the campaign against the gallows, Spear thought, "Now what a field is open before me." His newspaper, he believed, endowed him with "a mighty influence." With receipts from two books, he enjoyed a level of prosperity beyond any he had experienced before. The *Essays on Capital Punishment* opened doors for him; on a trip to New York, for example, the writer mingled with the "philanthropists of the day." By 1847, Spear had little trouble including himself among the assembly of "leading reformers" who gathered at Theodore Parker's house during anniversary week. Present at the meeting were Ralph Waldo Emerson, Lucretia Mott, William Lloyd Garrison, Wendell Phillips, Charles Sumner, Elizur Wright, Walter Channing, and others. That Spear took notes on the conversation but did not record saying anything himself suggests that, despite his success, he remained somewhat awed and intimidated by the gathering.[44]

But while social reform satisfied Spear's ambitions, it also inflamed them. After the seventh edition of *Essays on Capital Punishment* and sixteenth of the *Titles*, he confided discontent and wondered, "What will satisfy me?" Newly gained influence and visibility led him increasingly into conflict, and he became tormented with "fears and suspicions." He worried about losing control of his periodical and brooded as other organizations related to the welfare of the prisoner sprang up around him. A man deeply committed to moral purity, Spear had little comprehension of the internal politics of social reform. It stunned him when, at a meeting of the Boston Society for Discharged Convicts, for which Spear served as secretary, the president did not consult him and omitted his name from the new list of officers. Spear recorded, "Thus in the very movement in which I have been a prime mover I am set aside; and even my motives have been suspected. Such is the fate of the true Reformer!" On this occasion, the snubbed activist vowed to smash the society that thrust him aside; at other times, he despaired that the world had forgotten him.[45]

Although the splintering of reform associations was common in the antebellum years, Spear detested battles over tactics and leadership. How could Christian principles be applied to society if activists themselves did not adhere to them? Moral power, and not power struggles, he thought, would transform the world. Spear sickened of all associations and saw himself as "left alone to struggle on." The tendency toward feeling like a martyr, so pronounced in the psyche of social reformers, struck Spear in extreme form.[46] In 1846 he wrote one activist that "at present I must labour here in sickness and poverty; troubled on every side yet not distressed; perplexed but not in despair; persecuted, but not forsaken, cast down, but not destroyed." He never contemplated how his own ambitions, evident in so many reformers, created the very conditions that left him feeling isolated and unfulfilled.[47]

The financial drain of running a reform society full-time also took its toll. Acutely sensitive to pecuniary matters, Spear felt overwhelmed by the cost of publishing a periodical, of lecturing, of agitating in general. "How hard it is," he lamented, "to meet the expenses of a reform." He felt "exhausted and discouraged," the profit from selling books consumed by the cost of doing good.[48]

Spear's religious faith, like his ambition, was also strained and distorted by his calling to reform. Just as Universalism shaped his commitment to moral agitation, sectarianism undermined the progress of social reform. No social issue in antebellum American was as divided along sectarian lines as the question of capital punishment. Just as a belief in the benevolence of God, goodness of man, universal salvation and reformation—characteristic of Universalists and Unitarians—might lead one to oppose the death penalty, faith in retribution, innate depravity, and eternal punishment—tenets of more orthodox Congregationalists—generated supporters of capital punishment. For most of the 1840s, the debate over the death penalty thinly masked a rancorous, sectarian civil war.

The sectarian nature of the conflict over capital punishment troubled Spear. He desired an erosion of denominational barriers (along a liberal consensus, of course). At his most idealistic, the minister thought much was lost by not mingling with others, and he hoped that social reform would "break down the partition wall between the sects." With regard to Universalist and Unitarian activists, shared moral ideals probably did help paper over theological differences; Spear rejoiced when he was invited to preach in a Unitarian pulpit. But if social reform helped unite liberal sects, it served as the battleground on which liberal and orthodox beliefs collided.[49]

The anti-gallows activist reserved his most bilious comments for the orthodox ministers of Boston. One Calvinist clergyman, he commented, would sign the death warrant of his own child if he knew the child would descend straight into hell. In 1845, Spear organized a petition campaign against the Calvinist clergy, who were "up and doing to sustain the law of blood," to have them appointed executioners and to relocate the hanging to a place of public worship. One way to "impose a new moral order," Spear thought, was to wrest control of "our colleges, academies, and even our prisons" away from the orthodox.[50]

When not focusing on other denominations, Spear fixated on the reluctance of fellow Universalists to oppose capital punishment. He felt "ashamed at the backwardness" of Universalists and considered at times withdrawing from the denomination. The failure of Universalist Conventions to adopt resolutions denouncing the death penalty dismayed and disappointed him; at other times, he held hope that his brethren might still do something for humanity. His quandary of whether or not to leave the denomination over the question of a commitment to reform seemed especially acute on a Sabbath day in August 1844. That day he had to choose between going to Universalist Sabbath School or attending a celebration of West Indies Emancipation. Spear reflected that Universalism had once claimed his whole attention, but that was before he devoted himself to moral subjects. Now he was unhappy and distracted. On his return from Sabbath School he wrote that he enjoyed himself "very little.

Even the laughter of my children excited no joy within me." He thought he had better confine himself to the question of capital punishment for a while, and he prayed for guidance.[51]

Charles Spear's commitment to reform typified the motives and preoccupations of many social activists and moral schemers. Most of them shared deeply personal and millennial religious beliefs. Most craved recognition and joined associations, yet also envisioned themselves as martyrs, solitary visionaries ahead of their time. Most suffered both real and imagined illnesses and out of their fear of death pursued the abolition of all pain and suffering. If they did not succeed to the degree they expected, it was in part because the politics of social agitation splintered and distorted their visions even as moral reform promised to realize them.[52]

Spear's desire to be well thought of, to win the respect of "persons who once thought little" of him, was not quickly satisfied. His search for fame contributed to the splintering of reform associations; the competition between reformers seemed to make individual success less obtainable. By 1848 and 1849, Spear found it increasingly difficult to endure these tensions, and his anxiety over his health worsened. He lost the ability to speak publicly, which caused him "embarrassment" and made him feel even more unwell. He despaired about his health and, near the end of 1847, convinced himself that "disease is upon me."[53]

He survived the final sickness of 1847 and his last diary entry found him more hopeful. He reflected on the scenes he had passed through, how at the start of this volume of his diary he had just published the *Titles*. Now, he had interviewed Samuel Appleton, of the wealthy, mill-owning Appleton family. Spear hoped that he had found a new benefactor. At midnight he turned forty eight; he wished "to preserve in the future" and reflected again that "now an immense field is open before me."[54]

Spear returned repeatedly to the image of wide field opening before him, and, in the context of his commitment to reform, the phrase resonated with meanings. It captured the expansiveness of his desire to pursue and reap fame, influence, and comfort; it encapsulated his feeling that he could go on indefinitely, driven by the restlessness of ambition and the hope of escaping mortality; it worked as a ministerial image, an immense field for missionary labor; and, finally, it could be construed as a religious vision of the hereafter, an endless field opening up onto eternity.

Spear had fifteen more years ahead of him to labor in that immense field. In the end, despite his opposition to coercion and violence, despite his belief that, along with capital punishment, war should be abolished, despite his anxiety over his well-being, Charles Spear did what he could for the Union forces at the outbreak of the Civil War. Sometime after 1861, he left Boston for Washington, where he served as a chaplain in a hospital filling up with the wounded and the dying. In 1863, Spear wrote Longfellow that he was giving his time for the soldiers; still struggling to meet his expenses, he reminded the poet that, "at this period of our National Calamity," he must look to his Northern friends to sustain him. It was while in Washington, working alone, praying over the dead, and laboring through his fear of illness, that Spear became sick and died— a casualty of the war and a veteran of a greater campaign for justice, humanity, and salvation.[55]

7

The Conflict over
Capital Punishment
in Antebellum America

The subject of capital punishment, within a few months past has become widely discussed in the land, and is fast increasing in public interest.

WILLIAM LLOYD GARRISON
to HENRY CLARKE WRIGHT (1843)

On January 17, 1843, John L. O'Sullivan and George Barrell Cheever met at the Broadway Tabernacle, a cavernous free church and public meeting hall in New York City, to debate the question of capital punishment. The anticipation must have been great, for it had been less than two years since O'Sullivan, the fiery democratic legislator from New York, delivered a comprehensive report in favor of the abolition of capital punishment, and Cheever, Presbyterian minister at the Allen Street Church, issued his defense of punishment by death. The debate came at a time when public conflict over capital punishment was on the rise. Throughout the Northeast, legislatures considered bills and petitions for the elimination of the gallows, newspapers and periodicals featured numerous essays for and against the death penalty, and some professionals formed local and national societies for the abolition of capital punishment. The O'Sullivan-Cheever debate provides a window onto the conflict over capital punishment in the 1840s and 1850s, a conflict shaped by nothing less than competing visions of man and society.

I

As of 1843, the thirty-year-old O'Sullivan was one of the best-known opponents of capital punishment in the nation, and it was his *Report in*

141

Favor of the Abolition of the Punishment of Death by Law, presented to the New York legislature on April 14, 1841, that had helped establish his reputation. He came to the task already an accomplished lawyer and editor. A graduate of Columbia in 1834, O'Sullivan practiced law and founded the *United States Magazine and Democratic Review,* which he edited until 1843. It was O'Sullivan who most likely wrote the famous introductory statement of democratic principles that appeared in the premier issue of the review in 1837. In that essay, O'Sullivan restated in radical form the ideals of Jeffersonian democracy. He objected to strong, intrusive governments as a threat to liberty and the natural principle of self-government. Except for the administration of justice, protection of natural rights, and preservation of order, government should leave all else to "*the voluntary principle,*" to individual freedom. O'Sullivan made it clear the Democrats were opposed to "all precipitous radical changes in social institutions," but believed experimentation with new modes of governing for social betterment the key to progress. Was not the American Revolution the greatest of experiments? he asked. It was in this spirit of exploring democratic principles, of liberating the individual from all forms of tyranny, of promoting self-government, that O'Sullivan thought of democracy as "the cause of Humanity."[1]

In the most rousing paragraph of the statement, O'Sullivan declared that the object of democracy was "to emancipate the mind of the mass of men from the degrading and disheartening fetters of social distinctions and advantages . . . to war against all fraud, oppression, and violence by striking at their root, to reform all the infinitely varied human misery which has grown out of the old and false ideas by which the world has been so long misgoverned; to dismiss the hireling soldier; to spike the cannon, and bury the bayonet; to burn the gibbet, and open the debtors dungeon. . . ." It was an emotional call to reshape social relations by removing coercion, violence, and tyranny from daily existence, to experiment with the democratization and reformation of social institutions. Applied to the question of the right of government to take life, these principles helped sustain an opposition to capital punishment.[2]

O'Sullivan's *Report* began where every credible writer on capital punishment since Rush had started, with Scripture. He hurried through the familiar cant that the Mosaic code applied only to an earlier time, that the commandment "Thou shalt not kill" did not mean "Thou shall not commit murder—but mayest kill him who has committed murder," and that Genesis 9:6 was a prediction, not an imperative. Sullivan reported that the verse had been "mistranslated" and that an alternative reading of Genesis 9:6 would have it "whatsoever sheddeth man's blood, by man shall (or may) *its* blood be shed." Whatever the emphasis in the Old Testament, the New Testament, O'Sullivan argued, repudiated the principle of retribution.[3]

Knowing that he was preparing a legislative report, O'Sullivan apologized for including an extensive amount of scriptural analysis. Still, he thought it important to document the conclusion that the Bible neither demanded nor sanctioned capital punishment. He felt much less compelled to deal with the abstract question of whether society had the authority to take life, of whether individuals relinquished a right to the state that even they did not possess. In noting but passing over this part of the subject, O'Sullivan broke with scores of essayists before him who felt compelled to address the political theory of the social contract. O'Sullivan's desire to avoid the social contract question came at a time when the very idea of a social compact was being attacked as a "figment" by those who would have divine authority, not human consent, constitute the basis of government. The political culture of the 1780s necessitated some consideration of the rightful powers of the state, but critical aspects of the political culture of the 1840s were far more congenial to the notion of an unimpeachable authority. The legislator finessed the issue by arguing that, whether or not society had the abstract right of inflicting the death penalty, matters of "wisdom and policy" recommended strongly that society not exercise that right. It was to the failure of the death penalty as an effective punishment and deterrent to crime that O'Sullivan addressed the greater portion of his *Report*.[4]

Why did the death penalty fail as a punishment? With respect to criminals, it cut off all chance of a sincere repentance and jeopardized the "future state of the soul." Moreover, executions contradicted the principle that morals might be corrected, character purified. The punishment was irremediable; innocent men had been sent to their deaths. And capital punishment failed with respect to the community because it did not deter crime. To O'Sullivan, the question of deterrence was central to the argument against capital punishment. Why did executions not prevent crime? O'Sullivan offered two general answers: first, because the death penalty unleashed rather than harnessed those passions that caused crime, and, second, because imprisonment was most likely more effective as a deterrent.[5]

O'Sullivan's understanding of the causes of crime coincided with the psychological assumptions of Rush and Livingston. Executions, according to O'Sullivan, "harden and brutalize" man's finer instincts, and uncage those passions that seduce men into crime. Was not the demoralizing effect of capital punishment the reason for the abolition of public exe-

cutions? he inquired. And if public executions had little effect in preventing crime, then "the same penalty unseen, unfelt, unrealized, and to
a great extent unknown, must produce much less." O'Sullivan focused
specifically on what writers after Rush labeled "moral insanity." Insanity
could strike anyone, for it came about from being constantly subjected
"to the influence of a thousand unseen impairing causes over which we
can have no control, deranging, impairing, and often destroying . . . the
healthy action of that self-regulating moral power. . . ." If this were so,
O'Sullivan wondered, how could judges and juries distinguish intentional
criminal acts from those "which have had their true origin in little else
than an unconjectured internal derangement of the stomach or brain?"
Victims of moral insanity, O'Sullivan thought, were better fit for asylums
than for the gallows.[6]

In place of the death penalty, O'Sullivan proposed "solitary imprisonment for life with labor, placed beyond the reach of either Executive
or Legislative clemency." O'Sullivan's substitution marked a retreat from
a faith in the reformation of the criminal, which was paradoxical in light
of his emphasis on the environmental origins of crime. He unabashedly
advocated life imprisonment because it was more dreadful than death for
prospective criminals to contemplate: the "anticipation of such an imprisonment—perpetual, hopeless, and laborious—involving civil death,
with the total severance of all the social ties that bound the convicted
culprit to the world . . . would operate as a far more powerful control
and check, than the fear of a hundred deaths." Moreover, juries, O'Sullivan believed, would be more willing to convict as long as the punishment was not death. As for the criminal, perpetual solitary confinement
at labor would be more *severe* than death, but less *cruel*. Such punishment would at least spare the soul of the prisoner and "place him in a
position in which it is difficult to conceive the possibility of his long
remaining obdurate and inaccessible to the influences of a Christian ren-
ovation of heart." This repentance would neither open prospects for pardon nor mitigate the deterrent example of imprisonment but would "still
shed a sufficient light upon the solitary cell to make its darkness tolerable
to human powers of endurance."[7]

Repentance, then, could result as a byproduct of incarceration, but, in
O'Sullivan's scheme, it was not essential. Reformation in general hardly
figured in calculating punishments. As a consequence, O'Sullivan's proposal raised a number of questions. If lifetime imprisonment inadvertently
produced penitence but pardon was prohibited, then would not penitentiaries eventually become crowded with monk-like prisoners? Would not
these inmates be of greater use back in society? And if capital punishment

was inhumane, what was to be said about solitary imprisonment for life with labor? Beyond these problems, the central issue implicit in O'Sullivan's argument was the place of responsibility in a world seemingly governed by external influences. If environment, not depravity, caused crime, then was not society, rather than the individual, responsible for deviant behavior? It is perhaps a measure of the conservatism of the anti-gallows movement that O'Sullivan, like nearly every other essayist on capital punishment at the time, never considered that, if social and environmental conditions caused crime, society itself should be radically redesigned. This omission is particularly striking because in other concerns O'Sullivan and his democratic colleagues championed political and economic reforms. "If society is the criminal," one writer wondered, "were it not well to reform society?" The answer was yes, but in the 1840s and 1850s anti-gallows activists, like so many reformers, concentrated their efforts on influencinig individuals, not restructuring the political and economic spheres in which individuals lived.[8]

Leaving these tensions unexplored, the *Report* concluded that, as a matter of policy and humanity, it was time to try the experiment of abolition. The New York legislature, however, disagreed. In an evening session on May 24, 1841, legislators defeated O'Sullivan's bill by a vote of 52-46. Disappointed but undaunted, O'Sullivan introduced a new bill at the start of the January session. In the interim, a second edition of O'Sullivan's *Report* was published. Both Horace Greeley of the *Tribune* and William Cullen Bryant of the *Evening Post* endorsed abolition. Thousands of anti-gallows petitions were read into the legislative record. Yet once again the bill lost. Both in 1841 and 1842 the orthodox clergy played a crucial role in the bill's defeat. An *Evening Post* correspondent observed that "there is a violent opposition to this reform from a quarter where least of all it might have been looked for—the pastors of various denominations of churches." Another writer accounted for the defeat by the "machinations of those purblind and besotted priests who, generally twenty years behind their generation, feel it incumbent upon them to resist all the really elevated and good movements of the day." O'Sullivan as well was furious that the clergy had wielded "the thunders of their sacerdotal authority and spiritual power" against the abolition of capital punishment. O'Sullivan refused to permit his renomination to the legislature, and instead devoted himself to working at the popular rather than legislative level for reform. In the meantime, orthodox clergymen responded in print to O'Sullivan's *Report*.[9]

One of the first assaults on O'Sullivan's *Report* came from the Presbyterian minister Albert Baldwin Dod in the pages of the *Biblical Rep-*

ertory and Princeton Review. Dod assailed O'Sullivan's argument. How could it be, the minister asked, that O'Sullivan finds solitary imprisonment a more dreadful punishment than death but argues for the abolition of capital punishment on the grounds that it is inhumane and too severe? Dod also wondered how, if the gospel commanded man to love his enemies and return good for evil, imprisonment was any more permissible than hanging. Could not this reasoning lead to the abolition of punishment altogether?[10]

Dod also disagreed with O'Sullivan that deterrence served as the true end of punishment. By doing so, he articulated a fundamental philosophical difference between anti-gallows and pro-gallows essayists. In rejecting deterrent theory, Dod inquired, What right "have we to catch a man and hang him up because we have reason to believe that he will prove a scarecrow to frighten other men from mischief?" The right did not rest in considerations of the punishment's benefit to society; this was merely an attempt to base justice on utilitarian principles, a philosophy that sickened the minister. Rather than considerations of "the gratifications of the palate or the pinchings of cold and hunger," it was the "natural sentiment of justice," the "intrinsic ill-desert of crime," "the immutable and peremptory teachings of the moral sense" that authorized and commanded the death penalty. The source, then, for executing murderers was not considerations of deterrence, certainly not principles of reformation, but "the moral nature of man" which had always proclaimed the rightfulness of capital punishment.[11]

For Dod, the idea of the moral sense sustained capital punishment. In the last quarter of the eighteenth century, however, essayists such as Benjamin Rush had included moral sense philosophy in the array of intellectual traditions harnessed to oppose the death penalty. For Rush the moral sense, or moral faculty as he preferred to call it, was that "power in the human mind of distinguishing and chusing good and evil . . . virtue and vice." Mankind's benevolence and good will, guided by the moral sense, rejected capital punishment as barbarous, cruel, and revengeful. Moreover, Rush believed that external phenomena could injure one's moral sense, rendering it insensible. According to this understanding of human psychology, the execution spectacle deranged the moral sense and reoriented people toward vice rather than virtue.[12]

While anti-gallows essayists in the 1840s continued to write about the influence of external, or environmental, events on something akin to moral sense, they now ignored the argument that, when presented with the idea of capital punishment, the individual reflexively rejected it as a violation of man's moral nature. In the late eighteenth century, moral sense and moral nature served as intellectal tools in the dismantling of institutions associated with concentrated power. But in antebellum America, arguments from morality flowed directly from those who sought to re-establish the connection between the moral government of God and the secular polity of man. To be sure, O'Sullivan referred to "our natural instinctive repugnance to the cold and wilful shedding of human blood," but he attacked capital punishment primarily on utilitarian and political grounds rather than through moral sense arguments.[13]

In addition to Dod, a number of other writers argued that the moral sense sustained retributive punishment. Tayler Lewis, a member of the Dutch Reformed Church and a laywer in New York, staked out a similar position in the *Biblical Repository and Classical Review*. Lewis asserted that "the retributive power of human law is affirmed a priori by the moral sense." Intuitive moral ideas, he insisted, decided on the punishment of death not by utilitarian calculations, but on the question of "desert on intrinsic demerit"; the moral sense justified capital punishment not in terms of deterrence or reformation but in the eternal desire for justice and retribution. Leonard Bacon, a Congregationalist minister, disagreed with Lewis that retribution alone was an end that should be prized over the social good that results from punishment. But he, too, averred that "the expression of the moral sense of the state against the crime" authorized the death penalty.[14]

The readers of Dod's and Lewis's articles consisted primarily of orthodox clergymen and scriptural scholars. Another Presbyterian minister, George Barrell Cheever, reached a far wider audience. In the 1840s, Cheever served as the foremost proponent of capital punishment in America; he, too, assailed O'Sullivan's argument in print before the two men met publicly to debate the issue. Cheever's Calvinist credentials were impeccable. Graduate of Bowdoin and Andover Theological Seminary, Cheever, at age twenty-seven, established himself with a published assault on Unitarianism. He moved from New England to New York, where he became pastor of the Allen Street Presbyterian Church and, in 1845, editor of the *New York Evangelist*. His reputation in the 1840s rested on his impassioned defense of the death penalty. So renowned was he for his stance on this issue that a group of women from Jacksonville, Mississippi, considered Cheever "the most prominent champion of the Sacred Cause of Hanging" and sent him a bookmark embroidered with the silhouette of a person suspended from the gallows.[15]

Cheever's *Punishment by Death: Its Authority and Expediency* appeared in 1842. The Calvinist minister dedicated the work to the New York legislature. As one might expect, Cheever devoted the greatest portion of his book to proving the case for capital punishment from divine revelation. He argued that no legitimate reason existed for substituting "whatsoever" for "whosoever" in Genesis 9:6. The right of capital punishment, Cheever claimed, was universal. It belonged neither to "one dispensation nor another"; it was "neither Jewish, nor Gentile, nor Christian." Rather, the death penalty "is an ordinance of humanity and civil society the world over." The punishment of death was especially imperative in the case of murder because such a crime was not merely an "injury to man . . . but to God." The state not only had an obligation to maintain order and obedience to the law but also, according to Cheever, to avenge the blasphemy inherent in criminal activity. It was the divine authority of civil government that permitted rulers the exclusive right to take life. And it was human depravity that made such action necessary.[16]

In addition to Cheever, most advocates of capital punishment focused their defense of the gallows on this justification of punishment as revenge. Writers such as Leonard Bacon rejected completely "the absurd notion the design of punishment is the reformation of the criminal." And while most pro-gallows essayists were also concerned with deterrence, they thought the best way to achieve "the security of the community was to pit the nation against the murderer." Anything less would be a denial of the moral obligation of civil and divine government to exact justice.[17]

According to defenders of the death penalty, the moral imperative and "natural instinct" that the murderer be punished with death meant that, if the state did not revenge crime, the individual would. Abolish capital punishment, warned Leonard Bacon, and "you establish either the primeval barbarous rule of blood-revenge by the next friend of the murdered, or a horrible Lynch court." The abolition of capital punishment, predicted another minister, "would be followed by the semi-barbarous practice of carrying arms in the public streets. Individuals would feel that they must defend themselves when the law no longer threw around life the protection offered by its severest penalty." For pro-gallows essayists, then, man's moral nature demanded justice, and the state alone, through capital punishment, acted as the proper agent of revenge. When they responded, opponents of capital punishment decried the "*spirit of revenge*" as "foul and demoniac . . . evil in it nature . . . desecrating the idea of the inviolable sanctity of human life."[18]

For ministers such as Cheever, the claim that capital punishment coerced a false repentance was an assertion to be considered seriously. Cheever, however, inverted the argument and claimed that the death penalty promoted penitence and salvation, whereas life imprisonment probably did not. Cheever reasoned that, if the sentence of death failed to "rouse up the conscience of a hardened sinner," it was nearly certain that nothing else would. The interval between the sentence of death and its execution permitted the prisoner time enough for repentance. Life imprisonment, by comparison, allowed for infinite procrastination in the serious business of salvation. Rather than hurrying a soul unprepared to meet its maker, the death penalty, and not imprisonment, Cheever proclaimed, had the greatest regenerating influence.[19]

Cheever concluded his argument by noting the strangeness of the "humanity" of those who would substitute life imprisonment for death. Solitary confinement, he thought, "proved so terrible to the mind, so disastrous to the individual's nature" that it had in some cases led to insanity, hardly a beneficial mode of "reforming criminals and preparing them for heaven." Cheever agreed that suffering should be prevented, but that object was hardly accomplished by substituting imprisonment for hanging. Instead, the minister endorsed one suggestion that a "more humane, more instantaneous, more certain" mode of execution be substituted—decapitation.[20]

Generally, then, the defense of capital punishment centered on the belief that divine authority should govern human affairs, that religion should provide the principles of morality by which civil government operated. If capital punishment was a "divine institution," its abolition would result in the subversion of government. People might argue over what, precisely, divine government required of man, but few rejected the proposition that "human government ought to be administered on the same principles as the Divine." As we have seen, liberal and orthodox Protestants disagreed profoundly over what those principles entailed, but both groups shared the assumption that divine authority and civil rule were interrelated.[21]

The belief in a divine basis for civil government was nothing new in the 1840s. To the extent that it seemed jarring and reactionary, it was only as a result of the vitality of the language of natural rights and social compacts that captured the terms of public discourse in the ages of Jefferson and Jackson. Long before the Revolution, New England preachers spoke easily of legislative responsibility to God's precepts and the divine origins of civil government. Once again, in the middle decades of the nineteenth century, propelled by Christian politics and conservative fears, commentators assaulted democratic freedoms and inalienable rights with the weapons of moral government and inescapable obligation. Given what was at stake, nothing less than the language and direction of politics and society, it is not surprising that capital punishment, an issue that fractured debate along the fissures of individual reform versus divine revenge, gained considerable attention.[22]

II

Scores of legislative reports, newspaper articles, and essays on capital punishment flooded the reading public in the 1840s, but few of those works differed substantially from O'Sullivan's report and Cheever's book. When the Broadway Tabernacle in New York decided to sponsor a series of public debates, no question was as controversial as capital punishment and no two opponents as well known as O'Sullivan and Cheever.[23]

Public debates constituted a potent new cultural institution in the 1830s, '40s, and '50s. At a time when steam-driven and cylinder presses mass produced newspapers for a penny a piece, oral performances at lyceums and lecture halls became an inexpensive and popular entertainment for all classes. Individual lectures were the most common format, but many societies also sponsored debates. In January 1843 the Broadway Tabernacle announced a course in public debates intended to improve "facilities for Intellectual Culture and Acquirement." For a dollar for the series, or twelve cents an evening, citizens could attend "discussions of all topics of vital interest on which the community is divided." A faith in the supposedly democratic nature of such public events and a belief that, through discussion, conflict could be resolved helped lecture series such as these quickly gain legitimacy.[24]

For three evenings, January 27, February 3, and February 17, 1843, O'Sullivan and Cheever debated the question "Ought Capital Punishment to Be Abolished?" A prominent attorney, Hugh Maxwell, presided over the affair, and the debaters were joined on the platform by a number of "eminent literary, scientific, and clerical gentlemen." Because he was arguing the negative side of the question, Cheever insisted on speaking after O'Sullivan. Neither orator, as far as we can tell, drifted far from the arguments offered in their well-known works. The first evening's debate centered on scriptural arguments; the second, on the issue of expediency, the question of whether capital punishment should be inflicted regardless of any biblical injunction. The third was arranged to conclude the discussion left incomplete from the first two.[25]

It is difficult to determine how the audience reacted to the debate. As Horace Greeley pointed out in an editorial, "so much depends on the prepossessions of the hearer, and the disposition to give weight to the cogency of the facts, or to the preponderance of personal authority, the boldness of assumptions, and the felicity of rhetoric." The editor added that advocates of abolition were at a disadvantage because no one in the audience conceived of himself as a murderer, but everyone felt exposed to assault. Therefore, according to Greeley, people assume that executions increase personal security without personal risk, and out of "Self-love and fear," they support capital punishment.[26]

Following the second debate, on February 3, the proponents of capital punishment claimed victory, and an argument over oratorical style and debating tactics festered for the next month. In that second debate, O'Sullivan arrived, expecting this time to speak last. But Cheever refused to go first, claiming that he was not prepared to do so. O'Sullivan, "unwilling to deter the audience" further, agreed to begin provided he was given time for a rejoinder. O'Sullivan spoke extemporaneously, and, by one account, was not a particularly effective speaker. One listener complained that he was "too argumentative and metaphysical." Cheever's discourse was written out and the minister did not finish until a few minutes before ten o'clock, too late to allow further discussion. O'Sullivan, infuriated with Cheever, published a letter in the *Tribune* that requested "all judgements on the merits of the subjects be suspended" until the advocates of abolition had a fair chance to reply.[27]

A third evening of debate, however, did little for O'Sullivan's side. One writer to the *Tribune* reported that "a boast had been made in a certain quarter, that the negative achieved a great triumph in the last debate." Another letter, signed by "No Hangman," complained about Cheever's advantages in the debate: his "elaborately written discourse" and being allowed to go last. This correspondent challenged Cheever to a "fair and equal" debate of alternate half-hours with opportunity for rejoinder. "Justice" replied to "No Hangman" at length and claimed that O'Sullivan spoke longer than Cheever, that Cheever was never informed that he was to go first on the second evening, that a "practised lawyer" such as O'Sullivan should have found it an advantage that his opponent relied on a written text, and that, since Cheever had granted the challenge to a third evening of debate, why should he take time from his parish to debate the issue all over again?[28]

Tensions between O'Sullivan and Cheever and, by extension, proponents and opponents of abolition, escalated throughout March. O'Sullivan complained publicly about being made into an "object of no small amount of abuse." Cheever published a revised version of his reply at the Broadway Tabernacle and denied O'Sullivan's entreaties to permit a response in the Appendix so as to preserve the adversarial format of a debate. Finally, O'Sullivan published an essay in the *Democratic Review* that offended most of the clergy of New York. Entitled "The Gallows and the Gospel, an Appeal to Clergymen Opposing Themselves to the Abolition of the One, in the Name of the Other," the essay rebuked ministers for not recognizing the antagonism between the gallows and Christian principles. The New York legislator accused the clergy of assuming "the function of the very Bodyguard of the Hangman." O'Sullivan later admitted that the alliterative use of Gallows and Gospel was perhaps not in the best of taste, but stood by his position that a "*portion* of the clergy have undertaken a peculiar professional patronage and protection of the gallows and the executioner."[29]

By April, the public animosity between O'Sullivan and Cheever subsided, but the printed and oral debate between them encapsulated the conflict over capital punishment throughout the 1840s. The hostility between Unitarian and Universalist opponents of the gallows and Congregationalist and Presbyterian defenders of the death penalty grew especially acute. Convinced that Scripture did not authorize the death penalty and that the spirit of Christianity demanded its abolition, opponents of capital punishment tangled with orthodox ministers who believed that the bible authorized death and that civil government, as a representative of divine government, had an obligation to execute murderers. In Boston especially, the conflict with the clergy became public and vituperative. Anti-gallows activists there posted printed notices in the streets that read "Thou Shalt Not Kill" and included an engraving of the priest and the hangman standing on the scaffold together. Someone defaced these notices by scrawling across them in pencil, "Canonize murderers as saints! Give pensions to rascals! Let's have no punishment at all." The confrontation was not limited to street notices and speeches. Opponents of capital punishment launched a campaign to have the most "zealous advocates of judicial murder," the orthodox clergy, serve as hangmen. Calvinist clergymen responded by denouncing anti-gallows activists as impious, sacrilegious, and unchristian.[30]

The debate between O'Sullivan and Cheever also demonstrated the shift from an emphasis on reforming criminals to a preoccupation with the deterrent effect of punishment. Opponents of capital punishment argued that life in prison served as a powerful enough deterrent; defenders of the death penalty insisted that imprisonment could never deter as effectively as the threat of death. Absent from the discussion was any sign of an earlier devotion to the idea that prisons would serve as "schools of reformation," that "reformation is an end which should never be forgotten by society." At a time when the respectable classes feared social disorder and called for a return to moral government, the dream of reformation succumbed to the desire for deterrence.[31]

Nowhere was this fixation with whether capital punishment acted as a deterrent more evident than in a confrontation over the meaning of various statistics. O'Sullivan and others argued that, wherever the abolition experiment had been tried, it was followed by a decrease in the number of crimes for the offense no longer capital, even when crime was generally on the increase for other offenses. O'Sullivan pointed to Tuscany, Belgium, Russia, and even England. Evidence from Belgium revealed that, before 1830, when King Leopold abolished the death penalty for murder, murders averaged eight a year, but the five years after 1830 there were only four altogether. Another favorite statistic of O'Sullivan's was that in Belgium between 1824 and 1829 there were twenty-two executions and thirty-four murders; between 1829 and 1834, there were no executions and twenty murders. "What more can be required to satisfy the most obstinate preversion of prejudice" against abolition? he wondered.[32]

Cheever would have none of O'Sullivan's statistics and offered some data of his own. He claimed that in Belgium from 1830 to 1834 there were "6 poisonings, 60 infanticides, 119 assassinations" that O'Sullivan did not report. Cheever also asked why, of all the nations in the history of the world, only three had abolished capital punishment. No experiment, he insisted, had lasted long enough to permit valid generalizations about the relationship between the death penalty and murder. Moreover, even if crime rates fell, who was to say it was not the result of other "ameliorating influences" such as education and moral reform generally rather than the elimination of capital punishment. In conclusion, Cheever asserted that the statistical argument against capital punishment was "palpably false."[33]

The result was a tedious exchange over what other experiments in abolition had proven about the relationship between the death penalty and crime. But we should not allow the numbers to mask what was essentially competing visions of human nature. To be sure, opponents and proponents of capital punishment generally belonged to the same social and professional class. Each group was concerned with how best to punish crime, create social harmony, and harness the "humanitarian spirit of the age." Yet despite these similar backgrounds and concerns, opponents and defenders of the death penalty held radically opposed understandings of the nature of man and society.

Most anti-gallows activists viewed man as moral, reasonable, educable, and savable. They emphasized the material basis of experience, believed that social conditions contributed to crime, and focused on forging a new set of internal restraints for the individual. Rather than the use of coercion and brutality, opponents of capital punishment thought that individuals, once enlightened, would select self-control and self-discipline. Liberty was the decision to be temperate and industrious, virtuous and regulated; the fruit of that liberty would be an ordered society. The role of government, of all authority, was to promote self-government wherever possible. Opponents of capital punishment feared disorder, but were convinced that the gallows did not contribute to the stability of society.

Supporters of capital punishment, by comparison, thought of man as a sinful, depraved, and corrupt animal who had to be restrained by divine and civil laws. By these lights, no degree of environmental influence exculpated the criminal from his guilt, and the moral sense of the community demanded not the romantic ideal of reformation, not the practical goal of deterrence, but revenge. If for anti-gallows essayists a certain type of liberty would yield consensus and order, for pro-gallows writers only strict, disciplined order would permit any freedom at all. Civil government could not be separated artificially from the moral government of God, and divine government demanded that criminals be executed. This faith in the divine foundation of civil government blossomed in the 1840s and 1850s. In the context of the disordering transformations of the period, capital punishment promised a return to moral and religious order.

It is important to emphasize that both opponents and proponents of capital punishment desired an ordered, disciplined, crime-free society. Both groups shared in those beliefs and sensibilities that promoted the penitentiary, created private executions, and led them to join voluntary associations. Both groups represented a firmly entrenched middle-class culture of privacy and civility. But their opposing views of mankind and how best to achieve order in a democratic society shaped the debate over capital punishment and defined one boundary of conflict within Northeastern middle-class culture before the Civil War.

The competing visions of society were evident not only in the debate over capital punishment but also in the way advocates of the death penalty denounced anti-gallows activists. Pro-gallows essayists, primarily orthodox ministers and jurists, excoriated opponents of capital punishment as radicals and infidels, as anarchists and social levelers. One writer claimed that "the haunters of dramshops; the frequenters of brothels; those whose oaths shock you as they pass along the street—are generally in favor of the abolition of capital punishment." Another commentator divided anti-gallows activists into two classes: those actuated by "misguided philanthropy," and a more numerous group composed of "men of dissolute habits and violent passions, and far more hostile to punishments than crimes." To these writers, the desire to abolish capital punishment was one of the more "Vulgar Infidelity's" of the age, because in denying the right of civil government to take life, anti-gallows essayists necessarily rejected the authority of divine government as well. And if society cannot punish a criminal, asked one minister, then how could God?[34]

Proponents argued that, by rejecting the authority of civil and divine government, anti-gallows activists also advocated a "destructive radical-ism." One correspondent claimed that opponents of the gallows wanted to eliminate all restraints of law on the individual, that they regarded all laws as an "unwarrantable restriction of human liberty." But if they suc-ceeded in prying the individual loose from the state, in "uncag[ing] the lion of human depravity," the "total subversion of civil government" would follow. This "radical zeal" to liberate mankind from certain restraints would free men from both human and divine authority; its tendency, ac-cording to the pastor of one Congregationalist church, is to "anarchy and despotism."[35]

Another tactic used by proponents of capital punishment was to de-nounce the supposed "humanity," "justice," and "benevolence" of the anti-gallows cause. The battle over who could rightfully appropriate the language of humanity and claim it as their own illuminates a crucial aspect of antebellum reform. The politics of language was more than just a rhetorical competition. In the 1830s and 1840s, a word such as "hu-manity" carried talismanic power and the key to reform or anti-reform was to be identified as the rightful representative of a limited number of such words. One keen observer noted in 1846 that "nothing is more com-mon than for words to acquire new meanings"; proponents of the death penalty expended great effort in denouncing anti-gallows essayists for manipulating the true meaning of certain words.[36]

According to defenders of the gallows, the abolition of capital punish-ment was not "humane," "just," or "philanthropic," and the opponents of the death penalty offered nothing but "mock humanity," "rosewater philanthropy," and "morbid sentimentality." One minister warned that "there is no more cruel tyrant than Philanthropy run mad. There is no worse enemy to the public good than Benevolence untaught. And is it not an unenlightened benevolence which seeks to abolish the death pen-alty?" Another essayist defended capital punishment as truly benevolent. He insisted that "benevolence looks to the good of all, to the greatest good, and perceiving that the peace and security of the community at large will be sacrificed to the violence of the murderer, unless he is cut off, it demands his blood." This confrontation over whether opponents of capital punishment were anarchists and false prophets illustrates more than just the tactics of effective denunciation. Words such as "humanity" and "benevolence" was pitted at the core of middle-class attitudes and perceptions about their society.[37]

Needless to say, opponents of capital punishment were not as pro-gallows essayists depicted them. Although the two groups disagreed deeply over the nature of society, those opposed to the death penalty did not seek to loosen the bonds of society, overturn moral authority and government, or destroy civil order. E. H. Chapin, a Universalist minister best known as a lyceum lecturer, responded to the charges by pointing out that, whenever social evils are attacked, alarmists cry, "We are running into anarchy and licentiousness." But social reform in general, and the abolition of capital punishment in particular, "is not the result of this new dogma, or that new notion. It is not the effect of transcendentalism, or infidelity, or heresy. It is the legitimate result of republicanism and of protestantism."[38]

By invoking republicanism and Protestantism, Chapin reminded readers of the original source of the opposition to capital punishment dating back to the post-Revolutionary heritage. In the 1780s and 1790s, Benjamin Rush had argued against the death penalty as a violation of the republican gospel, as a repudiation of the republican ideal of virtue and the Protestant promise of salvation. In the 1840s, Chapin could still use these words against the death penalty, but with far less effect. Whereas patriots and politicians in the late eighteenth century fixated on the question of limiting and balancing a secular government, of guaranteeing inalienable rights, in the mid-nineteenth century, ministers and statesmen again extolled government as an expression of divine intention. The argument of social contract theorists that the individual had never relinquished his right over life to the state succumbed to the belief that individuals had no meaningful choice in the matter. If the religious identity of government loomed ever larger in antebellum America, so too did the orthodox component of religion. Rush and Chapin, both Universalists, stressed benevolence and salvation. But adherents of the orthodox side of Protestantism, emphasizing divine retribution and eternal punishment, proliferated in the 1840s. To be sure, evangelical Protestantism declared man a free moral agent, but it never promised life to those sinners who did not change. In antebellum America, conflict continued to rage in both the political and the religious arenas. But Chapin's two magical words, republicanism and Protestantism, enlisted few new converts in the campaign against capital punishment.

III

The debate over capital punishment persisted throughout the antebellum period; but in the early 1840s anti-gallows activists feared that the total abolition of the death penalty was still a long way off. Society, they felt, had progressed from the days of public executions for numerous capital crimes, but private hangings and death for first-degree murder seemed to disturb only a minority of Americans. Activists discovered that, although "no execution can take place without a very open demonstration of feeling against this form of punishment," public sentiment did not seem to support the total abolition of capital punishment. The faith in moral government and divine retribution would not permit any punishment other than death. Legislators remained convinced that the complete elimination of the gallows would "unkennel the bloodhounds of disorder . . . would seriously weaken the restraint of all law and perhaps overturn the very foundations of our political existence."[39]

As the debate over capital punishment started to drag, some activists shifted their attention elsewhere. Since most members of the societies for the abolition of capital punishment were as devoted to other reforms as to the anti-gallows cause, that was easy to do. Indeed, even as they shifted they did not envision themselves withdrawing from the anti-gallows movement. In the minds of abolitionists such as William Lloyd Garrison and Wendell Phillips, one campaign, against slavery or the gallows, was inseparable from another. Both slavery and capital punishment, they argued, represented systems of brutality that coerced individuals, and both institutions merited attack. They were pleasantly surprised when in 1847, and despite the general support for the gallows throughout the nation, Michigan became the first state to abolish capital punishment entirely.

When Congress admitted Michigan to statehood in 1838, the revised statutes of the state provided for death in cases of murder and treason. Corresponding to the abolition of public hangings, executions in Michigan were inflicted within the walls of the prison. The legislature intermittently reported and defeated bills to abolish capital punishment for murder until 1846 when, in revising the state's laws, the senate voted 9-2 and the house voted 21-14 to eliminate the death penalty and substitute solitary imprisonment at hard labor for life. The law went into effect on March 1, 1847.[40]

If there is a specific reason why Michigan first abolished capital punishment, we will never know it. The content of the debate over the death penalty in Michigan deviated little from debate in the East. The profile of the debaters was also the same. The Reverend George Duffield, a Presbyterian minister, led the defense of capital punishment; Universalists, Unitarians, and a Swedenborgian opposed it. The legislative debate was not particularly partisan, although Democrats tended to take the lead in opposing capital punishment. According to one account, of the 54 Democrats in 1846, 29 opposed the gallows, 21 favored it, and 4 did not vote. Nor does the Michigan case seem to be an example of transplanted New Englanders accomplishing in the West what they could not achieve in the East. Of those legislators with New England origins, 10 opposed capital punishment, whereas 9 supported the death penalty. It is possible that, after all those near misses in states such as Pennsylvania, New York, and Massachusetts, it was only a matter of time before some legislature would eventually succeed.[41]

Whatever the reasons for Michigan's experiment in abolition, anti-gallows activists in the East exulted over the legislation. One commentator exclaimed that "the sun has risen in the West," and hoped that "its rays will penetrate the darkness which has so long brooded over the East." Proponents of capital punishment in Michigan, however, did not relent easily, and the legislature considered re-enacting the death penalty in 1848, 1849, 1851, and 1859. With each murder came cries that, without the death penalty, violent crime was on the rise. J. Stebbins, a Unitarian minister, responded to the charges. He accused George Duffield, with his "keen relish for hanging," of looking for any pretext to alarm people. Men had been hanged for centuries without an end to murder. Why, he asked, blame the first murder after abolition on the new penal law? Moreover, Stebbins noted, intemperance figured prominently in the murders committed in Michigan. Clearly, rum, and not the new law, was responsible for the deaths. Finally, with the Mexican War in mind, Stebbins assailed the nation's "war-spirit" which by itself accounted for the increase in murder. "Is it any wonder," he asked, "that the vicious, the unprincipled and the revengeful, thus invited to and encouraged in scenes of carnage, should return ripe for murder?" Like capital punishment, war brutalized sensibilities and forced individuals to become slaves to "unbridled lust and passion." The experiment, Stebbins concluded, should be given a fair trial.[42]

Michigan did not reinstate capital punishment. By 1853 Rhode Island and Wisconsin had abolished it as well. But the issue of the death penalty was not to become a volatile public question again until after the Civil War. Throughout the 1850s, Eastern legislators studied new statistics from states without capital punishment and tried to divine the relation between the death penalty and the prevention of crime; activists continued to debate capital punishment, but in terms that were so familiar and repetitious that most people must have already formed an opinion on the subject; anti-gallows societies, like so many other reform associations, splintered and disbanded, leaving full-time activists in search of new approaches to reform.

As for O'Sullivan and Cheever, both men moved on to other concerns. O'Sullivan, "full of grand and world-embracing schemes," promoted Manifest Destiny and supported the Confederacy. Cheever worked in Bible education and, when he came out against slavery, found himself agreeing with his former antagonists, men such as Garrison and Phillips, about the most explosive issue of their times. When the war came, O'Sullivan and Cheever again found themselves on opposite sides of a conflict that was all about death.[43]

Epilogue

Although the ritual of execution day and conflict over capital punishment played an important part in the shift in American culture between the Revolution and the Civil War, the death penalty was not eliminated entirely. Michigan, Rhode Island, and Wisconsin abolished capital punishment, but Pennsylvania, New York, and Massachusetts, where anti-gallows activists concentrated their efforts, did not. On the eve of Civil War, the once youthful, ambitious generation of activists from the 1830s and 1840s felt drained by the slow pace of progress and distracted by the array of different causes. Some still pondered what to do with a troubled penitentiary system, but the discussion seemed half-hearted and confused, the vision clouded and obscured. With hangings institutionalized behind prison walls, anti-gallows activists could no longer alarm citizens by describing the damaging and brutalizing effect of executions. Having momentarily discovered a comfortable balance between public and private life, between concern for others and security for themselves, between social experimentation and cultural stability, middle-class Americans tried to consolidate the changes wrought over the previous half-century. In a culture that once again thought coercion as necessary as benevolence, revenge more desirable than reformation, the opposition to the death penalty lost much of its force.

If through the 1850s, as reform associations factionalized and national politics sectionalized, the abolition of capital punishment attracted little attention, it was nearly inconceivable during the Civil War. As one young activist, Marvin Bovee, informed one veteran, Wendell Phillips, "I am quietly resting on my oars waiting for the American conflict to cease that I may resume my labors on penal reform. . . . It is useless to talk of saving life when we are killing by thousands. Can't elevate mankind when government is debasing them."[1]

Following the war, the question of capital punishment recaptured a national audience, but in a manner that left opponents of the gallows on the defensive. The hanging of the Lincoln conspirators, attended by scores of men and women, drew little criticism. The lynchings of blacks and whites presented a chilling warning that, if the state refused to serve as

160

hangman, others would. In September 1881, a second President lay slain and the impending execution of Charles Guiteau, Garfield's assassin, provided another opportunity for proponents and opponents of the death penalty to state their cases. At least two of the adversaries were well acquainted with one another. George Barrell Cheever, seventy-five years old, and Wendell Phillips, seventy-one, were in the twilight of distinguished careers. They had fought on the same side to end slavery but had bitterly opposed one another on the issue of capital punishment. Now, with another presidential assassin awaiting death, they again offered their views on the death penalty.

It should come as no suprise that their finely honed positions came packaged in language addressed as much to the 1840s as to the 1880s. As he had done all his life, Cheever presented the scriptural argument for capital punishment. He repeated that the Bible authorized retributive punishments and that government, as a divine agency, had a responsibility to execute murderers. The social anxieties of this aged Calvinist minister punctuated his remarks. He argued that, without the death penalty, common thieves would murder their victims to eliminate witnesses to their crimes. He worried as well about those ghosts that haunted men like him after the Civil War: the threat posed by "the socialism of ignorant masses," the peril of "conflicting infidel speculations and political theories," and the danger of "suffrage universal." All of this, Cheever insisted, made it "inhumane, reckless, and unjust" to abolish "the divine law against murder."[2]

Phillips began by summarizing the lesson he had learned from over fifty years of agitating: "to get men to listen is half the battle, and the harder half, in all reforms." He went on, as he had done hundreds of times before, to deny that any biblical text authorized capital punishment, to reject the notion of divine government, and to emphasize the many successful experiments in abolition throughout the world. If for no other reason, the death penalty should be abolished, Phillips insisted, because hangings neither deterred crime nor attacked the causes of crime: poverty, heredity, and insanity, not depravity. Phillips concluded that Guiteau, "a pitiable and miserable wretch," was hardly responsible morally and that, if the state executed him, it would stand as a sorrowful example of "hot revenge . . . a blot on the justice of the American people . . . and evidence of how much actual barbarism lingers in the bosom of an intelligent and so-called Christian country."[3]

Since Phillips's and Cheever's time, legal and constitutional dilemmas rather than an exegesis of Biblical texts or a discourse on social contracts have dominated the public debate over capital punishment. In particular, the Supreme Court has considered and reconsidered questions of constitutionality in the imposition and administration of the death penalty. In 1972, the Court held in *Furman v. Georgia* that "the imposition and carrying out of the death penalty in these cases constitute cruel and unusual punishment in violation of the Eighth and Fourteenth Amendments." The decision marked the triumph of a decade-long campaign, spearheaded by the Legal Defense Fund and sustained by mounting public opposition to capital punishment between the mid-1950s and mid-1960s, to prevent the execution of anyone on death row. A belief in the inhumanity of the death penalty, an awareness that those most likely to suffer death were black or poor, and a commitment once again to rehabilitation rather than execution, forged in a cultural climate of social experimentation, had been fused to the Eighth and Fourteenth amendments to invalidate the laws governing capital punishment.[4]

The judicial abolition of the death penalty did not last long. Within several years of the decision in *Furman,* legislative reaction to judicial action helped reinvigorate capital punishment. Newly written statutes satisfied the Court's concern with procedural issues in the imposition of the death penalty. In *Gregg v. Georgia* (1976), the Court ruled that "the punishment of death does not invariably violate the Constitution," and noted "that a large proportion of American society continues to regard it [the death penalty] as an appropriate and necessary criminal sanction." A faith in deterrence and retribution, sustained by self-described representatives of a moral majority and advocates of social order, had resurrected capital punishment. By the mid-1980s, dozens of executions had taken place. With nearly two thousand prisoners on death row, and with most legal and constitutional arguments against the death penalty currently unaccepted, it is certain that the pace of executions will increase dramatically over the next decade.[5]

However many die, privacy is likely to remain the pre-eminent feature of executions. So powerful still is the belief that the public should be prevented from observing the execution, even television, which daily brings quivering images of sanitized death into the family room, is not permitted to broadcast the affair. On execution day, a dozen or so witnesses are allowed access to the inner recesses of the penitentiary; frequently, supporters of capital punishment gather outside to applaud the state's actions while opponents of the death penalty pass the night in candle-lit vigilance. The condemned is still wrapped in ritual—last meal, last words, last prayers—but no longer faces the procession to the gallows. In the past century, death in the electric chair, the gas chamber, and, most recently, on the prison gurney has replaced death by hanging. These new forms of execution embody the nation's faith in technological and medical palliatives; beneath the façade of humane execution, the state continues to impose private, isolated, anonymous death.

Notes

Introduction

1. Studies of the shift in rituals of punishment and origins of the penitentiary include Michel Foucault, *Discipline and Punish: The Birth of the Prison* (New York: Vintage Books, 1979); Michael Ignatieff, *A Just Measure of Pain: The Penitentiary in the Industrial Revolution, 1750–1850* (New York: Columbia University Press, 1978); Pieter Spierenburg, *The Spectacle of Suffering* (Cambridge: Cambridge University Press, 1984); John Bender, *Imagining the Penitentiary: Fiction and the Architecture of Mind in Eighteenth-Century England* (Chicago: University of Chicago Press, 1987); Patricia O'Brien, *The Promise of Punishment: Prisons in Nineteenth-Century France* (Princeton: Princeton University Press, 1982); and David Rothman, *The Discovery of the Asylum: Social Order and Disorder in the New Republic* (Boston: Little, Brown, 1971). For a general formulation of the shift toward privacy, see two volumes by Norbert Elias on *The Civilizing Process: The History of Manners* (New York: Pantheon, 1978) and *Power and Civility* (New York: Pantheon, 1982); also see Richard Sennett, *The Fall of Public Man* (New York: Vintage, 1978).

2. On criminal justice in seventeenth- and eighteenth-century England, see J. M. Beattie, *Crime and the Courts in England, 1660–1800* (Princeton: Princeton University Press, 1986); Joel B. Samaha, "Hanging for Felony: The Rule of Law in Elizabethan Colchester," *Historical Journal* 21 (December 1978): 763–782; Cynthia Herrup, "Law and Morality in Seventeenth-Century England," *Past and Present* (February 1985): 102–123; Douglas Hay, "Property, Authority, and the Criminal Law," in Hay et al., *Albion's Fatal Tree: Crime and Society in Eighteenth-Century England* (New York: Random House, 1975); John H. Langbein, "Albion's Fatal Flaws," *Past and Present* (February 1983): 96–120; Peter King, "Decision-makers and Decision-making in the English Criminal Law, 1750–1800," *Historical Journal* 27 (March 1984): 25–58. The historiography on criminal justice is discussed by Joanna Innes and John Styles, "The Crime Wave: Recent Writings on Crime and Criminal Justice in Eighteenth-Century England," *Journal of British Studies* 25 (October 1986): 380–435.

3. Quoted in Donald Veall, *The Popular Movement for Law Reform, 1640–1660* (Oxford: Clarendon Press, 1970), 127; Also see Robert Zaller, "The Debate over Capital Punishment during the English Revolution," *American Journal of Legal History* 31 (April 1987): 126–144; Leon Radzinowicz, *A History of English Criminal Law and Its Administration from 1750,* 4 vols. (London: Stevens,

1948–68); and Thomas Andrew Green, *Verdict According to Conscience: Perspectives on the English Criminal Trial Jury, 1200–1800* (Chicago: University of Chicago Press, 1985).

4. On middle-class formation and consciousness, see Paul Johnson, *A Shopkeeper's Millennium: Society and Revivals in Rochester, New York, 1815–1837* (New York: Hill and Wang, 1978); Mary P. Ryan, *Cradle of the Middle Class: A Case Study of Oneida County, New York, 1790–1865* (Cambridge: Cambridge University Press, 1981); John S. Gilkeson, Jr., *Middle-Class Providence, 1820–1940* (Princeton: Princeton University Press, 1986). Also see Myra Glenn, *Campaigns against Corporal Punishment: Prisoners, Sailors, Women, and Children in Antebellum America* (Albany: State University of New York Press, 1984). For a critique, consult Stuart Blumin, "The Hypothesis of Middle-Class Formation in the Nineteenth Century: A Critique of Some Proposals," *American Historical Review* 90 (April 1985): 299–338. These issues have not been as well developed for the South, although some evidence suggests similar patterns in attitudes toward punishment. See, for example, Edward Ayers, *Vengeance and Justice: Crime and Punishment in the 19th-Century American South* (New York: Oxford University Press, 1984). My discussion of the conflict over capital punishment and middle-class reform is largely restricted to the New England and Mid-Atlantic states.

5. Some central starting points for examining ritual, culture, and language are Clifford Geertz, *The Interpretation of Cultures* (New York: Basic Books, 1973); Victor Turner, *The Ritual Process* (Chicago: University of Chicago Press, 1969); and Quentin Skinner, "Meaning and Understanding in the History of Ideas," *History and Theory* 8 (1969): 3–53.

1. Ritual and Reform in Antebellum America

1. *Trial and Execution of Washington Goode* (Boston, 1849); *Boston Herald*, January 2, 1849. On blacks in antebellum Boston, see James Oliver Horton and Lois E. Horton, *Black Bostonians: Family Life and Community Struggle in the Antebellum North* (New York: Holmes and Meier, 1979).

2. Leonard W. Levy, *The Law of the Commonwealth and Chief Justice Shaw* (Cambridge, Mass.: Harvard University Press, 1957).

3. *Trial and Execution,* 2–4; *Boston Herald,* January 2, 1849.

4. *Boston Herald,* January 3, 1849; January 4, 1849.

5. *Boston Herald,* January 3, 1849.

6. *Boston Herald,* January 2, 1849.

7. *Boston Herald,* January 2–4, 1849.

8. Ibid.

9. *Boston Herald,* January 4, 1849.

10. Ibid.; *Trial and Execution,* 11–12; *Boston Herald,* January 4, 1849; *Trial and Execution,* 11–12.

11. *Boston Herald,* January 5, 1849; *Trial and Execution,* 13–14.

12. *Boston Herald,* January 4 and 5, 1849. For a discussion of the controversy over Shaw's instruction on the issue of malice in another case, see Levy, *Law of the Commonwealth,* 207–228.

13. *Boston Herald,* January 15, 1849; *Boston Courier* reprinted in the *Liberator,* January 26, 1849.

14. *Boston Courier* reprinted in the *Liberator,* January 26, 1849.

15. *Liberator,* March 30, 1849. For an overview of the campaign against the death penalty see David Brion Davis, "The Movement to Abolish Capital Punishment in America, 1787–1861," *American Historical Review* 63 (October 1957): 23–46.

16. "Shall He Be Hung?," broadside in uncatalogued broadside collection located at the American Antiquarian Society.

17. *Evening Herald,* January 17, 1849; *Boston Herald,* March 23, 1849.

18. "Shall He Be Hung?"; *Boston Herald,* March 23, 1849; "Shall He Be Hung?."

19. "Enthusiastic Meeting at the Tremont Temple in Behalf of Washington Goode," broadside in uncatalogued broadside collection located at the American Antiquarian Society; *Boston Herald,* April 9, 1849; Diary of Charles Spear, manuscript division, Boston Public Library, entry of April 6, 1849.

20. "Enthusiastic Meeting"; *Boston Herald,* April 9, 1849.

21. "Enthusiastic Meeting"; *Boston Herald,* April 9, 1849. For a recent biography of Phillips, see James Brewer Stewart, *Wendell Phillips: Liberty's Hero* (Baton Rouge: Louisiana State University Press, 1986).

22. "Enthusiastic Meeting"; *Boston Herald,* April 9, 1849.

23. "Enthusiastic Meeting"; *Boston Herald,* April 9, 1849.

24. *Prisoner's Friend,* May 1849, pp. 410–11, 417–18; Spear Diary, April 6, 1849.

25. *Prisoner's Friend,* April 1849, p. 364; Massachusetts Archives, Pardons File, 1849.

26. *An Exercise in Declamation in the Form of a Debate on Capital Punishment* (Boston: Charles Spear, 1849), 4–8; *Liberator,* May 4, 1849.

27. *Prisoner's Friend,* May 1849, pp. 417–18; *Liberator,* May 4, 1849. For a public referendum on capital punishment with a different result, see David Brion Davis, "Murder in New Hampshire," *New England Quarterly* 28 (June 1955): 147–163.

28. "Joint Special Committee on the Abolition of Capital Punishment," Commonwealth of Massachusetts, *House Documents,* Number 135, 1849 (Boston, 1849).

29. *Prisoner's Friend,* May 1849, pp. 395–399.

30. Ibid.

31. On reformers attitudes toward blacks, see Lawrence J. Friedman, *Gregarious Saints: Self and Community in American Abolitionism, 1830–1870* (Cambridge: Cambridge University Press, 1982), 160–195.

32. *Prisoner's Friend*, May 1849, pp. 485–486.

33. *Liberator*, May 25, 1849; *Prisoner's Friend*, July 1849, p. 485; *Liberator*, May 4, 1849.

34. *Liberator*, June 1, 1849.

35. Ibid.; *Evening Transcript*, May 25, 1849.

36. *Liberator*, June 1, 1849; *Prisoner's Friend*, July 1849, pp. 502–507.

37. *Herald Tribune*, May 25, 1849; *Liberator*, May 25, 1849.

38. *Boston Republican* quoted in *Prisoner's Friend*, May 1849, p. 394. For the general debate over the use of anesthesia in the nineteenth century, see Martin Pernick, *A Calculus of Suffering: Pain, Professionalism and Anesthesia in Nineteenth-Century America* (New York: Columbia University Press, 1985).

39. [G. W. Peck], "On the Use of Chloroform in Hanging," *American Whig Review* 2 (September 1848): 283–296.

40. Ibid.

41. On Victorian attitudes toward cruelty, see James Turner, *Reckoning with the Beast: Animals, Pain, and Humanity in the Victorian Mind* (Baltimore: Johns Hopkins University Press, 1980).

42. Wendell Phillips, *Speeches, Lectures, Letters*, 108–109; *Liberator*, June 29, 1849.

43. *Boston Daily Bee*, May 26, 1849; Spear's Diary, March 29, 1849.

44. *Boston Daily Bee*, May 26, 1849; *Boston Courier*, May 26, 1849.

45. *Boston Daily Bee*, May 26, 1849; *Boston Investigator*, May 30, 1849; *Boston Post*, May 26, 1849.

46. *Boston Daily Bee*, May 26, 1849; *Boston Herald*, May 26, 1849; *Boston Herald*, May 26, 1849.

47. *Boston Herald*, May 28, 1849.

48. *Liberator*, June 29, 1849; *Trial and Execution of Washington Goode*, 16.

2. The Design of Public Executions

1. James Dana, *The Intent of Capital Punishment, A Discourse Delivered in the City of New-Haven, October 20, 1790, Being the Day of the Execution of Joseph Mountain for a Rape* (New Haven: T. and S. Green, 1790), 21. Also see [David Daggett], *Sketches of the Life of Joseph Mountain, a Negro, who was executed at New-Haven, on the 20th Day of October, 1790, for a Rape* (New Haven: T. and S. Green, 1790).

2. Ezra Ripley, *Love to Our Neighbors Explained and Urged in A Sermon Delivered at Concord, Massachusetts, December 26, 1799, Being the Day on Which Samuel Smith was Executed for Burglary* . . . (Boston: Samuel Hall, 1800), 20; Nathan Strong, *The Reasons and Design of Public Punishments: A Sermon Delivered before the People Who Were Collected to the Execution of Moses Dunbar, Who Was Condemned for High Treason Against the State of*

Connecticut, and Executed March 19, 1777 (Hartford: Ebenezer Watson, 1777), 11.

3. John Shy, "The American Revolution: The Military Conflict Considered as a Revolutionary War," in Stephen G. Kurtz and James H. Hutson, eds., *Essays on the American Revolution* (New York: W. W. Norton, 1973), 150; Ronald Hoffman, "The Disaffected in the Revolutionary South," in Alfred F. Young, ed., *The American Revolution* (DeKalb: Northern Illinois University Press, 1976), 284; John Adams to Abigail Adams, July 3, 1776, in Jack P. Greene, ed., *Colonies to Nation, 1763–1789* (New York: W. W. Norton, 1975), 296–297.

4. On republican values, see Gordon Wood, *The Creation of the American Republic, 1776–1787* (Chapel Hill: University of North Carolina Press, 1969), especially 6–124; Elizabeth Cope Harrison, ed., *Philadelphia Merchant: The Diary of Thomas P. Cope, 1800–1851* (South Bend: Gateway Editions, 1978), 89.

5. Strong, *The Reasons and Design of Public Punishments*, 15–17.

6. William Cobbett, ed., *The Parliamentary History of England from the Earliest Period to the Year 1803* (London: T. C. Hansard, 1813), Vol. XVIII, p. 234.

7. "Harvard Commencement," *Worcester Magazine*, July 1787.

8. The most recent study of Shays's Rebellion is David P. Szatmary, *Shays' Rebellion: The Making of an Agrarian Insurrection* (Amherst: University of Massachusetts Press, 1980).

9. Thomas G. Amory, *Life of James Sullivan, with Selections from His Writings* (Boston: Phillips, Sampson, 1859), Vol. 1, pp. 205–207; Randall Conrad, "'A Captain with the Insurgents': Jason Parmenter of Bernardston," in Martin Kaufman, ed., *Shays' Rebellion: Selected Essays* (Westfield: Institute for Massachusetts Studies, 1987), 67–79. Also see *Hampshire Gazette*, December 1787.

10. Adams quoted in William V. Wells, *The Life and Public Services of Samuel Adams* (Boston: Little, Brown, 1866), Vol. 3, p. 246; Franklin B. Dexter, ed., *The Literary Diary of Ezra Stiles* (New York: Scribner's Sons, 1901), Vol. 3, entry for June 22, 1787, pp. 267–268.

11. For an analysis of the debate over capital punishment, see Chapter 3 below. Rush's argument can be followed in *An Enquiry into the Effects of Public Punishments upon Criminals and upon Society* (Philadelphia: Joseph James, 1787) and *Considerations on the Injustice and Impolicy of Punishing Murder by Death* (Philadelphia: Mathew Carey, 1792).

12. Bly was indicted for stealing a pistol, a powder horn, flint, bullets, and various other items including flute and fife. Rose was indicted for stealing two guns and a powder horn. Records of the Supreme Judicial Court, 1787, located at the Suffolk County Courthouse. See pp. 259, 260–261.

13. This account of Bly's activities is drawn from "Extracts from the Last Words and Dying Speeches of John Bly and Charles Rose, Who Were Executed at Lenox, Massachusetts for Burglary," *Worcester Magazine*, Second Week, January 1788.

14. Charles Rose, Petition for Clemency, November 1787, located at the Massachusetts State Archives.

15. Stephen West, *A Sermon Preached in Lenox, in the County of Berkshire, and Commonwealth of Massachusetts, December 6, 1787: at the Execution of John Bly and Charles Rose for Crimes of Burglary* (Pittsfield: Elijah Russell, 1788), 3, 10, 11.

16. "Extracts from the Last Words and Dying Speeches of John Bly and Charles Rose."

17. "Letter from Berkshire County," *Worcester Magazine*, Second Week, December 1787.

18. John Bly, Petition for Clemency, October 1787, and Charles Rose, Petition for Clemency, November 1787, located at the Massachusetts State Archives.

19. George Richards Minot, *The History of the Insurrections in Massachusetts* (Boston: James W. Burditt, 1810), 192; Amory, *Life of James Sullivan*, 200. Privately, Minot favored the "decapitation" of Shays. Diary of Minot quoted in Szatmary, *Shays' Rebellion*, xi.

20. *A Brief Narrative of the Life and Confession of Barnett Davenport . . .* (Hartford, 1780); *The Confession of John Battus, a Mulatto, Aged 19 Years, Who Was Executed at Dedham, November 8, 1804* (Dedham: Columbia Minerva Press, 1804); William Smith, *The Convict's Visitor; or, Penitential Offences Consisting of Prayers, Lessons, and Meditations, with Suitable Devotions before, and at the Time of Execution* (Newport: Peter Edes [1791]), 60–61.

21. [Daggett], *Sketches of the Life of Joseph Mountain*, 18. For a biographical sketch of Daggett, see Franklin Bowditch Dexter, *Biographical Sketches of the Graduates of Yale College*, Vol. 4: July 1778–June 1792 (New York: Holt, 1907), 260–264; *Life, Last Words, and Dying Speeches of John Sheehan, Who Was Executed at Boston, on Thursday November Twenty-Second, 1787, for Burglary* (Boston: E. Russell, 1787), broadside.

22. *The Last Words of William Huggins and John Mansfield, Who Are to Be Executed This Day, June 19, 1783, at Worcester for Burglary* (Worcester: Isaiah Thomas, 1783), broadside; *The Life and Confession of Johnson Green Who Is to Be Executed This Day, August 17th, 1786, for the Atrocious Crime of Burglary . . .* (Worcester: Isaiah Thomas, 1786), broadside; *Lives, Last Words, and Dying Speech of Ezra Ross, James Buchanan, and William Brooks Who Were Executed at Worcester . . .* (Worcester: Isaiah Thomas, 1778), broadside; *The Confession of John Battus.*

23. *Lives, Last Words, and Dying Speech of Ezra Ross, James Buchanan, and William Brooks; Life, Last Words, and Dying Confession of Rachel Wall . . . Executed at Boston, on Thursday, October 8, 1789 for Highway-Robbery* (Boston, 1789), broadside; *Life, Last Words, and Dying Confession of John Bailey . . . Executed at Boston, Thursday, October 14, 1790 for Burglary* (Boston, 1790), broadside; *The Confession, Last Words, and Dying Speech of John Stewart, a Native of Ireland* (Boston, 1797), broadside.

24. The sample for this statistic was derived from reading extant execution

sermons, last words and dying confessions, and gallows broadsides published between 1774 and 1812. Of nearly seventy such imprints, thirty-seven included the age of the prisoner at time of execution or provided a date of birth. Most of these imprints can be located in Charles Evans, *The American Bibliography* (New York: P. Smith, 1941–57). Also see Ronald A. Bosco, "Early American Gallows Literature: An Annotated Checklist," *Resources for American Literary Study* 8 (Spring 1978): 81–105.

25. *The Last Words of William Huggins and John Mansfield;* Henry Channing, *God Admonishing His People of Their Duty as Parents and Ministers. A Sermon Preached at the Execution of Hannah Ocuish, a Mulatto Girl, Aged 12 Years and Nine Months . . .* (New London: T. Green, 1786), 9.

26. *The Life, Last Words, and Dying Confession of Rachel Wall.* Also see *The Life and Confession of Johnson Green;* [Daggett], *Sketches of the Life of Joseph Mountain, 2; The Narrative and Confession of Thomas Powers, A Negro . . . Executed at Haverhill, in the State of New Hampshire, on the 28th of July 1796 for Committing a Rape* (Norwich: John Trumbull, 1796), 4.

27. Channing, *God Admonishing His People,* 11; Noah Worcester, *A Sermon Delivered at Haverhill, New Hampshire, July 28, 1796, at the Execution of Thomas Powers, Who Was Executed for a Rape, Committed at Lebanon on the 7th of December, 1795* (Haverhill: N. Coverly, 1796), 32–33.

28. Aaron Bancroft, *The Importance of Religious Education Illustrated and Enforced: A Sermon Delivered at Worcester, October 31, 1793, Occasioned at the Execution of Samuel Frost . . .* (Worcester: Isaiah Thomas, 1793), 7. On student riots, see Steven J. Novak, *The Rights of Youth: American Colleges and Student Revolts, 1798–1815* (Cambridge, Mass.: Harvard University Press, 1977).

29. Jay Fliegelman, *Prodigals and Pilgrims: The American Revolution Against Patriarchal Authority* (Cambridge: Cambridge University Press, 1982); David Hackett Fischer, *Growing Old in America* (expanded edition; New York: Oxford University Press, 1978); Edwin G. Burrows and Michael Wallace, "The American Revolution: The Ideology and Psychology of National Liberation," *Perspectives in American History* 6 (1972): 167–306.

30. Dana, *The Intent of Capital Punishment,* 26, 28; *The Narrative and Confession of Thomas Powers,* 5; Dana, *The Intent of Capital Punishment,* 28.

31. Bancroft, *The Importance of Religious Education,* 18, 11; Worcester, *A Sermon Delivered,* 28.

32. Worcester, *A Sermon Delivered,* 22–24; Uzal Ogden, "The Reward of Iniquity: A Sermon Delivered at Newark, in the New Presbyterian Church, May 6, 1791, at the Execution of William Jones for Murder," in David Austin, ed., *The American Preachers* (Elizabethtown, 1791), Vol. 3, p. 193.

33. *The Last Words and Dying Speech of Robert Young; Who Was Executed at Worcester on Thursday Last, November 11, 1779, for a Rape* (Worcester: Isaiah Thomas, 1779), broadside; *The Last Words of William Huggins and John Mansfield; A Brief Narrative of the Life and Conversion of Barnett Davenport,* 15. On American anxieties over the standing army, see Lawrence Delbert Cress,

Citizens in Arms: The Army and the Militia in American Society to the War of 1812 (Chapel Hill: University of North Carolina Press, 1982).

34. For data base, see note 24. Lawrence Towner has pointed to a similar pattern between 1702 and 1776. Of some eighty-five people executed in New England, "sixty-six were outsiders." See his article "True Confessions and Dying Warnings in Colonial New England," in *Sibley's Heir: A Volume in Memory of Clifford Kenyon Shipton* (Boston: Colonial Society of Massachusetts, 1982), 537.

35. Perez Fobes, *The Paradise of God Opened to a Penitent Thief . . .* (Providence: Bennett Wheeler, 1784), Appendix.

36. See, for example, Increase Mather, *Wicked Mans Portion* (Boston, 1675), and Cotton Mather, *The Sad Effects of Sin* (Boston, 1713), *Pillars of Salt* (Boston, 1699); Cotton Mather, *Tremenda* (Boston, 1721), 4–5; Smith, *The Convict's Visitor*; Mather, *Wicked Mans Portion*, 23. On executions in the seventeenth century, see Wayne C. Minnick, "The New England Execution Sermon, 1639–1800," *Speech Monographs* 35 (March 1968): 77–89; Ronald A. Bosco, "Lectures at the Pillory: The Early American Execution Sermon," *American Quarterly* 30 (1978): 156–176; Richard Slotkin, "Narratives of Negro Crime in New England, 1676–1800," *American Quarterly* 25 (1973): 3–31; and Towner, "True Confessions and Dying Warnings."

37. West, *A Sermon Preached in Lenox*, 8; Nathaniel Fischer, *A Sermon Delivered at Salem, January 14, 1796, Occasioned by the Execution of Henry Blackburn on That Day for the Murder of George Wilkinson* (Boston: S. Hall, 1796), 6; West, *A Sermon Preached in Lenox*, 8.

38. William Andrews, *A Sermon Delivered at Danbury, November 13, 1817, Being the Day Appointed for the Execution of Amos Adams for the Crime of Rape* (New Haven: T. E. Woodward, 1817), 18.

39. Ogden, *The Reward of Iniquity*, 197; Perez Fobes, *The Paradise of God*, 6–8.

40. Worcester, *A Sermon Delivered*, 5.

41. *The Narrative of the Life of Francis Uss, Who Was Executed at Poughkeepsie, in the County of Dutchess, on Friday the 31 of July 1789* (Poughkeepsie [?], 1789), 6; *Worcester Magazine*, Second Week, January 1788; *The Confession, &c. of Thomas Mount, Who Was Executed at Little-Rest in the State of Rhode Island, on Friday, the 27th of May 1791 for Burglary* (Newport, 1791), 15; *The Last Words and Dying Speech of Robert Young*.

42. Maccarty, *The Guilt of Innocent Blood Put Away* (Worcester: Thomas, 1778), title page; on conversion experience in prison, see, for example, *A Narrative of the Life and Conversion of Alexander White, AET 23, who was Executed at Cambridge, November 18, 1784 . . .* (Boston: Powars and Willis, 1784); *The Life, Last Words, and Dying Speech of Dirick Grout, a Dutchman . . . and Francis Coven, a Frenchman . . . Who Were Executed This Day for Burglary* (n.p., 1784), broadside. On ministerial authority, see Donald M. Scott, *From Office to Profession: The New England Ministry, 1750–1850* (Philadelphia: Uni-

versity of Pennsylvania Press, 1978); Maccarty, *The Guilt of Innocent Blood,* 30; *A Narrative of the Life and Conversion of Alexander White,* 21.

43. Dana, *The Intent of Capital Punishment,* 22; *The Confession and Dying Words of Samuel Frost, Who Is to Be Executed This Day, October 31, 1793, for the Horrid Crime of Murder* (Worcester: Isaiah Thomas, 1793); Bancroft, *The Importance of Religious Education,* 24.

44. Joshua Spalding, *A Sermon Delivered at Salem, Previous to the Execution of Isaac Coombs, an Indian . . .* (Salem: Dabney and Cushing, 1787), 22; William Bentley, *The Diary of William Bentley, D.D., pastor of the East Church Salem, Massachusetts* (Salem: Essex Institute, 1905–1914), Vol. I, p. 48.

45. David Sutherland, *A Sermon Delivered at Haverhill, New Hampshire, August 12, 1806, at the Execution of Josiah Burnham . . .* (Haverhill: Moses Davis, 1806), 12; Fobes, *The Paradise of God,* 34; Leland Howard, *A Sermon Delivered at Woodstock, Vermont, February 13, 1818, at the Execution of Samuel E. Godfrey . . .* (Windsor: A. and W. Spooner, 1818), 13.

46. Aaron Bascom, *A Sermon, Preached at the Execution of Abiel Converse . . . July 6, 1788 . . .* (Northampton: William Butler, 1788), 22; [Daggett], *Sketches of the Life of Joseph Mountain,* 18.

47. Fobes, *The Paradise of God*; Spalding, *A Sermon Delivered at Salem,* 5; Nathan Strong, *A Sermon Preached in Hartford, June 10, 1797, at the Execution of Richard Doane* (Hartford: Elisha Babcock, 1797), 4.

48. Spalding, *A Sermon Delivered at Salem,* 21; Timothy Hilliard, *Paradise Promised by a Dying Saviour to the Penitent Thief on the Cross: A Sermon Delivered at Cambridge on Thursday, the Eighteenth of November, immediately Preceding the Execution of Alexander White, Richard Barrick, and John Sullivan* (Boston: E. Russell, 1785), 24; Dana, *The Intent of Capital Punishment,* 12.

49. David Field, *Warning Against Drunkeness: A Sermon Preached in the City of Middletown, June 20, 1816, the Day of the Execution of Peter Lung . . .* (Middletown: Seth Richards, 1816), 28; *The Last Words of Tully Who Was Executed for Piracy at South-Boston, December 10, 1812* (Boston: N. Coverly, 1812), broadside.

50. *Worcester Magazine,* Second Week, December 1787 (italics mine); Fobes, *The Paradise of God,* 26.

51. *The Herald, A Gazette for the Country,* August 19, 1797.

52. William Bentley, *The Diary of William Bentley,* Vol. 2, p. 170; Unknown Diary, 1796, Diary Entry, January 14, 1796, Essex Institute Manuscript Collection.

3. The Opposition to Capital Punishment

1. Rush to Elizabeth Graeme Ferguson, January 18, 1793, in Lyman H. Butterfield, ed., *Letters of Benjamin Rush,* 2 vols. (Princeton: Princeton University

Press, 1951), vol. 2, pp. 627–628 (hereafter cited *Letters*). In this letter, Rush confessed his hope that the legislature would soon abolish capital punishment entirely.

2. Charles de Secondat Montesquieu, *The Spirit of Laws*, Volume 1, especially Books 6 and 12.

3. See article by Louis de Jaucourt on "Crime" in the *Encyclopédie, ou Dictionaire Raisonné Des Sciences, Des Arts et Des Métiers* (Neufchastel: Samuel Faulche, 1765), Vol. 4, p. 467. Beccaria described the writers who influenced him in a letter to Morellet. See Leon Radzinowicz, *A History of the English Criminal Law and Its Administration from 1750. Volume 1: The Movement for Reform* (London: Stevens and Sons, 1948), 279n.

4. On Beccaria, see Coleman Phillipson, *Three Criminal Law Reformers: Beccaria, Bentham, Romilly* (London: J. M. Dent and Sons, 1923); Marcello T. Maestro, *Voltaire and Beccaria as Reformers of the Criminal Law* (New York: Columbia University Press, 1942); and Maestro, *Cesare Beccaria and the Origins of Penal Reform* (Philadelphia: Temple University Press, 1973).

5. The publication history of Beccaria's essay is discussed in Paul M. Spurlin, "Beccaria's *Essay on Crimes and Punishments* in Eighteenth-Century America," *Studies on Voltaire and the Eighteenth Century*, 27 (1963): 1489–1504. For serialization, see *New-Haven Gazette and the Connecticut Magazine*, February 23 through August 3, 1786.

6. Franklin B. Dexter, ed., *The Literary Digest of Ezra Stiles* (New York: Scribner's Sons, 1901), Vol. 3, entry for September 10, 1788, p. 328. For other questions relating to capital punishment, see entries for April 20 and June 29, 1784. As at Yale, Princeton commencement exercises first began to address questions related to punishment in the mid-1780s. In 1786, an oration on "the evils of severe penal laws" was delivered. In 1787, commencement included a "disquisition on the disadvantages of public punishments." An oration on the impolicy of "sanguinary punishments" was included in 1796. Princeton University Archives, *Sources for Commencement Notices* and *Faculty Minutes*.

7. Cesare Beccaria, *An Essay on Crimes and Punishments*, 5th edition revised and corrected (London: E. Hodson, 1801), 41.

8. Ibid., 102, 105, 107.

9. Benjamin Rush, *An Enquiry into the Effects of Public Punishments upon Criminals and upon Society* (Philadelphia: Joseph James, 1787), 14; also see Rush, "Rejoinder to a Reply to the Enquiry into the Justice and Policy of Punishing Murder by Death," *American Museum* 5 (January and February 1789), 63–65 and 121–123; Rush, *Considerations on the Injustice and Impolicy of Punishing Murder by Death* (Philadelphia: Mathew Carey, 1792), 13; William Bradford, *An Enquiry into How Far the Punishment of Death Is Necessary in Pennsylvania* (Philadelphia: T. Dobson, 1793), 3.

10. Thomas Jefferson to John Norvell, June 11, 1807, in Thomas Jefferson Randolph, ed., *Memoir, Correspondence, and Miscellanies, from the Papers of Thomas Jefferson* (Charlottesville: F. Carr, 1829), Vol. 4, pp. 79–82; Randolph,

Memoir, Correspondence, and Miscellanies, Vol. 1, p. 37. For the books in Jefferson's library, consult E. Millicent Sowerby, comp., *Catalogue of the Library of Thomas Jefferson,* 5 vols. (Washington, D.C.: Library of Congress, 1952–1959). An edition of Beccaria in Jefferson's possession is listed in Vol. 3, p. 21. Jefferson also abstracted Beccaria's essay in Italian in his commonplace book. Gilbert Chinard, ed., *The Commonplace Book of Thomas Jefferson* (Baltimore: Johns Hopkins University Press, 1926), 298–317. For Jefferson's "Bill for Proportioning Crimes and Punishments in Cases Heretofore Capital," see Julian P. Boyd, ed., *The Papers of Thomas Jefferson* (Princeton: Princeton University Press, 1950), Vol. 2, pp. 492–507.

11. *Pennsylvania Journal,* June 28, 1775.

12. James Thacher, *A Military Journal during the Revolutionary War, from 1775 to 1783* (Boston: Richardson and Lord, 1823), 25, 57–58. Rush related this story in a letter to John Adams. Rush to Adams, July 20, 1811, in *Letters,* Vol. 2, p. 1090. In another letter to Adams, Rush wrote that Gerry confirmed the incident. Rush to Adams, September 4, 1811, in *Letters,* Vol. 2, p. 1102. A similar version of this anecdote was repeated in John Sanderson, *Biography of the Signers of the Declaration of Independence* (Philadelphia: R. W. Pomeroy, 1827), Vol. 8, p. 147.

13. *New York Packet,* March 28, 1776, quoted in Frank Moore, *Diary of the American Revolution from Newspapers and Original Documents,* 2 vols. (New York: Charles Scribner, 1860), Vol. 1, p. 222; *Pennsylvania Packet,* August 7, 1775, quoted in Moore, *Diary of the American Revolution,* Vol. 1, p. 111.

14. Abigail Adams to Mercy Warren, August 14, 1777, in *Warren-Adams Letters,* 2 vols. (Boston: Massachusetts Historical Society, 1917–1925; AMS Press edition, 1972), Vol. 1, p. 358. John Adams observed, "I left Congress on the 11th of November, 1777, that year which the Tories said, had three gallows in it, meaning the three sevens." Adams quoted in John S. Pancake, *1777: The Year of the Hangman* (University, Ala.: University of Alabama Press, 1977), opposite p. 1. *Pennsylvania Evening Post,* April 24, 1777, cited in Moore, *Diary of The American Revolution,* Vol. 1, pp. 419–422.

15. Petition in Larry Gerlach, ed., *New Jersey in the American Revolution, 1763–1783* (Trenton: New Jersey Historical Commission, 1975), 393–394. For a discussion of loyalist raiders, see John Shy, *A People Numerous and Armed* (New York: Oxford University Press, 1976), 183–192. On Associated Loyalists, see Edward H. Tebbenhoff, "The Associated Loyalists: An Aspect of Militant Loyalism," *New-York Historical Quarterly* 63 (April 1979): 115–144.

16. L. Kinvin Wroth recounts the Huddy episode in "Vengeance: The Court-Martial of Captain Richard Lippincott, 1782," in Howard H. Peckham, ed., *Sources of American Independence: Selected Manuscripts from the Collection of the William L. Clements Library* (Chicago: University of Chicago Press, 1978), 499–532.

17. "To Sir Guy Carleton," in Philip Foner, ed., *The Complete Writings of Thomas Paine* (New York: Citadel, 1945), Vol. 1, p. 218. This letter was dated

May 31, 1782, and formed one of the additional numbers of Paine's Crisis Letters. These letters were reprinted widely. See, for example, the *New Jersey Gazette,* June 12 1782. Rush wrote Nathaniel Greene that Paine's "Crisis did as much mischief to the enemy, & as much service to the friends of liberty as it has been in the power of any one man to render this country with any other weapon short of the sword." Benjamin Rush to Nathaniel Greene, September 4, 1781, in Lyman H. Butterfield, "Further Letters of Benjamin Rush," *Pennsylvania Magazine of History and Biography* 78 (January 1954): 18.

18. George Washington to the General and Field Officers of the Army, April 19, 1782, in John C. Fitzpatrick, ed., *The Writings of George Washington,* (Washington, D.C.: United States Government Printing Office, 1938), Vol. 24, p. 136; George Washington to the President of Congress, April 20, 1782, in ibid., 145; George Washington to Sir Henry Clinton, April 21, 1782, in ibid., 146; ibid., 306n.

19. "To Sir Guy Carleton," in Foner, *The Complete Writings of Thomas Paine,* Vol. 1, pp. 218–219.

20. *The American Crisis, VI,* in ibid., 132–133. Thacher, *A Military Journal,* 137; Joseph Plumb Martin, *Private Yankee Doodle. Being a Narrative of Some of the Adventures, Dangers and Sufferings of a Revolutionary Soldier,* George F. Scheer, ed. (Boston: Little, Brown, 1962), 180.

21. Alexander Hamilton to Henry Knox, June 7, 1782, in Harold Syrett, ed., *The Papers of Alexander Hamilton* (New York: Columbia University Press, 1962), Vol. 3, 91–93. Also see Hamilton's letter to John Laurens, October 11, 1780, following the execution of John Andre in ibid., Vol. 2, pp. 460–470.

22. Henry Knox to Alexander Hamilton, July 24, 1782, in ibid., Vol. 3, p. 118.

23. Fitzpatrick, *The Writings of George Washington,* Vol. 24, p. 308. On the Asgill affair see Kathleen Mayo, *General Washington's Dilemma* (New York: Harcourt, Brace, 1938). In September 1776, the Articles of War expanded the number of capital crimes from three to eleven. See Robert Harry Berlin, "The Administration of Military Justice in the Continental Army during the American Revolution, 1775–1783" (unpublished Ph.D. dissertation, University of California at Santa Barbara, 1976), 71.

24. On the relationship between war and violence, see Robin Brooks, "Domestic Violence in America's Wars: An Historical Interpretation," in Hugh Davis Graham and Ted Robert Gurr, eds., *Violence in America* (New York: Anchor, 1969), 503–521.

25. Kathryn Preyer, "Crime, the Criminal Law, and Reform in Post-Revolutionary Virginia," *Law and History* 1 (Spring 1983): 53–85. On the problem of crime control, see also Adam J. Hirsch, "From Pillory to Penitentiary: The Rise of Criminal Incarceration in Early Massachusetts," *Michigan Law Review* 80 (May 1982): 1228–46; *Massaschusetts Centinel,* October 16, 1784, quoted as well in Hirsch, "From Pillory to Penitentiary," 1235.

26. *The Confession, &c. of Thomas Mount, who was Executed at Little-Rest in the State of Rhode Island, on Friday, the 27th of May 1791 for Burglary* (Newport, 1791).

27. *Weekly Monitor* (Litchfield, Conn.), October 25, 1790.

28. Noah Worcester, *A Sermon Delivered at Haverhill, New Hampshire, July 28, 1796, at the Execution of Thomas Powers, Who Was Executed for a Rape, Committed at Lebanon on the 7th of December, 1795* (Haverhill: N. Coverly, 1796), 21.

29. The literature of republicanism is vast. For a historiographical review, see two essays by Robert Shalhope: "Toward a Republician Synthesis: The Emergence of an Understanding of Republicanism in American Historiography," *William and Mary Quarterly*, 3rd Ser., 29 (January 1972): 49–80, and "Republicanism and Early American Historiography," *William and Mary Quarterly*, 3rd Ser. (April 1982): 334–354. Three works that dominate thinking on the subject are J. G. A. Pocock, *The Machiavellian Moment: Florentine Political Thought and the Atlantic Republican Tradition* (Princeton: Princeton University Press, 1975); Bernard Bailyn, *The Ideological Origins of the American Revolution* (Cambridge, Mass.: Harvard University Press, 1967); and Gordon Wood, *The Creation of the American Republic, 1776–1787* (Chapel Hill: University of North Carolina Press, 1969). On the problem of republics and the virtue of the people, see, especially, Wood, *The Creation of the American Republic*, 46–124. John Howe points out that "virtue was one of those marvelously vague yet crucially important concepts that dotted late-eighteenth-century moral and political thought." John R. Howe, Jr., "Republican Thought and the Political Violence of the 1790's," *American Quarterly* 19 (Summer 1967): 155.

30. John Adams to Mercy Warren, April 16, 1776, *Warren-Adams Letters*, 222; Article XIV of "A Declaration of the Rights of the Inhabitants of the State of Pennsylvania, Constitution of Pennsylvania, 1776," in Francis Newton Thorpe, ed., *The Federal and State Constitutions, Colonial Charters, and Other Organic Laws*, 7 vols. (Washington, D.C.: Government Printing Office, 1909), Vol. 5, p. 3083; Wood, *The Creation of the American Republic*, 47. Rush's list of "anti-republican vices" included "ignorance, venality, luxury, and idolatry." Rush to William Gordon, December 10, 1778, *Letters*, Vol. 1, p. 222.

31. Julian P. Boyd, ed., *The Papers of Thomas Jefferson*, (Princeton: Princeton University Press, 1950), Vol. 2, pp. 493–507; Jared Sparks, ed., *The Works of Benjamin Franklin* (Boston: Hilliard, Gray, 1840), Vol. 2, p. 479; Charles F. Hobson and Robert A. Rutland, eds., *The Papers of James Madison* (Charlottesville: University Press of Virginia, 1981), Vol. 13, pp. 67–70 and 93–94.

32. For a fine, brief biographical sketch of Rush, see James McLachlan, "Benjamin Rush," *Princetonians, 1748–1768, A Biographical Dictionary* (Princeton: Princeton University Press, 1976), 318–325. The most recent biography of Rush is David Freeman Hawke's *Benjamin Rush: Revolutionary Gadfly* (Indianapolis: Bobbs-Merrill, 1971), which unfortunately concludes at 1790. For a superb study

of Rush's thought, see Donald J. D'Elia, "Benjamin Rush: Philosopher of the American Revolution," *Transactions of the American Philosophical Society*, new series, Vol. 64, Part 5, 1974.

33. In addition to the works cited in note 9 above, see Rush, "An Enquiry into the Justice and Policy of Punishing Murder by Death," *American Museum* 4 (July 1788): 78–81; "An Oration Intended to Have Been Spoken at a Late Commencement, on the Unlawfulness and Impolicy of Capital Punishment, and the Proper Means of Reforming Criminals," *American Museum* 6 (January–April, 1790): 8–9, 69–71, 135–137, 193–195; Alfred, "Thoughts on Crimes and Punishments," *American Museum* 4 (May 1788): 395–402; Valentine, "Letter," *New-York Magazine, or Literary Repository* (January 1794): 35–37; An Humble Inquirer, "On Punishment by Death," *Weekly-Magazine* 3 (August 11, 1798): 40–45.

34. Benjamin Rush, *Considerations on the Injustice and Impolicy . . .* (1792), 13.

35. George W. Corner, ed., *The Autobiography of Benjamin Rush: His "Travels Through Life" together with His Commonplace Book for 1789–1813* (Princeton: Princeton University Press for the American Philosophical Society, 1948), 40–78, 89.

36. Rush to John Adams, July 21, 1789, *Letters*, Vol. 1, p. 523; Rush to Richard Price, May 25, 1786, *Letters*, Vol. 1, p. 388.

37. Rush to Horatio Gates, September 5, 1781, *Letters*, Vol. 1, p. 265.

38. Rush, *An Enquiry into the Effects of Public Punishments*, title page. Thomas Paine wrote the rules and regulations for the Society. Foner, *The Complete Writings of Thomas Paine*, Vol. 2, pp. 41–43. For Rush's thoughts on monarchy see *Autobiography*, 197–200; Rush to John Adams, July 21, 1789, *Letters*, Vol. 1, p. 522.

39. Rush, *An Enquiry into the Effects of Public Punishments*, 10 and passim. One writer argued that "cultivating the precepts of Humanity" resulted in "virtuous, honorable, and useful members of the Community." "On Humanity," *Weekly Magazine* 3 (March 30, 1799): 355.

40. Rush to Anthony Wayne, September 24, 1776, *Letters*, Vol. 1, p. 114; Rush to David Ramsay, March or April 1788, *Letters*, Vol. 1, p. 454.

41. Rush, *Considerations on the Injustice and Impolicy*, 18–19. For a similar argument, see Bradford, *An Enquiry into How Far the Punishment of Death Is Necessary*, 5, and Valentine, "Letter," 36.

42. Thomas Paine, *The Rights of Man* (1791), in Foner, *The Complete Writings of Thomas Paine*, Vol. 1, pp. 265–266. Rush applauded Paine's response to Burke. Rush to Belknap, June 6, 1791, *Letters*, Vol. 1, p. 583, and Rush to Belknap, June 21, 1792, *Letters*, Vol. 2, p. 620.

43. Rush to John Adams, July 21, 1789, *Letters*, Vol. 1, p. 523; Rush to Granville Sharp, March 31, 1801, in John A. Woods, ed., "The Correspondence of Benjamin Rush and Granville Sharp, 1773–1809," *Journal of American Studies* 1 (April 1967): 34; Rush to Elhanan Winchester, November 12, 1791, *Letters*,

Vol. 1, p. 611; Rush to Jefferson, August 22, 1800, *Letters,* Vol. 2, pp. 820–821.

44. Rush to Belknap, June 21, 1792, *Letters,* Vol. 1, p. 620; Rush, *An Enquiry into the Effects of Public Punishments,* 16; Rush to Belknap, June 6, 1791, *Letters,* Vol. 1, p. 584. For the argument that the spirit of Christianity is opposed to the gallows, also see "An Oration Intended to have Been Spoken at a Late Commencement," 69–70; Samuel Whelpley, *Letters Addressed to Caleb Strong, Esq.* (Providence: Miller and Hutchens, 1818), 18 and passim; *Moral Advocate* I (February 1822), 127–130; and Roland Diller, *Discourse on Capital Punishment* (New Holland, Pennsylvania, 1825), 7 and passim.

45. Benjamin Rush, "An Enquiry into the Justice and Policy . . ." (July 1788), 79.

46. Rush to Thomas Eddy, October 19, 1803, *Letters,* Vol. 2, p. 875; Rush, *An Enquiry into the Effects of Public Punishments,* 15. "Rejoinder to a Reply . . ." (January 1789), 65; "Rejoinder to a Reply . . ." (February 1789), 122.

47. Rush, "An Enquiry into the Justice and Policy," 81; Rush to Elizabeth Ferguson, January 18, 1793, *Letters,* Vol. 2, p. 628; *Considerations on the Injustice and Impolicy . . .* (1792), 6–7. Jay Fliegelman points out that in the post-Revolutionary years the Old Testament was printed far less frequently than the New. From 1777 to 1800 there were 33 editions of the entire bible but "nearly eighty separate printings of the New Testament." *Prodigals and Pilgrims: The American Revolution Against Patriarchal Authority, 1750–1800* (Cambridge: Cambridge University Press, 1982), 170.

48. Rush to Thomas Eddy, October 19, 1803, *Letters,* Vol. 2, p. 875; on Cain, see *Considerations on the Injustice and Impolicy . . .* (1792), 8–9. Also see Valentine, "Letter," 36.

49. For an introduction to the tenets of liberal theology, see Conrad Wright, *The Beginnings of Unitarianism in America* (Boston: Starr King Press, 1955). On nineteenth-century Unitarianism in New England, see Daniel Walker Howe, *The Unitarian Conscience: Harvard Moral Philosophy, 1805–1861* (Cambridge, Mass.: Harvard University Press, 1970). Ann Douglas, in *The Feminization of American Culture* (New York: Avon, 1977), 143–155, offers a penetrating analysis of the shift in interpretation of the doctrine of the atonement. On Rush's religious beliefs, see *Autobiography,* 162–166, and *Letters,* Vol. 1, pp. 418–420, 581–584, 611–612. Donald J. D'Elia's study provides the most detailed analysis of Rush's theology.

50. Rush to Belknap, June 6, 1791, *Letters,* Vol. 1, p. 584.

51. This is not to suggest that all who entertained a liberal theological position opposed capital punishment or that those with orthodox principles defended it. But it is clear that there was a correlation between one's position on the death penalty and one's theology. In New England, in the antebellum period, denominations used the issue of capital punishment as a platform from which to assault one another.

52. Philochorus [Robert Annan], "Observations on Capital Punishment: Being

a Reply to an Essay on the Same Subject," *American Museum* 4 (November and December 1788): 444–448, 558 on "liberality," and 443 on "divine appointment."

53. Rush to Belknap, October 7, 1788, *Letters,* Vol. 1, p. 490. Earlier, Rush had written Belknap that his *Enquiry* "staggered many Old Testament saints and Legislators." August 19, 1788, *Letters,* Vol. 1, p. 481; Rush to Richard Price, June 2, 1787, *Letters,* Vol. 1, p. 419.

4. The Dream of Reformation and the Limits of Reform

1. [duc de Rochefoucauld-Liancourt], *On the Prisons of Philadelphia* (Philadelphia: Moreau de Saint-Mey, 1796), 33.

2. For experiments in continental reform, see Leon Radzinowicz, *A History of English Criminal Law and Its Administration from 1750. Volume 1, The Movement for Reform* (London: Stevens and Sons, 1948), 285–292; the Pennsylvania Acts are contained in *The Statutes at Large of Pennsylvania* (Harrisburg, 1911), Vol. 12, pp. 280–290, and Vol. 15, pp. 174–181; on congressional action see *Annals of the Congress of the United States,* Fourth Congress, First Session, December 15, 1795, p. 144, and December 31, 1795, p. 185.

3. The texts of the state constitutions can be found in Frances Newton Thorpe, ed., *The Federal and State Constitutions, Colonial Charters, and Other Organic Laws,* 7 vols. (Washington: Government Printing Office, 1909), Vol. 3, p. 1688; Vol. 5, p. 3090; Vol. 7, p. 3813; Vol. 4, p. 2456.

4. See Gilbert Chinard, ed., *The Commonplace Book of Thomas Jefferson* (Baltimore: Johns Hopkins Press, 1926), 298–317. For Jefferson's Bill, see Julian P. Boyd, ed., *The Papers of Thomas Jefferson* (Princeton: Princeton University Press, 1950), Vol. 2, pp. 492–507. Also see Jefferson's letter to George Wythe, pp. 229–231. Near the end of his life, Jefferson wondered "how this last revolting principle [the lex talionis] came to obtain our approbation." Thomas Jefferson Randolph, ed., *Memoir, Correspondence, and Miscellanies, from the Papers of Thomas Jefferson* (Charlottesville: F. Carr, 1829), Vol. 1, p. 35.

5. For Jefferson's views on laws and republicanism, see his *Notes on the State of Virginia* (New York: Harper Torchbooks Edition, 1964), 131; Edmund Pendleton to Thomas Jefferson, August 10, 1776, in David John Mays, ed., *The Letters of Edmund Pendleton* (Charlottesville: University Press Virginia, 1967), Vol. 1, p. 198.

6. *The Statutes at Large of Pennsylvania,* Vol. 12, pp. 280–290.

7. Benefit of clergy was a common law doctrine that mitigated the death sentence in the case of first offense felonies. Studies of the administration of the criminal law are more prevalent for England than America. See J. M. Beattie, *Crime and the Courts in England, 1660–1800* (Princeton: Princeton University Press, 1986); Douglas Hay, "Property, Authority and the Criminal Law," in Hay

et al., *Albion's Fatal Tree: Crime and Society in Eighteenth Century England* (New York: Pantheon, 1975), 17–63; John Langbein, "Albion's Fatal Flaws," *Past and Present* 98 (February 1983): 96–120; Peter King, "Decision-makers and Decision-making in the English Criminal Law, 1750–1800," *The Historical Journal* 27 (1984): 25–58. On America, consult Linda Kealey, "Patterns of Punishment: Massachusetts in the Eighteenth Century," *American Journal of Legal History* 30 (April 1986): 163–176. A list of Pennsylvania executions can be found in Negley Teeters, "Public Executions in Pennsylvania, 1682–1834," *Journal of the Lancaster County Historical Society* 64 (Spring 1960): 85–164.

8. William Bradford, *An Enquiry into How Far the Punishment of Death Is Necessary in Pennsylvania* (Phildelphia: T. Dobson, 1793), 20.

9. A. Ruth Fry, *John Bellers, 1654–1725: Quaker Economist and Social Reformer* (London: Cassell and Company, 1935), 75, 166

10. Elbert Russell, *The History of Quakerism* (New York: Macmillan, 1942), 90; Rush to John Coakley Lettsom, August 16, 1788, in Lyman H. Butterfield, ed., *Letters of Benjamin Rush*, 2 vols. (Princeton: Princeton University Press for the American Philosophical Society, 1951), Vol. 1, pp. 479–481 (hereafter cited as *Letters*).

11. For indictments, see *Minutes of the Supreme Executive Council of Pennsylvania* (Harrisburg: Theo. Fenn and Co., 1852), Vol. 11, pp. 601–606; on legal issues raised by the case, see Steven R. Boyd, "Political Choice—Political Justice: The Case of the Pennsylvania Loyalists," in Michael R. Belknap, ed., *American Political Trials* (Westport: Greenwood Press, 1981), 43–56.

12. *Pennslyvania Archives* (Philadelphia: Joseph Severns and Company, 1853), Vol. 7, pp. 39, 24, 55.

13. Henry Biddle, ed., *Extracts from the Journal of Elizabeth Drinker, 1759–1807* (Philadelphia: Lippincott and Company, 1889), 112; Samuel L. Knapp, *The Life of Thomas Eddy* (London: Edmund Fry and Son, 1826), 32–33. Samuel Rowland Fisher, an imprisoned Quaker loyalist, commented that another execution, that of David Dawson for treason on November 25, 1780, seemed to him "a greater act of Cruelty in the present Rulers than anything they have heretofore done." "Extracts from the Journal of Samuel Rowland Fisher," *Pennsylvania Magazine of History and Biography* 41 (1917): 327.

14. *Statutes at Large of Pennsylvania*. Vol. 12, p. 280. For a general history of penal reform in Pennsylvania, see two works by Harry Elmer Barnes, *The Repression of Crime: Studies in Historical Penology* (New York: George Doran Co., 1926) and *The Evolution of Penology in Pennsylvania: A Study in American Social History* (Indianapolis: Bobbs-Merrill, 1927). Also see Michael Meranze, "The Penitential Ideal in Late Eighteenth-Century Philadelphia," *Pennsylvania Magazine of History and Biography* 108 (October 1984): 419–450. Two valuable contemporary accounts are Bradford, *An Enquiry*, and James Mease, *The Picture of Philadelphia* (Philadelphia: B. and T. Kite, 1811), 158–186.

15. See John Locke, *An Essay Concerning Human Understanding* (1690) and

Some Thoughts Concerning Education (1693). A fine introduction to Lockean thought is offered by Neal Wood, *The Politics of Locke's Philosophy: A Social Study of "An Essay Concerning Human Understanding"* (Berkeley: University of California Press, 1983). Jay Fliegelman discusses Locke's influence in America in *Prodigals and Pilgrims: The American Revolution against Patriarchal Authority, 1750–1800* (New York: Cambridge University Press, 1982); Tunis Wortman, *An Oration on the Influence of Social Institutions upon Human Morals and Happiness* (New York, 1796), 4–5.

16. On Scottish Philosophy see Gladys Bryson, *Man and Society: The Scottish Inquiry of the Eighteenth Century* (Princeton: Princeton University Press, 1945). David Hartley developed his theory of associationist psychology in his *Observations on Man* (1749). For a thoughtful consideration of Hartley's influence on Rush, see Donald J. D'Elia, "Benjamin Rush, David Hartley, and the Revolutionary Uses of Psychology," *Proceedings of the American Philosophical Society* 114 (April 1970): 109–118.

17. A Citizen of Maryland, "An Oration . . . on the Unlawfulness and Impolicy of Capital Punishment, and the Proper Means of Reforming Criminals," *American Museum,* March 1790, p. 137.

18. "A Citizen of the World," in *Pennsylvania Mercury,* November 27, 1788; for suggestions see *American Museum,* April 1790, p. 193; Knapp, *Life of Thomas Eddy,* 43.

19. *Statutes at Large of Pennsylvania,* Vol. 12, pp. 280–281, 284. Also see Susan Dillwyn to William Dillwyn, quoted in *Letters,* Vol. 1, p. 416n.

20. Caleb Lownes, *An Account of the Alteration and Present State of the Penal Laws of Pennsylvania,* added to Bradford, *An Enquiry,* 76–77; Randolph, *Memoir of Thomas Jefferson,* Vol. 1, p. 37; Mease, *The Picture of Philadelphia,* 161.

21. Benjamin Rush, *An Enquiry into the Effects of Public Punishments upon Criminals and upon Society* (Philadelphia: Joseph James, 1787), 4–5, 6–7.

22. Ibid., 9, 12; also see *Independent Gazette,* July 10, 1787.

23. Rush, *An Enquiry,* 12, 10–11. For other accounts of the emergence and meaning of the penitentiary in America, see W. David Lewis, *From Newgate to Dannemora: The Rise of the Penitentiary in New York* (Ithaca: Cornell University Press, 1965); Adam J. Hirsch, "From Pillory to Penitentiary: The Rise of Criminal Incarceration in Early Massachusetts," *Michigan Law Review* 80 (May 1982): 1179–1269; David J. Rothman, *The Discovery of the Asylum: Social Order and Disorder in the New Republic* (Boston: Little, Brown, 1971); Christopher Lasch, "Origins of the Asylum," in his *The World of Nations: Reflections on American History, Politics, Culture* (New York: Alfred A. Knopf, 1973), 3–17.

24. Rush, *An Enquiry,* 11–14. Rush also cited Howard's classic work on prisons. See p. 13.

25. Rush to John Coakley Lettsom, September 28, 1787, *Letters,* Vol. 1, p. 443; Minutes of the Pennsylvania Society for Alleviating the Miseries of Public Prisons, Vol. 1, 1787–1809, Historical Society of Pennsylvania; account of es-

cape in *Maryland Gazette,* October 21, 1788; for situation in New York, see account in *Maryland Journal and Baltimore Advertiser,* January 2, 1789. In October 1789, authorities in New York executed several former wheelbarrow men and made it clear that the Pennsylvania experiment in penal reform was not entirely to their liking: "Executions which have taken place in this city yesterday, will deter the villains who have through the lenity of the laws in some other states been suffered to escape from the hands of justice, from emigrating into the state of New-York, where they seldom are suffered to escape the gallows." *Maryland Gazette,* November 6, 1789; October 31, 1788.

26. Henry Fielding, *A Proposal for Making Effectual Provision for the Poor* (London: A. Miller, 1753), 153–154; for a discussion of prison architecture, see Nikolaus Pevsner, *A History of Building Types,* Bollingen Series XXXV.19 (Princeton: Princeton University Press, 1976), 159–168, and Robin Evans, *The Fabrication of Virtue: English Prison Architecture, 1750–1840* (Cambridge: Cambridge University Press, 1982); Joseph Hanway, *Solitude in Imprisonment* (London: 1776). For an account of Beevor's efforts, see *American Museum,* September 1789, pp. 223–226.

27. *American Museum,* April 1790, p. 194; Benjamin Rush, *An Enquiry into the Influence of Physical Causes upon the Moral Faculty* (Philadelphia: Charles Cist, 1786), 24.

28. Rush to Enos Hitchcock, April 24, 1789, *Letters,* Vol. 1, p. 512.

29. Robert J. Turnbull, *A Visit to the Philadelphia Prison* (Philadelphia: Budd and Bartram, 1796), 58.

30. The phrase "counterfeit contrition" is William Bradford's, *An Enquiry,* 46; Rochefoucauld-Liancourt, *On the Prisons,* 11.

31. Rush to John Coakley Lettsom, September 28, 1787, *Letters,* Vol. 1, p. 441; Rush, *An Enquiry into the Effects of Public Punishments,* 12; "Report of the Board of Inspectors of the Prison for the City and County of Philadelphia in the Year 1791," in William Roscoe, *Observations on Penal Jurisprudence, and the Reformation of Criminals* (London: T. Cadell and W. Davies, 1819), Appendix, p. 2; Lownes, *An Account,* 81.

32. Rochefoucauld-Liancourt, *On the Prisons,* 11.

33. *Maryland Gazette,* October 31, 1788.

34. William Paley, *The Principles of Moral and Political Philosophy* (Philadelphia: Thomas Dobson, 1788), 414; Enoch Edwards, "Charge Delivered to a Grand Jury for the County of Philadelphia," *Universal Asylum and Columbian Magazine,* March 1791, pp. 158–161; *Maryland Gazette,* July 3, 1789.

35. Rush, for example, wrote that "a wheelbarrow, a whipping post, nay even a gibbet, are all light punishments compared with letting a man's conscience loose upon him in solitude." Rush to Enos Hitchcock, April 24, 1789, *Letters,* Vol. 1, p. 512. Under the pseudonym Philochorus, Robert Annan, pastor at the Scot's Presbyterian Church in Philadelphia, assailed the opponents of capital punishment for hypocrisy, among other things. For the exchange between Annan and

Rush, see the *Pennsylvania Mercury,* September 25 and 30, October 2, 4, 7, 21, and 23, 1788. Also see the *American Museum,* November and December 1788 and January 1789.

36. "Extracts from the Diary of Ann Warder," *Pennsylvania Magazine of History and Biography* 18 (1894): 61.

37. *Massachusetts Centinal,* October 16, 1784.

38. Alexander Hamilton to James McHenry, July 29, 1799, in Harold Syrett, ed., *The Papers of Alexander Hamilton* (New York: Columbia University Press, 1970), Vol. 23, p. 293. Hamilton goes on to observe that public opinion "should not have too much infuence."

39. Charles Lincoln, ed., *State of New York: Messages from the Governors, Vol. 2, 1777–1822* (Albany: Lyon Company, 1909), 350, 363; see Knapp, *Life of Thomas Eddy,* 43 and passim.

40. George Keith Taylor, *Substance of a Speech Delivered in the House of Delegates in Virginia, on the Bill to Amend the Penal Laws of This Commonwealth* (Richmond: Samuel Pleasants, 1796), 31; Randolph, *Memoir of Thomas Jefferson,* Vol. 1, p. 38.

41. On Rochefoucauld-Liancourt in Paris, see Gordon Wright, *Between the Guillotine and Liberty: Two Centuries of the Crime Problem in France* (New York: Oxford University Press, 1983), 53 and passim; on penal reform in England, in addition to Radzinowicz, see Coleman Phillipson, *Three Criminal Law Reformers* (London: J. M. Dent and Sons, 1923).

42. On the legislative history of penal reform in New York, see Philip English Mackey, "Anti-Gallows Activity in New York State, 1776-1861" (Ph.D. dissertation, University of Pennsylvania, 1969), chapter two. Quote is from *Greenleaf's New York Journal,* 60.

43. *Memoirs of Stephen Burroughs* (Hanover: Benjamin True, 1798), 126.

44. Gustave de Beaumont and Alexis de Tocqueville, *On the Penitentiary System in the United States, and Its Applications in France,* Francis Lieber, trans. (Philadelphia: Carey, Lea, and Blanchard, 1833), 47.

45. Roscoe, *Observations on Penal Jurisprudence,* Appendix, p. 2.

46. *Report on the Penitentiary System in the United States* (New York: Mahlon Day, 1822), 18; "Description and Historical Sketch of the Massachusetts State Prison," in Roscoe, *Observations on Penal Jurisprudence,* Appendix, p. 84.

47. Characteristics of reformation in Roscoe, *Observations on Penal Jurisprudence,* 172; see "Report of the Commonwealth of Massachusetts," in ibid., Appendix, p. 90; *Memoirs of Stephen Burroughs,* 224.

48. Quoted in Adam J. Hirsch, "From Pillory to Penitentiary: The Rise of Criminal Incarceration in Early Massachusetts," *Michigan Law Review* 80 (May 1982): 1255; [Thomas Eddy], *An Account of the State Prison or Penitentiary-House, in the City of New York* (New York: Isaac Collins, 1801), 12.

49. Rush to Thomas Eddy, October 19, 1803, *Letters,* Vol. 2, p. 875; Rush to John Adams, June 10, 1806, *Letters,* Vol. 2, p. 919.

50. George W. Corner, ed., *The Autobiography of Benjamin Rush* (Princeton: Princeton University Press for the American Philosophical Society, 1948), 161; Rush to James Madison, February 27, 1790, *Letters,* Vol. 1, p. 540; Rush to John Adams, July 11, 1806, *Letters,* Vol. 2, pp. 922–923.

51. Rush to John Adams, September 16, 1808, *Letters,* Vol. 2, pp. 976–979.

52. Beaumont and Tocqueville, *On the Penitentiary System in the United States,* 202.

5. The Origins of Private Executions in America

1. *Prisoner's Friend,* April 23, 1845; May 7, 1845.

2. *Trial and Execution of Thomas Barrett Who Was Hung at Worcester, January 3, 1845* (Boston: Skinner and Blanchard, 1845); *Hangman,* February 19, 1845, and *Last Days of Gordon: Being the Trial of John and William Gordon . . . Together with Full Particulars of the Execution of John Gordon on the 14th of February, 1845* (Boston: Skinner and Blanchard, 1845); *New York Evening Post,* May 10, 1845, and *Hangman,* May 28, 1845.

3. *Laws of the General Assembly of the State of Pennsylvania, Passed at the Session 1833–1834* (Harrisburg: Henry Welsh, 1834), Act No. 127, pp. 234–35.

4. For the vote in Pennsylvania, see *Journal of the Forty-fifth House of Representatives* (Harrisburg, 1834), 446–447. *Report on the Expediency of Abolishing Public Executions* (Harrisburg: Henry Welsh, 1833), 4.

5. On the meaning of the penitentiary, see Michel Foucault, *Discipline and Punish: The Birth of the Prison* (New York: Vintage Books, 1979), and Michael Ignatieff, *A Just Measure of Pain: The Penitentiary in the Industrial Revolution, 1750–1850* (New York: Columbia University Press, 1978).

6. Benjamin Rush, *An Enquiry into the Effects of Public Punishments upon Criminals and upon Society* (Philadelphia: Joseph James, 1787), 12; Philochorus [Robert Annan], *Pennsylvania Mercury,* October 7, 1788.

7. *Escritor,* December 1, 1826, p. 359; Roland Diller, *Discourse on Capital Punishment* (New Holland, Pennsylvania, 1825), 27; Jonathan Going, *A Discourse Delivered at Worcester, December 11, 1825, the Sabbath after the Execution of Horace Carter* (Worcester: W. Manning, 1825), 11.

8. Nicholas B. Wainwright, ed., "The Diary of Samuel Breck, 1814–1822," *Pennsylvania Magazine of History and Biography* 102 (October 1978): 485; H. E. Scudder, ed., *Recollections of Samuel Breck* (Philadelphia: Porter and Coales, 1877), 37.

9. Jacob Cassat, *Journal of the Thirty-fourth House of Representatives of the Commonwealth of Pennsylvania* (Harrisburg: John Weistling, 1823–24), 577; *The Dying Confession of John Lechler, Made in the Presence of Samuel Car-*

penter, Mayor of the City of Lancaster, and Others (Lancaster, S. C. Stambaugh, 1822). Also see Albert Post, "Early Efforts to Abolish Capital Punishment in Pennsylvania," *Pennsylvania Magazine of History and Biography* 68 (January 1944): 43–44 and passim.

10. *Lancaster Gazette,* November 6, 1822; *Lancaster Journal,* October 25, 1822; *Lancaster Intelligencer,* November 2, 1822; *New York Evening Post,* October 30, 1822.

11. *Yorktown Gazette* quoted in Edward Livingston, "Introductory Report to the Code of Crimes and Punishments," *The Complete Works of Edward Livingston on Criminal Jurisprudence* (New York: National Prisons Association, 1873), Vol. 1, p. 200.

12. Cassat, *Journal of the Thirty-fourth House,* 706–709.

13. Livingston also seized on the Lechler case. In 1827 he wrote to Roberts Vaux, the Quaker penal reformer and secretary of the Philadelphia Society for Alleviating the Miseries of Public Prisons, for information about the execution of Lechler and its aftermath. A year before, Vaux himself had suggested that the death penalty might better "be visited upon the unhappy culprit within the jail yard." Edward Livingston to Roberts Vaux, November 3, 1827, Vaux Papers, Historical Society of Pennsylvania; Roberts Vaux, *Letters on the Penitentiary System of Pennsylvania Addressed to William Roscoe* (Philadelphia, 1826), 63.

14. See Livingston's "Report on the Plan of a Penal Code," in *Complete Works,* Vol. 2, p. 39 and passim, and his "Introductory Report to the Code of Crimes and Punishments," p. 199 and passim.

15. The secondary literature on phrenology is sparse and uneven. For an introduction, see John D. Davies, *Phrenology: Fad and Science—A Nineteenth-Century American Crusade* (New Haven: Yale University Press, 1955), and D. A. DeGiustino, "Phrenology in Britain: A Study of George Combe and His Circle" (Ph.D. dissertation, University of Wisconsin at Madison, 1969). Combe explains phrenology in *A System of Phrenology* (Boston: March, Capen, and Lyon, 1834) and *Lectures on Phrenology* (New York: S. Colman, 1839).

16. George Combe, "Capital Punishment," in *Moral and Intellectual Science Applied to the Elevation of Society* (New York: Fowles and Wells, 1848), 207, 209, 214, 211. For Combe's reaction to an execution he witnessed, see Charles Gibbon, *The Life of George Combe* (London: Macmillan, 1878), Vol. 1, pp. 32–34.

17. "Humanity," "Observations on the Curiosity of Those Who Go to Witness Public Executions," in *The Record of Crimes in the United States* (Buffalo: H. Faxton and Co., 1833), pp. V, VIII, IX, X.

18. Charles Caldwell, *Thoughts on the Impolicy and Injustice of Capital Punishment* (Louisville: G. H. Monsarrant, 1848).

19. Critiques of phrenology can be found in David Meredith Reese, *Humbugs of New York: Being a Remonstrance Against Popular Delusions* (New York: John S. Taylor, 1836), 63–88; G. Bradford, "Phrenology," in *North American Review* 37 (July 1833): 59–83.

20. Horace Mann, Lecture Notes 64, n.d., Mann Papers, Massachusetts Historical Society.

21. *Liberator,* August 15, 1835; *Liberator,* September 14, 1835; *American Quarterly Review* 17 (March 1835), 209.

22. The literature on crowd behavior and popular violence is vast. A synthesis of the literature that challenges dominant historiographical models is Thomas Paul Slaughter, "Mobs and Crowds, Riots and Brawls: The History of Early American Political Violence" (unpublished paper, 1985). Also see Paul A. Gilje, "'The Mob Begins to Think and Reason': Recent Trends in Studies of American Popular Disorders, 1700–1850," *The Maryland Historian* 12 (Spring 1981): 25–36.

23. On the transformation of the eighteenth-century crowd, see Slaughter, "Mobs and Crowds," 20 and passim; Paul A. Gilje, "The Baltimore Riots of 1823 and the Breakdown of the Anglo-American Mob Tradition," *Journal of Social History* 13 (1980): 547–564, and Gilje, "Mobocracy: Popular Disturbances in Post-Revolutionary New York City, 1783–1829" (Ph.D. dissertation, Brown University, 1980); *Pennsylvania Magazine,* August 4, 1786; William Bentley, *The Diary of William Bentley, D.D., Pastor of the East Church at Salem, Massachusetts* (Salem: The Essex Institute, 1905–1914), Vol. 2, p. 165; Samuel Eliot in *City Records,* XV, September 18, 1837, quoted in Roger Lane, *Policing the City, Boston 1822–1885* (Cambridge, Mass.: Harvard University Press, 1967), 30–31.

24. See Paul O. Weinbaum, *Mobs and Demagogues: The New York Response to Collective Violence in the Early Nineteenth Century* (Ann Arbor: UMI Research Press, 1979), 22–30; on Boston, see Theodore M. Hammett, "Two Mobs of Jacksonian Boston: Ideology and Interest," *Journal of American History* 63 (1976): 845–868. Horace Mann, incidentally, belonged to the legislative group commissioned to investigate the riot; on Philadelphia, see John Runcie, "'Hunting the Nigs' in Philadelphia: The Race Riot of August 1834," *Pennsylvania History* 39 (April 1972): 187–218; Allan Nevins, ed., *The Diary of Philip Hone, 1828–1851* (New York: Dodd, Mead and Company, 1936), 169; Channing quoted in Hammett, "Two Mobs," 853; on the riot act in Massachusetts, see Michael S. Hindus, "A City of Mobocrats and Tyrants: Mob Violence in Boston, 1747–1863," *Issues in Criminology* 6 (Summer 1971): 70.

25. *Christian Observer* quoted in Paul Boyer, *Urban Masses and Moral Order in America, 1820–1920* (Cambridge, Mass.: Harvard University Press, 1978), 35; on the cholera epidemic, see Charles E. Rosenberg, *The Cholera Years: The United Staes in 1832, 1849, and 1866* (Chicago: University of Chicago Press, 1962).

26. *Report on the Expediency of Abolishing Public Executions* (Harrisburg: Henry Welsh, 1833), 8.

27. Norbert Elias, *The Civilizing Process: The History of Manners* (New York: Pantheon, 1978) and *The Civilizing Process: Power and Civility* (New York: Pantheon, 1982); Jay Fliegelman, *Prodigals and Pilgrims: The American Revolution Against Patriarchal Authority, 1750–1800* (Cambridge: Cambridge Uni-

versity Press, 1982); Lawrence Stone, *The Family, Sex and Marriage in England, 1500–1800* (New York: Harper and Row, 1977); Richard Sennett, *The Fall of Public Man: On the Social Psychology of Capitalism* (New York: Vintage Books, 1978); John McManners, *Death and the Enlightenment* (New York: Oxford University Press, 1981).

28. See Betsey Blackmar, "Re-walking the 'Walking City': Housing and Property Relations in New York City, 1780–1840," *Radical History Review* 21 (Fall 1979): 131–148; Paul E. Johnson, *A Shopkeeper's Millennium: Society and Revivals in Rochester, New York, 1815–1837* (New York: Hill and Wang, 1978); David Grimsted, *Melodrama Unveiled: American Theatre and Culture, 1800–1850* (Chicago: University of Chicago Press, 1968), 52–56; Karen Halttunen, *Confidence Men and Painted Women: A Study of Middle-Class Culture in America, 1830–1870* (New Haven: Yale University Press, 1982); Mary P. Ryan, *Cradle of the Middle Class: The Family in Oneida County, New York, 1790–1865* (Cambridge: Cambridge University Press, 1981); John F. Kasson, "Civility and Rudeness: Urban Etiquette and the Bourgeois Social Order in Nineteenth-Century America," in Jack Salzman, ed., *Prospects*, Vol. 9 (Cambridge: Cambridge University Press, 1984): 143–167, David E. Stannard, "Where All Our Steps Are Tending: Death in the American Context," in Martha Pike and Janice Armstrong, eds., *A Time to Mourn: Expressions of Grief in Nineteenth-Century America* (Stony Brook: Museums at Stony Brook, 1980), 19–28. Also see Myra Glenn, *Campaigns Against Corporal Punishment: Prisoners, Sailors, Women, and Children in Antebellum America* (Albany: State University of New York Press, 1984).

29. Valentine, "Letter on Capital Punishment," *New York Magazine; or Literary Depository*, January 1794, p. 36; "Conversion Most Difficult on the Hour of Death," *The Christian's Scholars and Farmers Magazine*, December and January 1789–1790, p. 585; Caldwell, *Thoughts on the Impolicy and Injustice of Capital Punishment*, 28; Roland Diller, Discourse on Capital Punishment (New Holland, Pennsylvania, 1825), 16.

30. Halttunen, *Confidence Men and Painted Women*, passim.

31. Herman Melville, *The Confidence-Man: His Masquerade* (New York: W. W. Norton, 1971), 111. For a discussion of the theme of the confidence man in literature, see Gary Lindberg, *The Confidence Man in American Literature* (New York: Oxford University Press, 1982).

32. Francis Bacon, "Capital Punishment," *Christian Examiner* (March 1832), 29, 28.

33. Eliza Cope Harrison, ed., *Philadelphia Merchant: The Diary of Thomas P. Cope, 1800–1851* (South Bend: Gateway Editions, 1971), 357.

34. William Sullivan, Robert Rantoul, Thomas Kendell, and Oliver Holden, "Report on Punishment by Death," Commonwealth of Massachusetts, *House Documents*, Number 15, June 1831 (Boston, 1831), 14–16.

35. Andrew Preston Peabody, "Capital Punishment," *Christian Examiner*, July 1833, pp. 312–313.

36. Thomas Upham, *The Manual of Peace* (New York: Leavitt, Lord, 1836), 234–235.

37. *Laws of the State of New-York Passed at the Fifty-eighth Session of the Legislature* (Albany: E. Croswell, 1835), 299; *Prisoner's Friend,* April 23, 1845; *Christian Messenger* quoted in the *Hangman,* May 28, 1845; *Boston Traveller* quoted in the *National Aegis,* May 30, 1849.

38. *Christian Messenger* quoted in the *Hangman,* May 28, 1845; *Boston Evening Traveller,* August 30, 1850; *Liberator,* December 3, 1858.

39. Sean Wilentz, ed., "Crime, Poverty and the Streets of New York City: The Diary of William H. Bell, 1850–51," *History Workshop* 7 (Spring 1979): 148.

40. Thomas Sergeant Perry, ed., *The Life and Letters of Francis Lieber* (Boston: James R. Osgood, 1882), 170; John L. O'Sullivan, *Report in Favor of the Abolition of the Punishment of Death by Law* (New York: J. & H. G. Langley, 1841), 62; William Lloyd Garrison quoted in the *Hangman,* January 15, 1845.

41. Going, *A Discourse Delivered at Worcester,* 11; *Nile's Weekly Register* 39 (November 20, 1830): 202; Lucy Colman, "Execution of Ira Stout," *Liberator,* December 3, 1858. Both the proponents and opponents of capital punishment opposed the presence of women at executions. Lydia Maria Child, *Letters from New York* (New York: C. S. Francis, 1844), 221.

42. "The Punishment of Death," *Philadelphia Gazette,* December 23, 1841; Edward Hubbell Chapin, *Three Discourses upon Capital Punishment* (Boston: Trumpet Office, 1843), 42–43; Wendell Phillips, *Speeches, Lectures, Letters* (Boston: Lee and Shepard, 1891), 99.

43. "The Address of the United States Anti-Masonic Convention (1830)," in David Brion Davis, ed., *The Fear of Conspiracy* (Ithaca: Cornell University Press, 1971), 77. Also see Davis's seminal article, "Some Themes of Counter-subversion: An Analysis of Anti-Masonic, Anti-Catholic, and Anti-Mormon Literature," *Mississippi Valley Historical Review* 47 (September 1960): 205–224; Frederyck Marryat, *A Diary in America, with Remarks on Its Institutions* (Philadelphia: Carey and Hart, 1839), 49; *Report on the Expediency of Abolishing Public Executions,* 8.

44. *New York Herald* quoted in the *Hangman,* September 3, 1845.

45. See Michael Shudson, *Discovering the News: A Social History of American Newspapers* (New York: Basic Books, 1978), and Frank Luther Mott, *American Journalism* (New York: Macmillan, 1947).

46. Alexander Saxton, "Problems of Class and Race in the Origins of the Mass Circulation Press," *American Quarterly* 36 (Summer 1984): 211–234; Dan Schiller, *Objectivity and the News: The Public and the Rise of Commercial Journalism* (Philadelphia: University of Pennsylvania Press, 1981).

47. *New York Sun,* November 20, 1835; *New York Herald,* November 20, 1835.

48. Senate Document No. 79 in *Documents of the Senate of the State of New-*

York, Fifty-eighth Session, 1835, (Albany: E. Croswell, 1835), Vol. 2, pp. 4, 10.

49. Senate Document No. 79, pp. 8–10.

6. Anti-Gallows Activists and the Commitment to Moral Reform

1. *Pennsylvania Freeman,* March 14, 1844.

2. "Report of Committee on Capital Punishment," Commonwealth of Massachusetts, *House Documents,* Number 196, April 27, 1848 (Boston, 1848), 18.

3. On reformers' careers, see Donald M. Scott, "Abolition as a Sacred Vocation," in Lewis Perry and Michael Fellman, eds., *Antislavery Reconsidered: New Perspectives on the Abolitionists* (Baton Rouge: Louisiana State University Press, 1979), 51–74; Lewis Perry, *Childhood, Marriage, and Reform: Henry Clarke Wright, 1797–1870* (Chicago: University of Chicago Press, 1980); Lawrence J. Friedman, *Gregarious Saints: Self and Community in American Abolitionism, 1830–1879* (Cambridge: Cambridge University Press, 1982).

4. Donald M. Scott, "The Popular Lecture and the Creation of a Public in Mid-Nineteenth Century America," *Journal of American History* 66 (March 1980): 791–809; Michael Shudson, *Discovering the News: A Social History of American Newspapers* (New York: Basic Books, 1981); Dan Schiller, *Objectivity and the News: The Public and the Rise of Commercial Journalism* (Philadelphia: University of Pennsylvania Press, 1981); Donald M. Scott, *From Office to Profession: The New England Ministry, 1750–1850* (Philadelphia: University of Pennsylvania Press, 1978); Mary P. Ryan, *Cradle of the Middle Class: The Family in Oneida County, New York, 1790–1865* (Cambridge: Cambridge University Press, 1981).

5. "Capital Punishment Meeting," undated in book of clippings on the death penalty in Pennsylvania, Historical Society of Pennsylvania, Manuscripts Division.

6. Biographical and occupational information on these men can be found in *Biographical Encyclopedia of Pennsylvania of the Nineteenth Century* (Philadelphia: Galaxy Publishing, 1874); *McElroy's Philadelphia Directory for 1842* (Philadelphia: C. Rogers, 1842); Henry Simpson, *The Lives of Eminent Philadelphians Now Deceased* (Philadelphia: William Brotherhead, 1859).

7. *Tribune,* February 5, 1844. In March, O'Sullivan began a monthly publication devoted to providing information on the death penalty. Titled *Anti-Draco,* the periodical was not a success.

8. On political ideology in the antebellum period, see John Ashworth, *Agrarians & Aristocrats: Party Political Ideology in the United States, 1837–1846* (London: Royal Historical Society, 1983); Marvin Meyers, *The Jacksonian Persuasion: Politics and Belief* (Stanford: Stanford University Press, 1957); Daniel Walker Howe, *The Political Culture of the American Whigs* (Chicago: University of Chicago Press, 1979); Herbert Ershkowitz and William G. Shade, "Consensus

or Conflict? Political Behavior in the State Legislature during the Jacksonian Era," *Journal of American History* 58 (December 1971): 591–621; Major L. Wilson, *Space, Time, and Freedom: The Quest for Nationality and the Irrepressible Conflict, 1815–1861* (Westport: Greenwood Press, 1974).

9. *Hangman,* October 8, 1845. Societies for the abolition of capital punishment formed in other states as well. See Philip English Mackey, "'The Result May be Glorious'—Anti-Gallows Movement in Rhode Island, 1838–1852," *Rhode Island History* 33 (1974): 19–30.

10. Lydia Maria Chid to Ellis Gray Loring, March 6, 1843, New York Public Library, Manuscript Division; Child, *Letters from New York,* (New York: C. S. Francis, 1844), 220; 224.

11. Petition on Capital Punishment, January 23 to March 5, 1847, Library Company of Philadelphia, Manuscript Collection.

12. On these general shifts, see Paul Boyer, *Urban Masses and Moral Order in America, 1820–1920* (Cambridge, Mass.: Harvard University Press, 1978); Paul Johnson, *A Shopkeeper's Millennium: Society and Revivals in Rochester New York, 1815–1837* (New York: Hill and Wang, 1978); Sean Wilentz, *Chants Democratic: New York City and the Rise of the American Working Class, 1788–1850* (New York: Oxford University Press, 1984); Ryan, *Cradle of the Middle Class.*

13. There is no single, interpretive synthesis of antebellum reform that addresses these issues. For specific movements, see Ian Tyrrell, *Sobering Up: From Temperance to Prohibition in Antebellum America, 1800–1860* (Westport: Greenwood Press, 1979); Jed Dannenbaum, *Drink and Disorder: Temperance Reform in Cincinnati from the Washingtonian Revival to the WCTU* (Urbana: University of Ilinois Press, 1984); Michael B. Katz, *The Irony of Early School Reform: Educational Innovation in Mid-Nineteenth Century Massachusetts* (Cambridge, Mass.: Harvard University Press, 1968); Ronald G. Walters, *The Antislavery Appeal: American Abolitionism after 1830* (Baltimore: Johns Hopkins University Press, 1976); David J. Rothman, *The Discovery of the Asylum: Social Order and Disorder in the New Republic* (Boston: Little, Brown, 1971); on evangelical Protestantism and reform, see James H. Moorhead, "Social Reform and the Divided Conscience of Antebellum Protestantism," *Church History* 48 (December 1979): 416–430.

14. Spear's diary, or journal as he called it, covers the period from November 1, 1841, through April 30, 1849. There is a gap from August through November 1845. The original is located in the manuscripts division of the Boston Public Library. Spear maintained a journal throughout his adult life, but this is the only volume that has been located. For an obituary of Spear, see the *Boston Daily Evening Transcript,* April 14, 22, 1863. The following references are to the date of entry in the unpaginated journal.

15. December 13, November 10, 25, 1841.

16. November 2, 1841; January 18, 1842; December 14, 1841.

17. December 14, 1841. On Unitarianism, see Daniel Walker Howe, *The Un-*

itarian Conscience: Harvard Moral Philosophy, 1805–1861 (Cambridge, Mass.: Harvard University Press, 1970).

18. November 6, 1841; January 26, 1843; May 1, 1848.

19. The Lane story unfolds from the following entries: November 1, 1841; January 3, 1842; January 10, 1842; January 24, 25, 1842; and February 5, 1842. At an antislavery meeting on May 10, 1842, Lane appeared with his family, whom he purchased for $2500. According to Spear, Lane "had been shamefully treated at the South. Though he had a permit to remain twenty days, yet he was tried, forcibly taken from the ears, tarred and feathered, and barely escaped with his life! The bill of sale was read and all the family was there. It was a joyous occasion."

20. *Essays on Imprisonment for Debt* (Hartford: B. Sperry, 1833) 5, 8, 20, 17–18. A good historical survey of the debt question is Peter J. Coleman, *Debtors and Creditors in America: Insolvency, Imprisonment for Debt, and Bankruptcy, 1607–1900* (Madison: State Historical Society of Wisconsin, 1974).

21. Spear Diary, November 25, 1841.

22. May 16, 1843, January 17, 1844.

23. On Universalism, see Stephen Marini, *Radical Sects of Revolutionary New England* (Cambridge, Mass.: Harvard University Press, 1982); Richard Eddy, *Universalism in America. A History* (Boston: Universalist Publishing House, 1884–1886); Ernest Cassara, comp., *Universalism in America: A Documentary History* (Boston: Beacon Press, 1971); Russell E. Miller, *The Larger Hope: The First Century of the Universalist Church in America, 1770–1870* (Boston, 1978).

24. Thomas Whittemore, *Life of the Rev. Hosea Ballou*, 4 vols. (Boston: J. M. Usher, 1854–55).

25. Spear Diary, February 20, 1842; June 12, 1843.

26. September 19, 1847.

27. May 27–29, 1845; October 10, March 6, May 23–26, September 21, 1842.

28. June 1, 1844; October 31, 1843; February 22, 1842; June 7–9, 1843; May 27, 1844.

29. *Essays on the Punishment of Death* (Boston: Charles Spear, 1844).

30. Spear Diary, November 25, 1842; May 10, 1842.

31. July 4, 1846; September 30, 1847; Lydia Maria Child to Ellis Gray Loring, May 16, 1844, New York Public Library, Manuscript Division; Spear Diary, May 1, 1846.

32. November 25, 1841; May 21, 1844.

33. March 8, 1842.

34. February 4, 1843.

35. November 26, 1841.

36. August 15, 1842; Thomas Upham, *Manual of Peace* (New York: Leavitt, Lord and Company, 1836).

37. Spear Diary, August 15, 1842.

38. Entry for January 27, 1843 summarizes this argument.

39. *Essays on the Punishment of Death*, passim and 29, 91.

40. Spear Diary, February 22, 1842; May 1, 1845.

41. *The Hangman* began as a weekly newspaper devoted to the abolition of capital punishment. The first series ran for thirteen issues, January 1–March 26, 1845. From the start, some anti-gallows activists criticized the name of the paper. One correspondent suggested that from the title alone readers might first suppose that it was designed to defend the gallows. Spear reacted defensively, at first, to this criticism. He reasoned that "by constantly keeping the name before the public we may arouse the community to this dangerous form of punishment." (See issues of February 19 and April 23, 1845). Starting with the issues published on January 7, 1846, however, the weekly was now called *The Prisoner's Friend*.

42. Spear Diary, February 17, March 22, 1844.

43. April 16, 1845.

44. May 1, 1844; June 30, 1845; May 24–28, 1847.

45. July 31, 1844; April 30, 1848; May 23, October 10, 1847.

46. Hazel Catherine Wolf, *On Freedom's Altar* (Madison: University of Wisconsin Press, 1952), contains a discussion of the martyr complex among abolitionists.

47. Spear Diary, July 21, 1848; Charles Spear to Richard D. Webb, July 16, 1846, Manuscripts Division, Boston Public Library.

48. Spear Diary, September 11, 1848.

49. May 22, 1842.

50. *The Hangman,* January 7 and March 12, 1845; Spear Diary, August 19, 1845; February 16, January 21, 1844.

51. June 7–9, 1843; May 28, 1842; September 16–19, 1845; August 1, 1844.

52. For patterns of thought and behavior similar to Spear's, see, for example, Walter M. Merrill and Louis Ruchames, eds., *The Letters of William Lloyd Garrison, 1822–1879,* 6 vols. (Cambridge, Mass.: Harvard University Press, 1971–1981); Gilbert H. Barnes and Dwight L. Dumond, *The Letters of Theodore Dwight Weld, Angelina Grimke Weld, and Sarah Grimke, 1822–1844,* 2 vols. (New York: D. Appleton-Century, 1934); Irving H. Bartlett, ed., "New Light on Wendell Phillips: The Community of Reform, 1840–1880," *Perspectives in American History* 12 (1979): 3–251.

53. Spear Diary, December 16, 1848; October 31, 1845; September 30, 1847.

54. April 30, 1849.

55. Charles Spear to Henry Longfellow, January 7, 1863, Longfellow Papers, Houghton Library, Harvard University.

7. The Conflict over Capital Punishment in Antebellum America

1. "Introduction," *United States Magazine and Democratic Review* (October 1837), 1–15, reprinted in Joseph L. Blau, ed., *Social Theories of Jacksonian Democracy* (Indianapolis: Bobbs-Merrill, 1954), 21–37.

2. Blau, *Social Theories,* 32–33.

3. John L. O'Sullivan, *Report in Favor of the Abolition of the Punishment of Death by Law* (New York: J. & H. G. Langley, 1841), 20 and passim.

4. Ibid., 29, 44; "Capital Punishment," *New Englander* 1 (January 1843): 29.

5. O'Sullivan, *Report,* 34, 52.

6. Ibid., 85, 63, 110–112, 116.

7. Ibid., 70, 135.

8. Lydia Maria Child, *Letters from New York* (New York: C. S. Francis, 1844), 207.

9. On the legislative history of the campaign against capital punishment in New York, see Philip English Mackey, "Anti-Gallows Activity in New York State, 1776–1861" (Ph.D. dissertation, University of Pennsylvania, 1969), especially chapters Four and Five; *Evening Post,* March 30, 1842; *Evening Post,* April 2, 1842.

10. [Albert Baldwin Dod], "Capital Punishment," *Biblical Repertory and Princeton Review* 14 (April 1842): 310–311, 325. Leonard Bacon expressed similar fears in "Shall Punishment Be Abolished?," *New Englander* 4 (October 1846): 563-588.

11. Dod, "Capital Punishment," 300–333. David Brion Davis notes the use of a moral-sense argument by proponents of capital punishment in "The Movement to Abolish Capital Punishment in America, 1787–1861," *American Historical Review* 63 (October 1957): 38.

12. See Rush's *Enquiry into the Influence of Physical Causes upon the Moral Faculty* (Philadelphia: Charles Cist, 1786), and his *Considerations on the Injustice and Impolicy of Punishing Murder by Death* (Philadelphia: Mathew Carey, 1792). For an introduction to the Scottish Enlightenment, see Gladys Bryson, *Man and Society: The Scottish Inquiry of the Eighteenth Century* (Princeton: Princeton University Press, 1945).

13. O'Sullivan, *Report,* 136.

14. Tayler Lewis, "Human Justice; or, Government a Moral Power," *Biblical Repository and Classical Review* 3 (January and April 1847): 214; Bacon, "Shall Punishment Be Abolished?," 579–583.

15. Jacksonville Women to George Barrell Cheever, May 4, 1846, in Cheever Family Papers, American Antiquarian Society; on Cheever's career, see Robert M. York, *George B. Cheever, Religious and Social Reformer 1807–1890* (Orono: Maine University Press, 1955), and Philip English Mackey, "Reverend George Barrell Cheever: Yankee Reformer as Champion of the Gallows," *Proceedings of the American Antiquarian Society* 82 (1972): 323–342. Also see Cheever's *The Course and System of the Unitarians Plainly and Solemnly Surveyed* (Boston: W. Peirce, 1834).

16. George Barrell Cheever, *Punishment by Death: Its Authority and Expediency* (New York: M. W. Dod, 1842), 34–35, 60.

17. "Capital Punishment," *New Englander* 1 (January 1843): 36; William T. Dwight, *A Discourse on the Rightfulness and Expediency of Capital Punishments* (Portland: Printed at the Temperance Office, 1843).

18. Leonard Bacon, "Shall Punishment Be Abolished?," 587; William H. Buddington, *Capital Punishment: A Discourse Occasioned by the Murder of the Late Warden of the Massachusetts State Prison* (Boston: Marvin, 1843), 14; O'Sullivan, *Report,* 92–93n.

19. Cheever, *Punishment by Death,* 108–114.

20. Ibid., 134, 143.

21. "Capital Punishment," 30; Joseph Parrish Thompson, *The Right and Necessity of Inflicting the Punishment of Death for Murder* (New Haven: J. M. Patten, 1842); Milo D. Codding, *Capital Punishment: A Violation of the Principles of Divine Government* (Rochester: Jerome and Brothers, 1846), 41.

22. Daniel T. Rodgers, *Contested Truths: Keywords in American Politics Since Independence* (New York: Basic Books, 1987), 112–143.

23. For reviews of Sullivan's and Cheever's arguments, see, in addition to the works discussed above, F. W. Holland, "Abolition of Capital Punishment," *Christian Examiner* 43 (November 1847): 355–373; E. B. Hall, "The Punishment of Death," *North American Review* 62 (January 1846): 40–70; and "Capital Punishment," *Southern Quarterly Review* 4 (July 1843): 81–97.

24. *Tribune,* January 25 and 28, 1843; on the lecture system, see Donald M. Scott, "The Popular Lecture and the Creation of a Public in Mid-Nineteenth Century America," *Journal of American History* 66 (March 1980): 791–809.

25. For accounts, see *Herald,* January 28, 1843; *Tribune,* January 28, February 6, 7, 9, 11, March 2, 17, 18, 20–24 and passim, 1843; *New York Evangelist,* February 2, 9, 16, 23, and March 23, 1843.

26. *Tribune,* February 6, 1843.

27. *Herald,* January 28, 1843; *Tribune,* February 9, 1843.

28. *Tribune,* March 17, 18, 24, 1843.

29. *Tribune,* March 27, 1843; see Cheever, *A Defense of Capital Punishment* (New York: Wiley and Putnam, 1846); "The Gallows and the Gospel," *United States Magazine and Democratic Review* 12 (March 1843): 227–236; *Tribune,* March 27, 1843.

30. *Hangman,* July 30, 1845; *Tribune,* March 2, 1843.

31. "Capital Punishments," *The Christian Disciple* 5 (March 1817): 77.

32. *Tribune,* February 6, 1843; O'Sullivan, *Report,* 108–109. For statistical argument also see "Capital Punishment," in *American Jurist and Law Magazine* 18 (October 1837): 334–374, and *Hon. Robert Rantoul's Letters on the Death Penalty* (Boston: 1846). A discussion of the American obsession with numbers is provided by Patricia Cline Cohen, *A Calculating People: The Spread of Numeracy in Early America* (Chicago: University of Chicago Press, 1982), esp. 150–226.

33. *New York Evangelist,* February 16 and 23, 1843.

34. Bacon, "Shall Punishment Be Abolished?," 564; "Capital Punishment" (*New Englander*), 28–34.

35. "Capital Punishment," in the *North American,* no date, in book of clippings on the death penalty in Pennsylvania, Historical Society of Pennsylvania; Thompson, *The Right and Necessity,* 53.

36. *United States Magazine and Democratic Review* (August 1846) quoted in Lewis, "Human Justice," 69.

37. George Barrell Cheever in the *New York Evangelist,* February 23, 1843; Bacon, "Shall Punishment Be Abolished?," 573; Thompson, *The Right and Necessity,* 52; "Capital Punishment," (*New Englander*), 31.

38. Edward Hubell Chapin, *Three Discourses on Capital Punishment* (Boston: Trumpet Office, 1843), 69.

39. Quoted in Edwin Powers, *Crime and Punishment in Early Massachusetts, 1620–1692, a Documentary History* (Boston: Beacon Press, 1966), 311; "Capital Punishment," Commonwealth of Massachusetts, *House Documents,* number 73, March 7, 1843 (Boston, 1843).

40. On the abolition of capital punishment in Michigan, see Albert Post, "Michigan Abolishes Capital Punishment," *Michigan History Magazine* 29 (January 1945): 44–50; Edward W. Bennett, "The Reasons for Michigan's Abolition of Capital Punishment," *Michigan History* (November/December 1978): 42–55. On criminal law on the frontier generally, see William Wirt Blume, "Criminal Procedure on the American Frontier," *Michigan Law Review* 57 (December 1958): 195–257, and Blume, "Legislation on the American Frontier," *Michigan Law Review* 60 (January 1962): 317–372.

41. See, for example, George Duffield, *The Divine Organic Law Ordained for the Human Race, or Capital Punishment for Murder Authorized by God and Sustained by Reason* (Detroit: Garrett and Geiger, 1848); legislative voting data in Bennett, "The Reasons for Michigan's Abolition," 44 and passim. Also see Ronald Formisano, *The Birth of Mass Political Parties: Michigan, 1827–1861* (Princeton: Princeton University Press, 1971), 125.

42. *Prisoner's Friend,* May 13, 1846; Phillips quoted in *Prisoner's Friend,* July 8, 1846; "Death Penalty in Michigan," *Prisoner's Friend,* January 1849, pp. 184–186.

43. Julian Hawthorne on O'Sullivan, quoted in Julius W. Pratt, "John L. O'Sullivan and Manifest Detiny," *New York History* 14 (July 1933): 219.

Epilogue

1. Marvin Bovee to Wendell Phillips, n.d., Blagden Collection, Houghton Library, Harvard University.

2. "The Death Penalty," *North American Review* 133 (1881): 534–541. For a discussion of the concept of criminal insanity in the late nineteenth century,

see Charles Rosenberg, *The Trial of the Assassin Guiteau: Psychiatry and Law in the Gilded Age* (Chicago: University of Chicago Press, 1968).

3. "The Death Penalty," 550–559.

4. *Furman v. Georgia,* 408 U.S. 238 (1972). Also see Michael Meltsner, *Cruel and Unusual: The Supreme Court and Capital Punishment* (New York: William Morrow, 1974); Hugo Adam Bedau, ed., *The Death Penalty in America,* 3rd ed. (New York: Oxford University Press, 1982); William J. Bowers, *Legal Homicide: Death as Punishment in America, 1864–1982* (Boston: Northeastern University Press, 1984); and Franklin E. Zimring and Gordon Hawkins, *Capital Punishment and the American Agenda* (Cambridge: Cambridge University Press, 1986).

5. *Gregg v. Georgia,* 428 U.S. 153 (1976). For one Justice's perspective on the Supreme Court and capital punishment, see William J. Brennan, "Constitutional Adjudication and the Death Penalty: A View from the Court," *Harvard Law Review* 100 (December 1986): 313–331.

Index

199